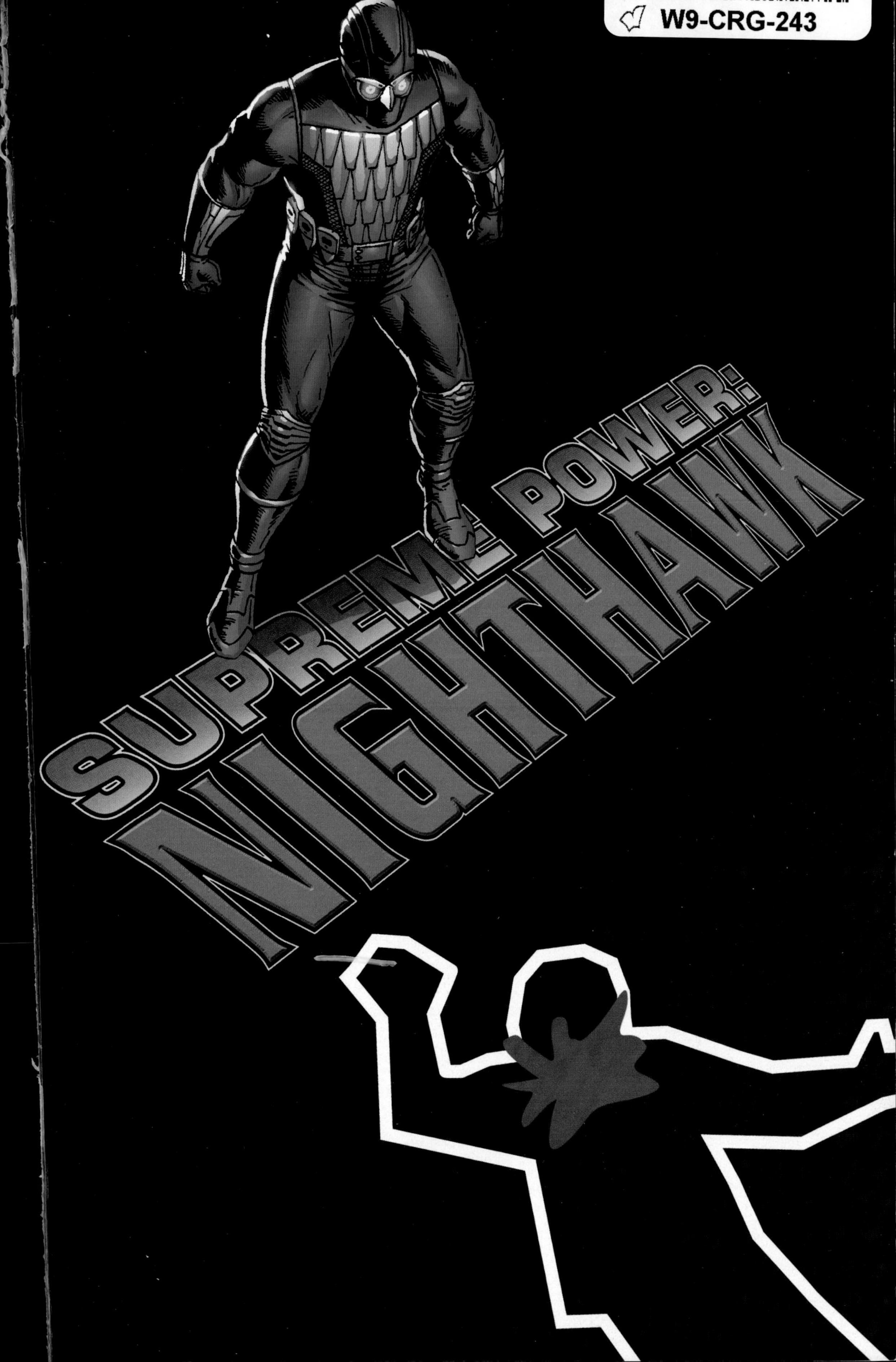
SUPREME POWER:
NIGHTHAWK

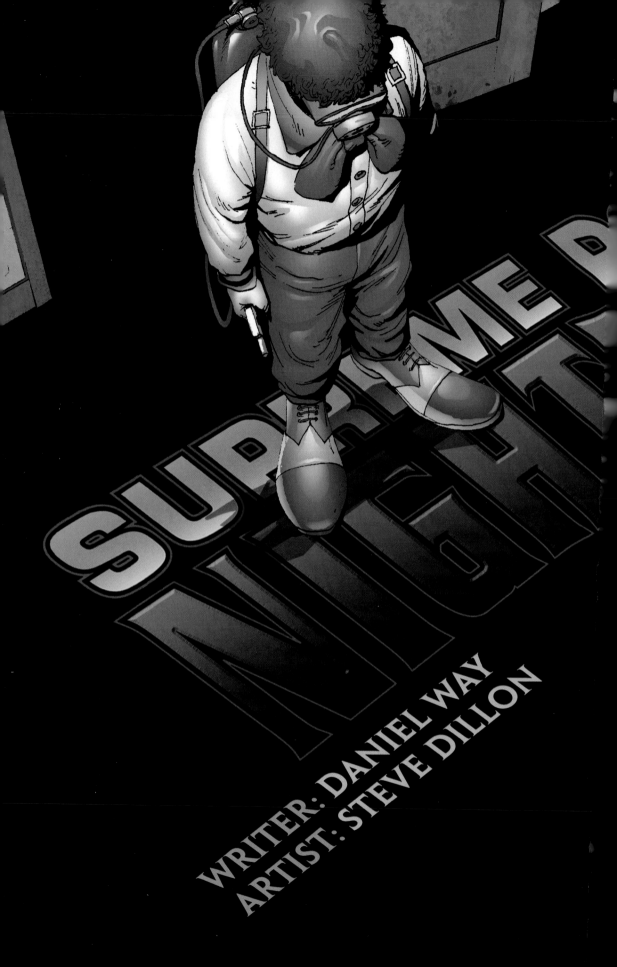

SUPREME POWER
NIGHT

WRITER: DANIEL WAY
ARTIST: STEVE DILLON

COLORS: AVALON'S DAN KEMP
LETTERS: VIRTUAL CALLIGRAPHY'S JOE CARAMAGNA
ASSOCIATE EDITOR: CORY SEDLMEIER
EDITOR: AXEL ALONSO

COLLECTION EDITOR: **JENNIFER GRÜNWALD**
ASSISTANT EDITOR: **MICHAEL SHORT**
SENIOR EDITOR, SPECIAL PROJECTS: **JEFF YOUNGQUIST**
VICE PRESIDENT OF SALES: **DAVID GABRIEL**
BOOK DESIGNER: **JHONSON ETENG**
VICE PRESIDENT OF CREATIVE: **TOM MARVELLI**

EDITOR IN CHIEF: **JOE QUESADA**
PUBLISHER: **DAN BUCKLEY**

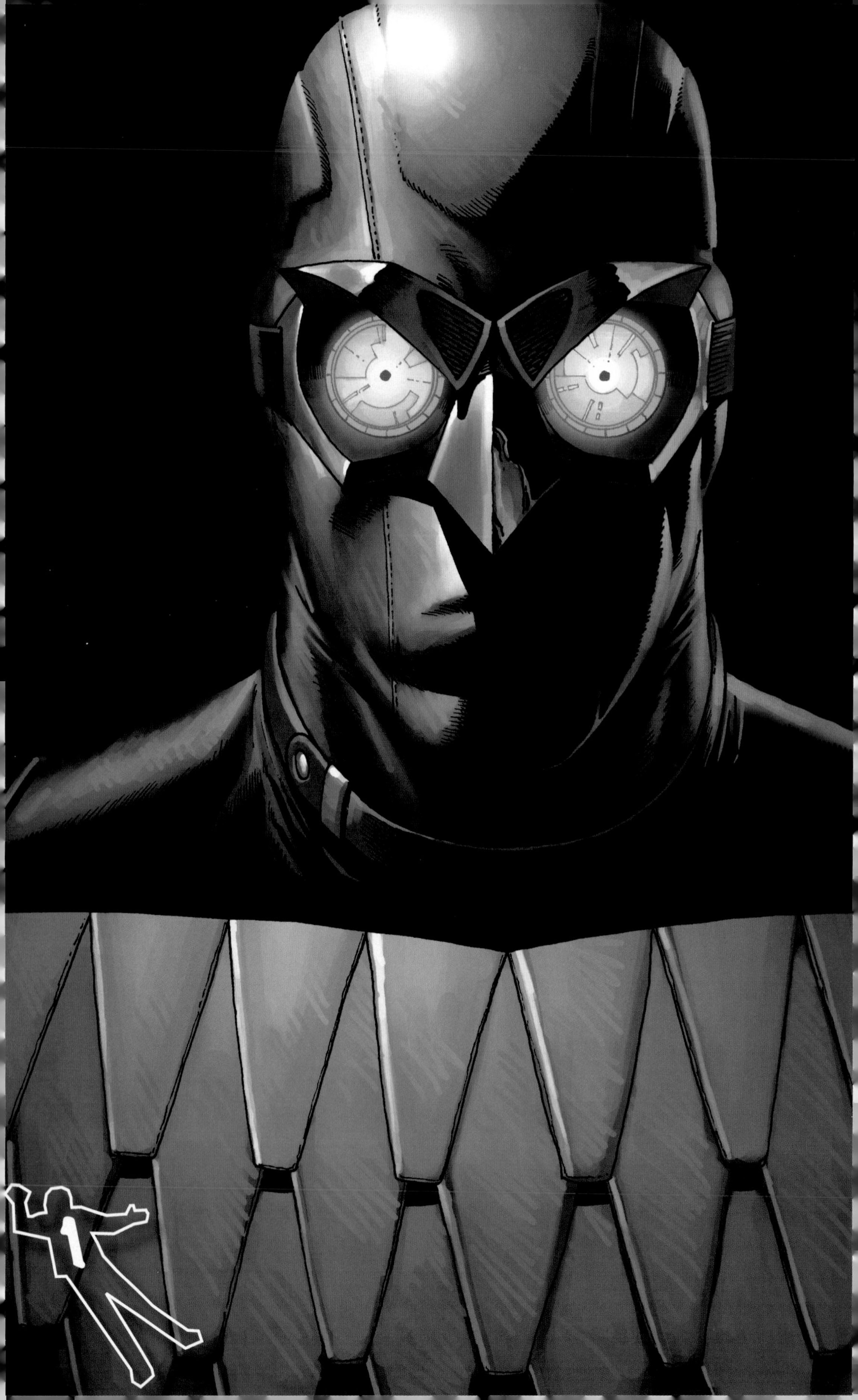

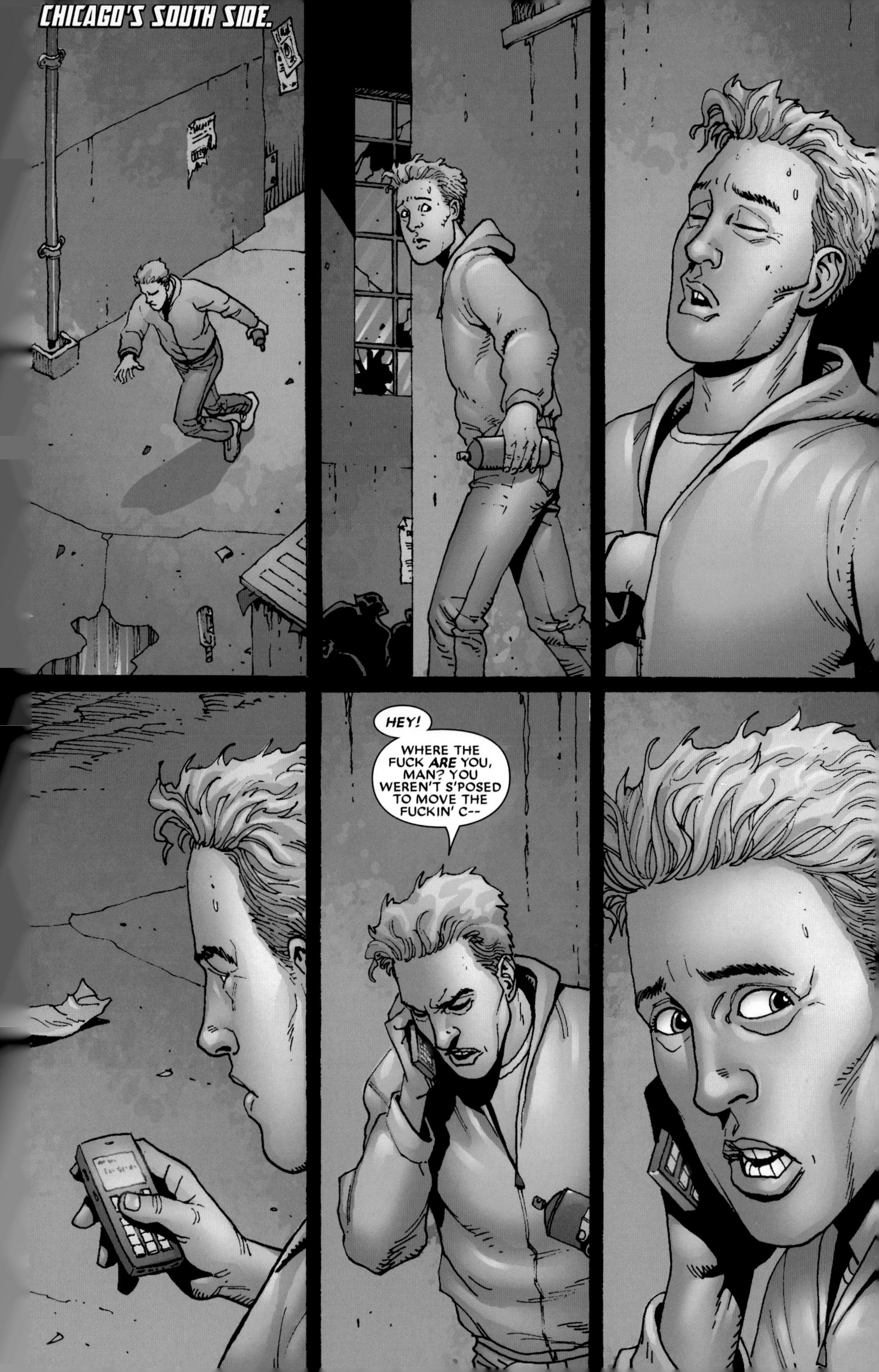
CHICAGO'S SOUTH SIDE.
HEY!
WHERE THE FUCK ARE YOU, MAN? YOU WEREN'T S'POSED TO MOVE THE FUCKIN' C--

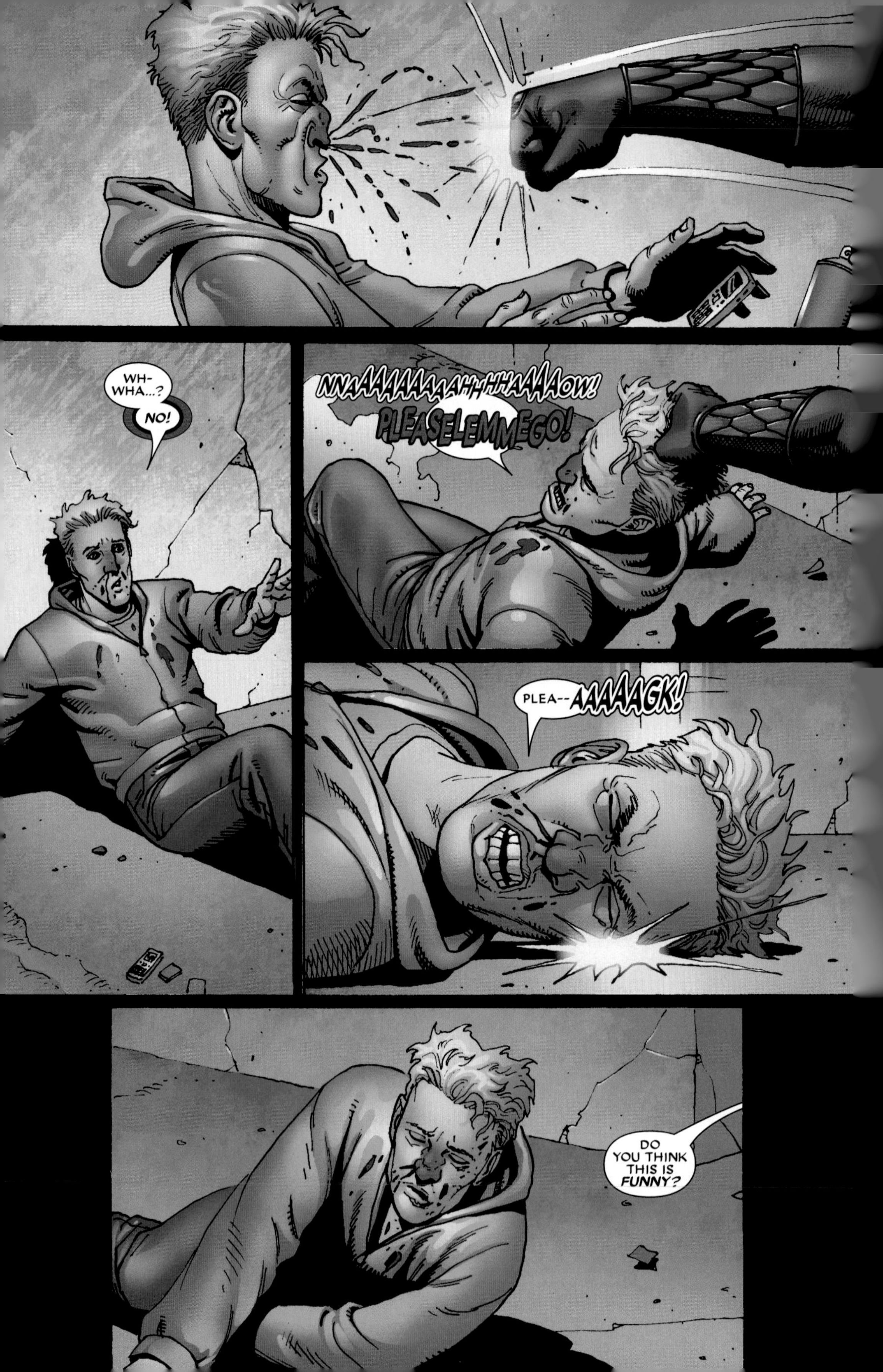
WH-
WHA...?
NO!
NNAAAAAAAAAHHHHAAAAOW!
PLEASELEMMEGO!
PLEA--AAAAAGK!
DO YOU THINK THIS IS FUNNY?

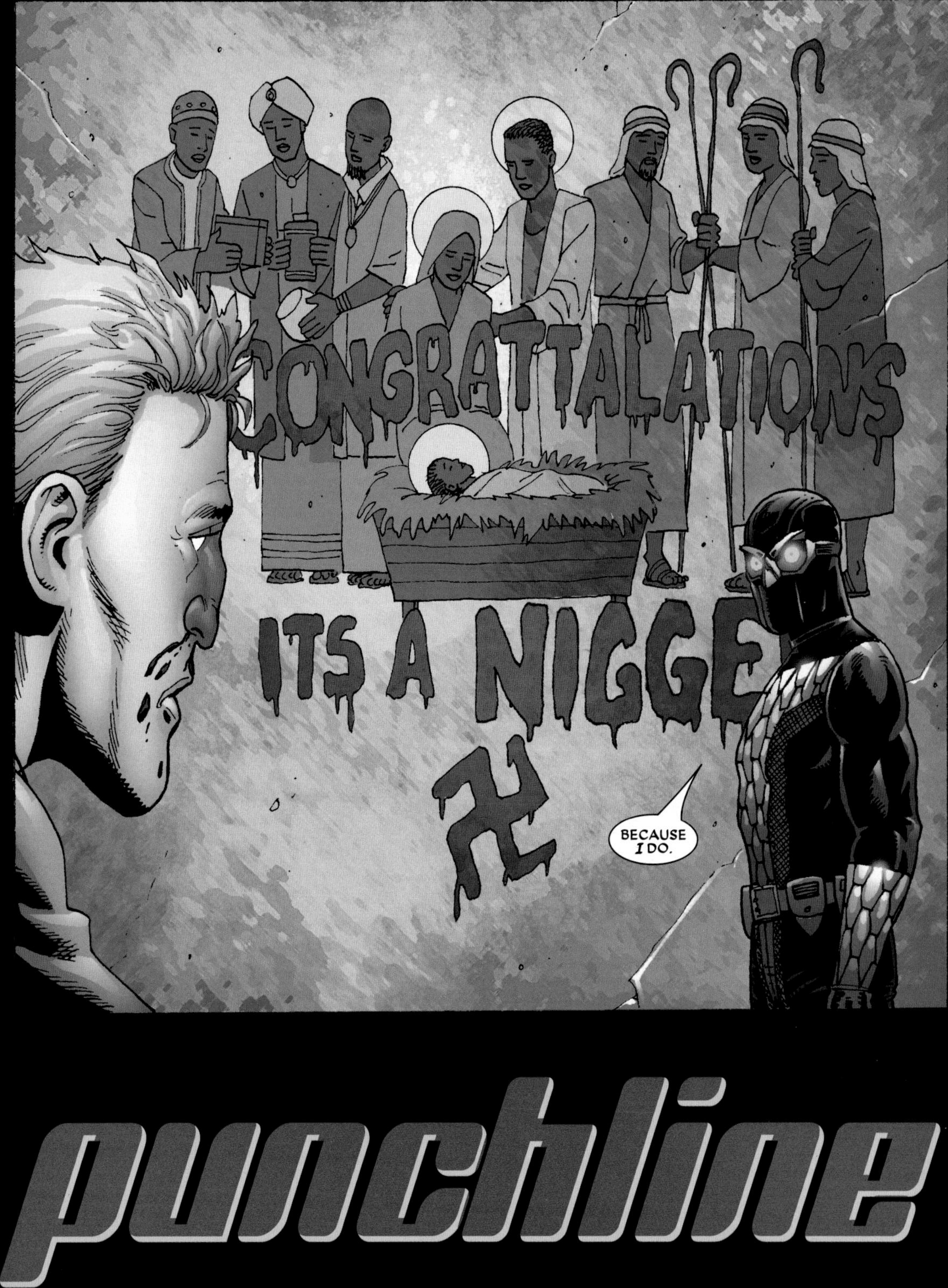
CONGRATTALATIONS
ITS A NIGGE
BECAUSE I DO.

punchline

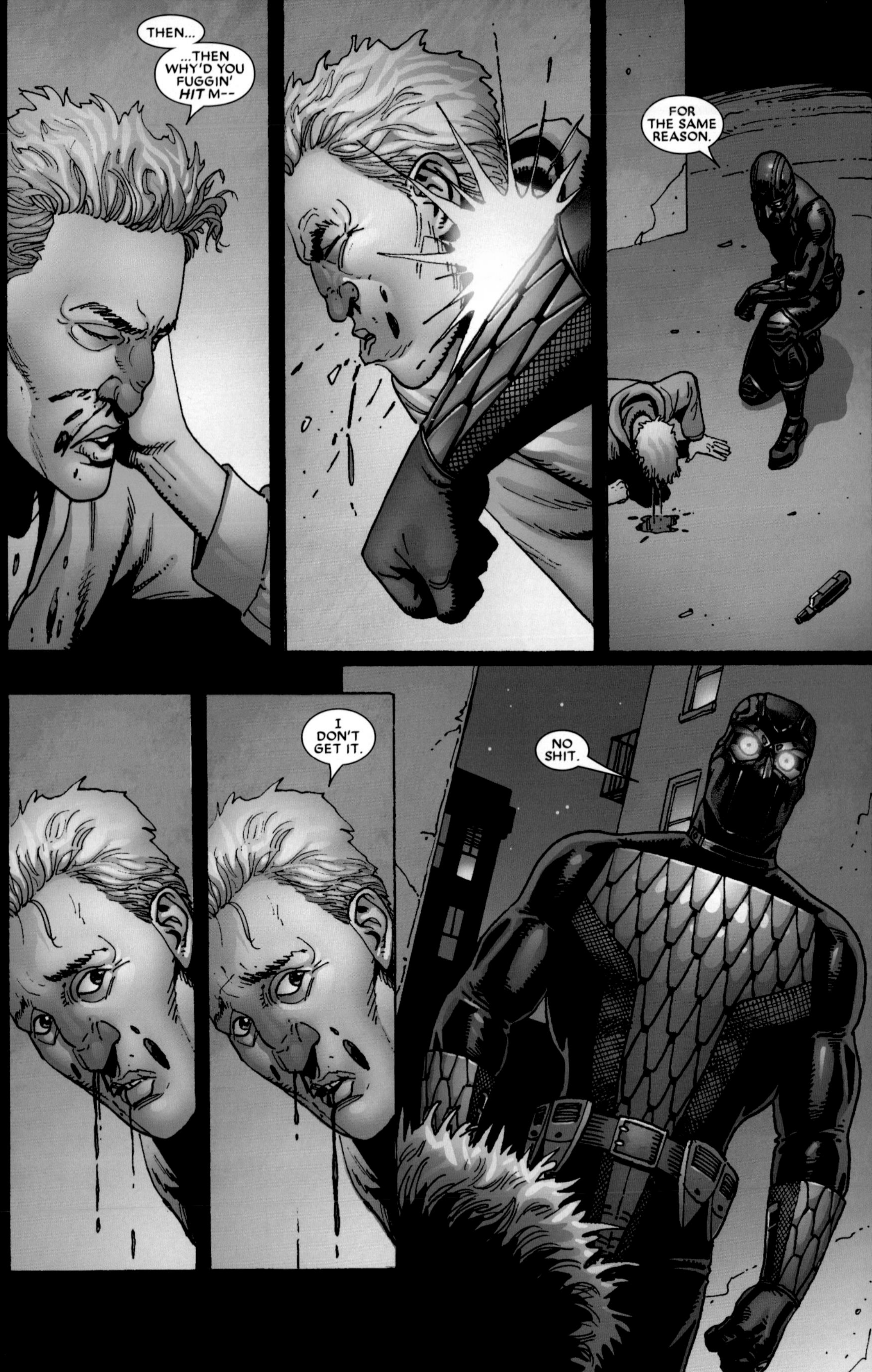
THEN...
...THEN WHY'D YOU FUGGIN' *HIT* M--
FOR THE SAME REASON.
I DON'T GET IT.
NO SHIT.

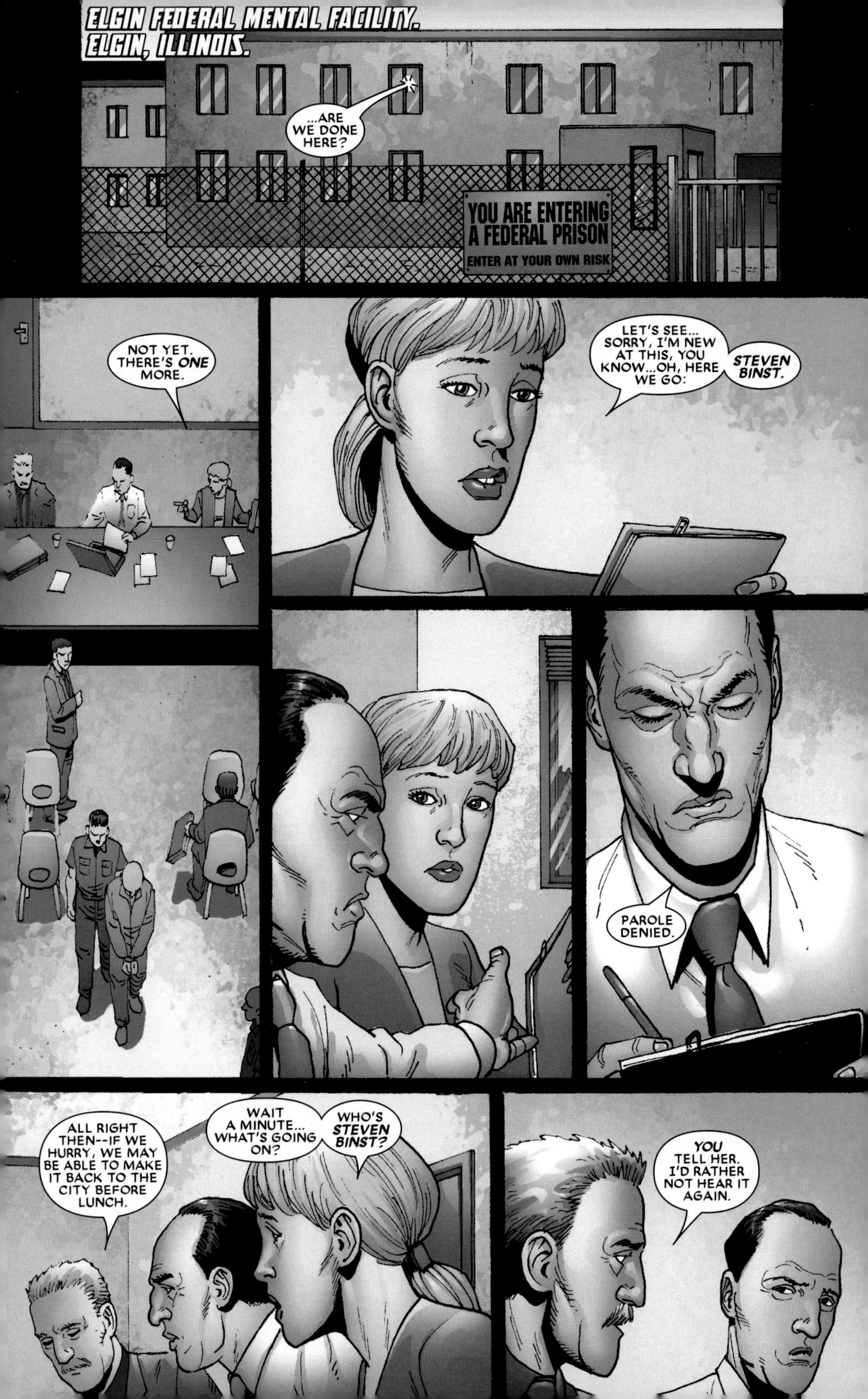
ELGIN FEDERAL MENTAL FACILITY.
ELGIN, ILLINOIS.
...ARE WE DONE HERE?
YOU ARE ENTERING A FEDERAL PRISON
ENTER AT YOUR OWN RISK
NOT YET. THERE'S ONE MORE.
LET'S SEE... SORRY, I'M NEW AT THIS, YOU KNOW...OH, HERE WE GO:
STEVEN BINST.
PAROLE DENIED.
ALL RIGHT THEN--IF WE HURRY, WE MAY BE ABLE TO MAKE IT BACK TO THE CITY BEFORE LUNCH.
WAIT A MINUTE... WHAT'S GOING ON?
WHO'S STEVEN BINST?
YOU TELL HER. I'D RATHER NOT HEAR IT AGAIN.

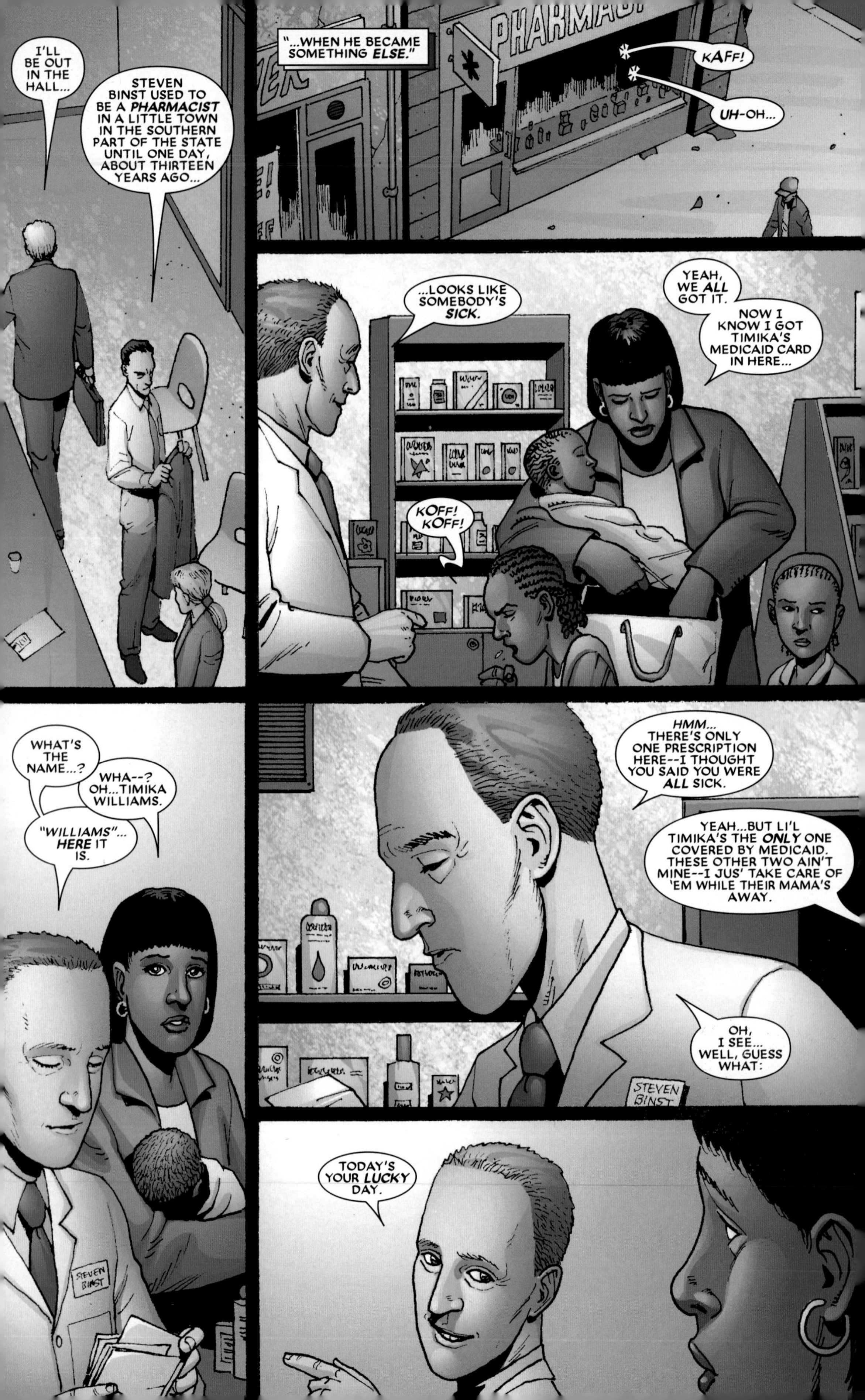
I'LL BE OUT IN THE HALL...
STEVEN BINST USED TO BE A *PHARMACIST* IN A LITTLE TOWN IN THE SOUTHERN PART OF THE STATE UNTIL ONE DAY, ABOUT THIRTEEN YEARS AGO...
"...WHEN HE BECAME SOMETHING *ELSE*."
PHARMACI
KAFF!
UH-OH...
...LOOKS LIKE SOMEBODY'S *SICK.*
YEAH, WE *ALL* GOT IT.
NOW I KNOW I GOT TIMIKA'S MEDICAID CARD IN HERE...
KOFF! KOFF!
WHAT'S THE NAME...?
WHA--? OH...TIMIKA WILLIAMS.
"WILLIAMS"... HERE IT IS.
STEVEN BINST
HMM... THERE'S ONLY ONE PRESCRIPTION HERE--I THOUGHT YOU SAID YOU WERE *ALL* SICK.
YEAH...BUT LI'L TIMIKA'S THE *ONLY* ONE COVERED BY MEDICAID. THESE OTHER TWO AIN'T MINE--I JUS' TAKE CARE OF 'EM WHILE THEIR MAMA'S AWAY.
OH, I SEE... WELL, GUESS WHAT:
STEVEN BINST
TODAY'S YOUR *LUCKY* DAY.

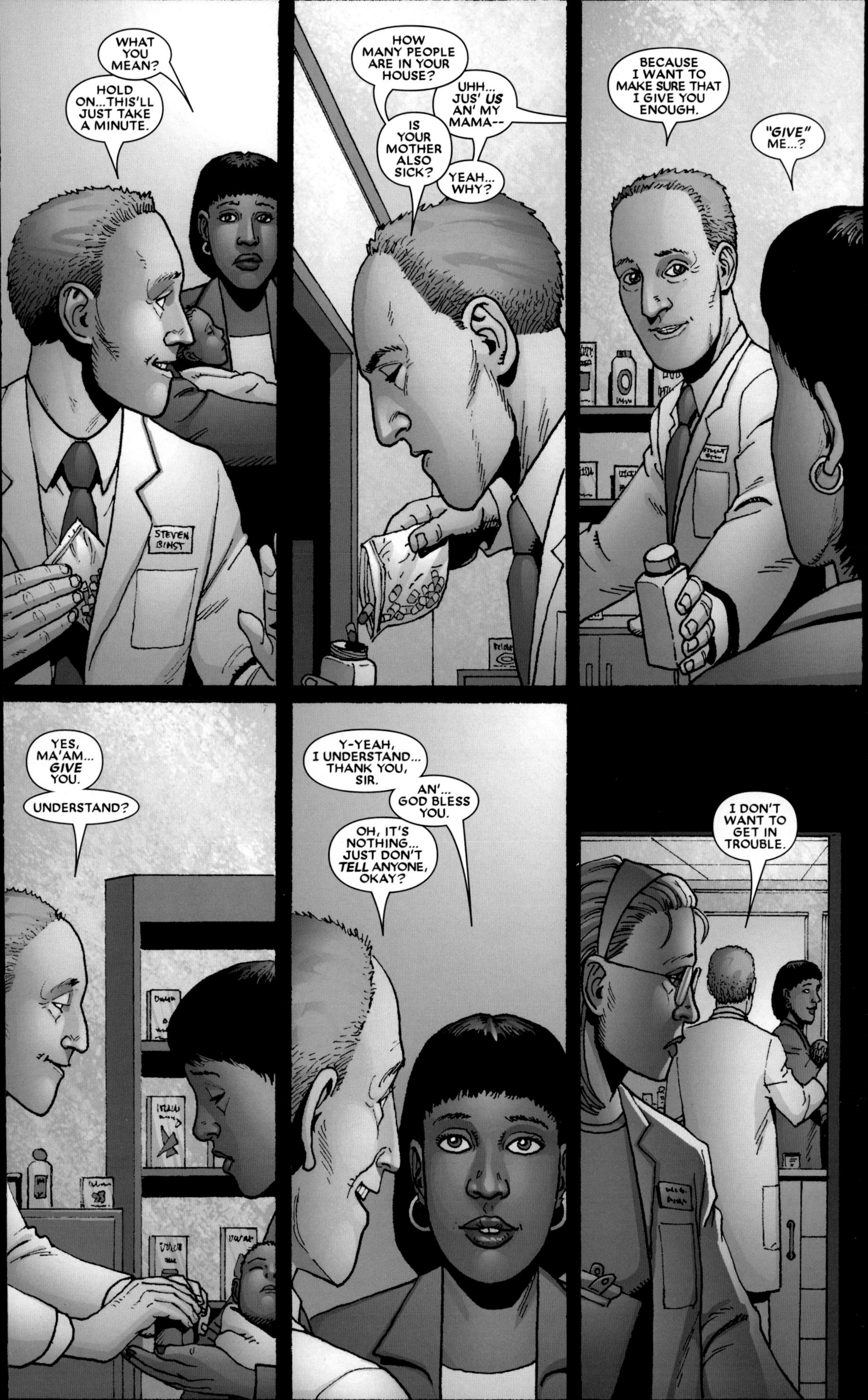
WHAT YOU MEAN?
HOLD ON...THIS'LL JUST TAKE A MINUTE.
STEVEN BINST
HOW MANY PEOPLE ARE IN YOUR HOUSE?
UHH... JUS' *US* AN' MY MAMA--
IS YOUR MOTHER ALSO SICK?
YEAH... WHY?
BECAUSE I WANT TO MAKE SURE THAT I GIVE YOU ENOUGH.
"*GIVE*" ME...?
YES, MA'AM... *GIVE* YOU.
UNDERSTAND?
Y-YEAH, I UNDERSTAND... THANK YOU, SIR.
AN'... GOD BLESS YOU.
OH, IT'S NOTHING... JUST DON'T *TELL* ANYONE, OKAY?
I DON'T WANT TO GET IN TROUBLE.

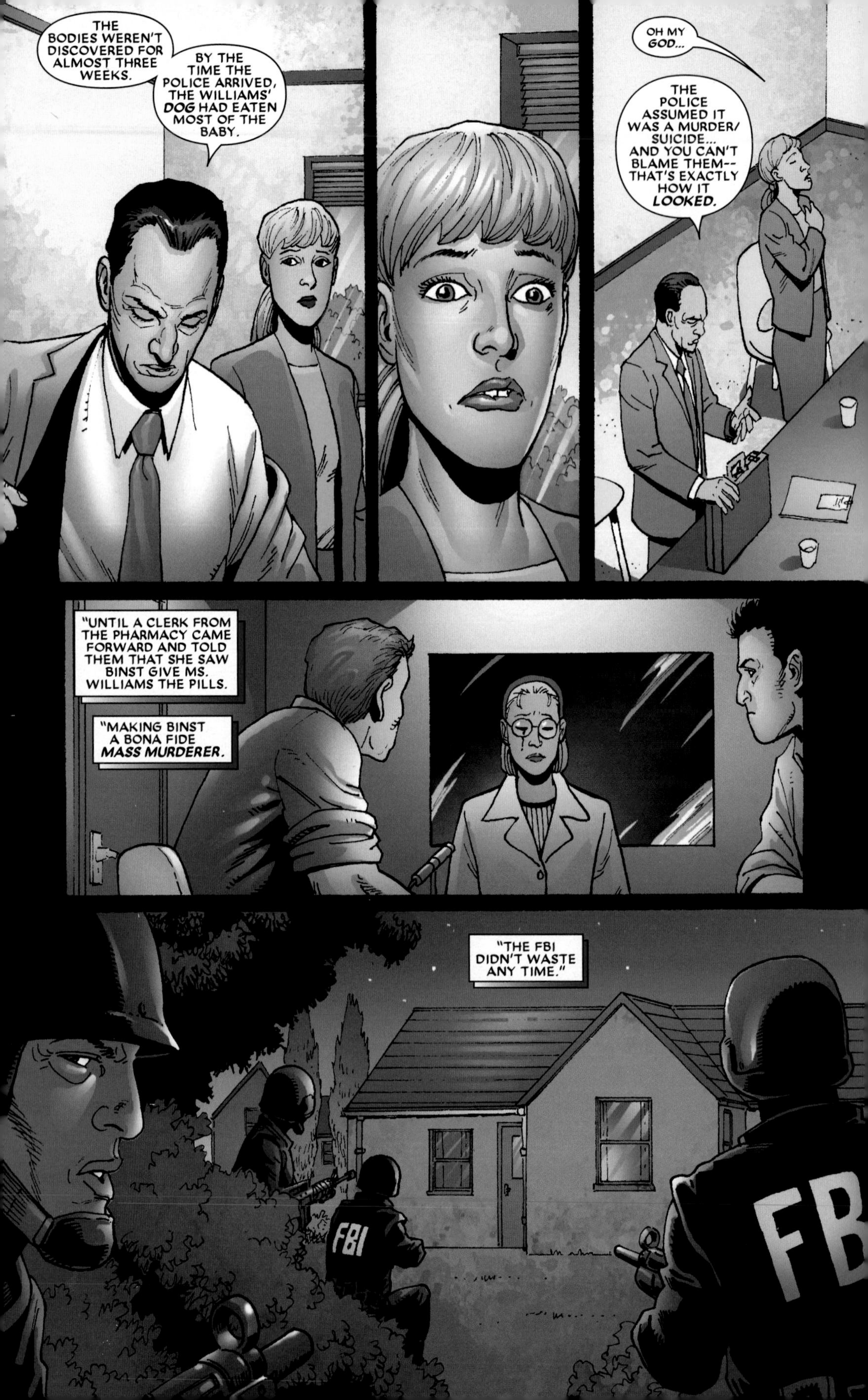
THE BODIES WEREN'T DISCOVERED FOR ALMOST THREE WEEKS.
BY THE TIME THE POLICE ARRIVED, THE WILLIAMS' *DOG* HAD EATEN MOST OF THE BABY.
OH MY *GOD...*
THE POLICE ASSUMED IT WAS A MURDER/ SUICIDE... AND YOU CAN'T BLAME THEM-- THAT'S EXACTLY HOW IT ***LOOKED.***
"UNTIL A CLERK FROM THE PHARMACY CAME FORWARD AND TOLD THEM THAT SHE SAW BINST GIVE MS. WILLIAMS THE PILLS.
"MAKING BINST A BONA FIDE ***MASS MURDERER.***
"THE FBI DIDN'T WASTE ANY TIME."
FBI
FB

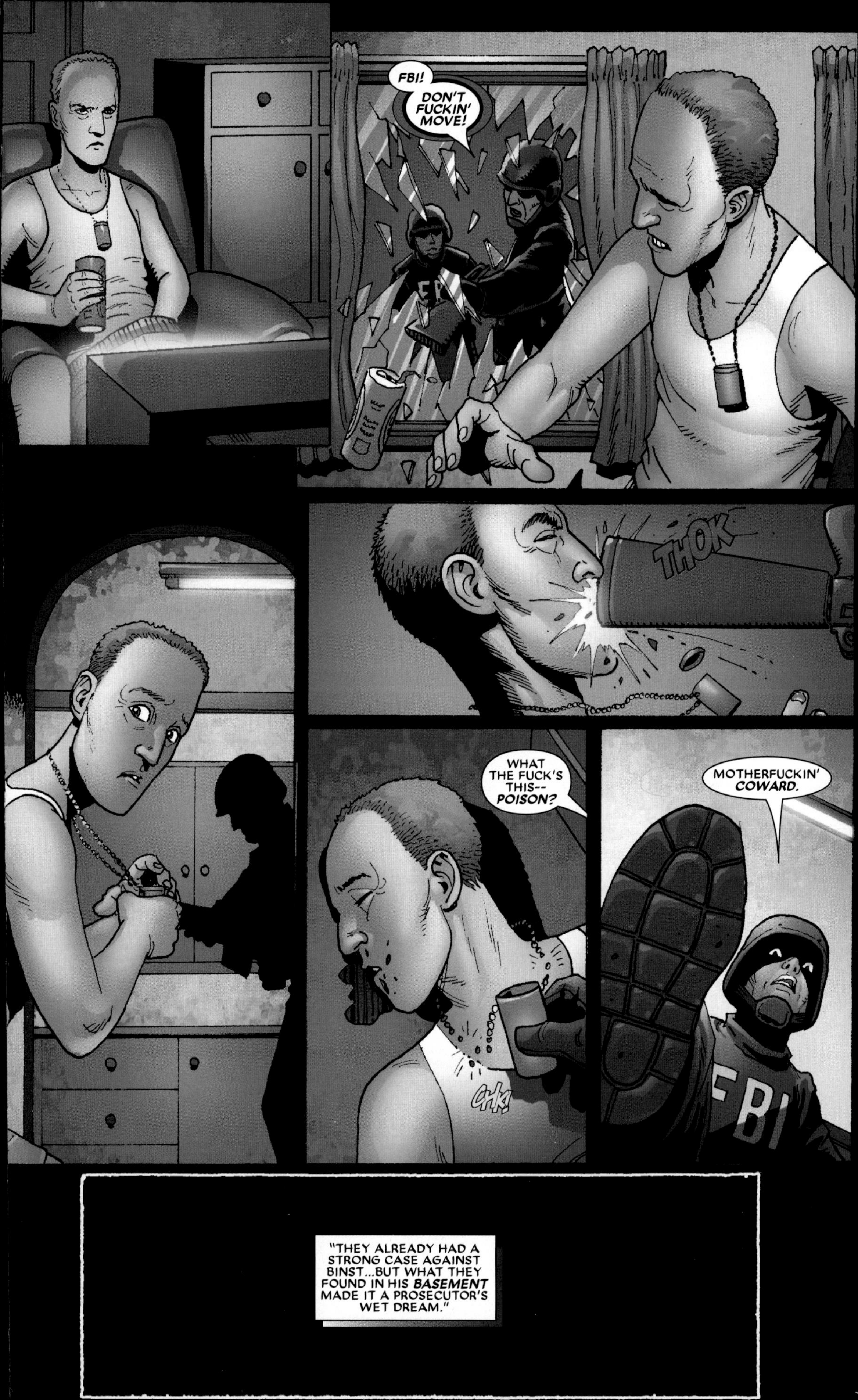
FBI!
DON'T FUCKIN' MOVE!
THOK
WHAT THE FUCK'S THIS-- POISON?
CHK!
MOTHERFUCKIN' COWARD.
"THEY ALREADY HAD A STRONG CASE AGAINST BINST...BUT WHAT THEY FOUND IN HIS BASEMENT MADE IT A PROSECUTOR'S WET DREAM."

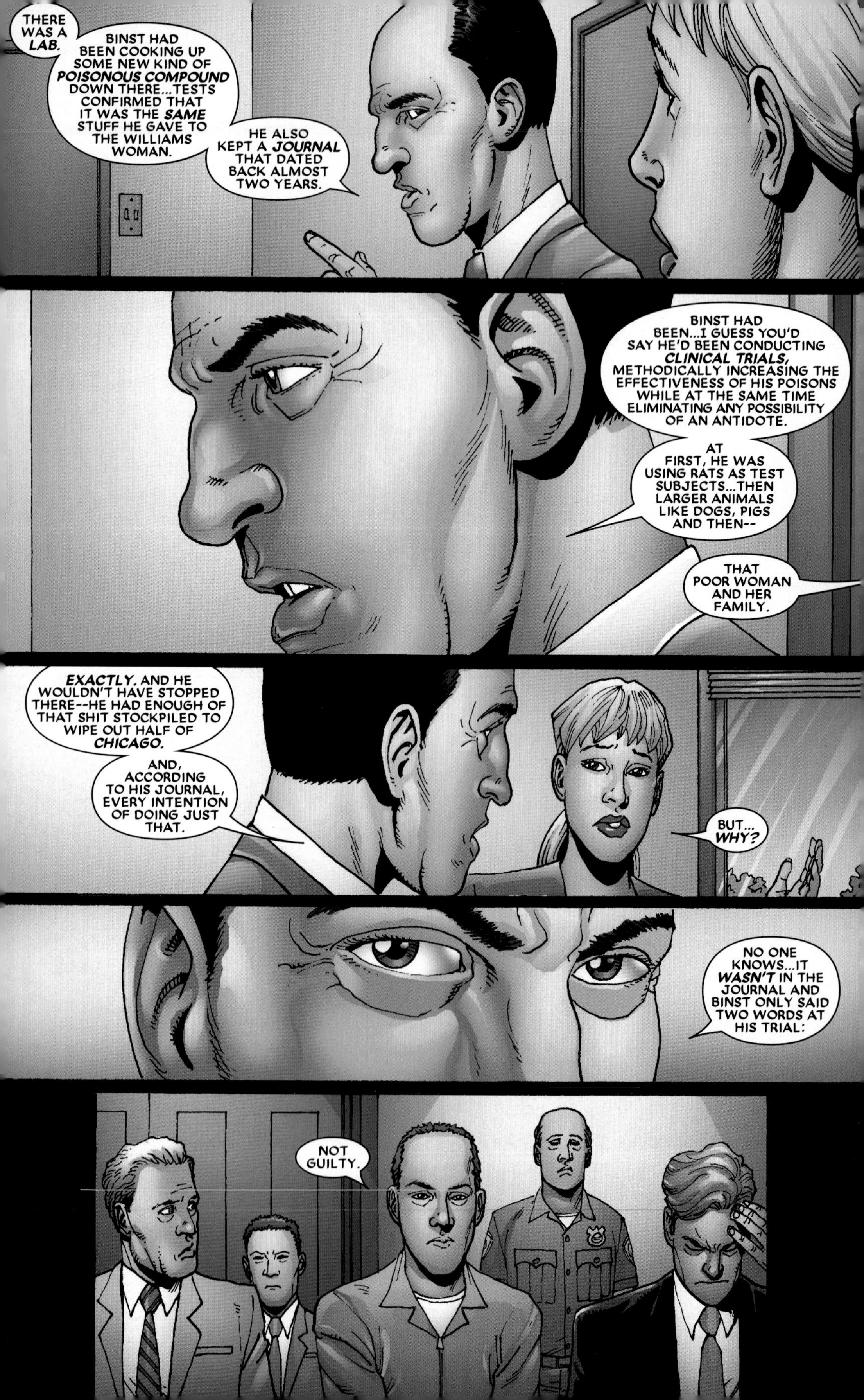
THERE WAS A *LAB.*
BINST HAD BEEN COOKING UP SOME NEW KIND OF *POISONOUS COMPOUND* DOWN THERE...TESTS CONFIRMED THAT IT WAS THE *SAME* STUFF HE GAVE TO THE WILLIAMS WOMAN.
HE ALSO KEPT A *JOURNAL* THAT DATED BACK ALMOST TWO YEARS.
BINST HAD BEEN...I GUESS YOU'D SAY HE'D BEEN CONDUCTING *CLINICAL TRIALS,* METHODICALLY INCREASING THE EFFECTIVENESS OF HIS POISONS WHILE AT THE SAME TIME ELIMINATING ANY POSSIBILITY OF AN ANTIDOTE.
AT FIRST, HE WAS USING RATS AS TEST SUBJECTS...THEN LARGER ANIMALS LIKE DOGS, PIGS AND THEN--
THAT POOR WOMAN AND HER FAMILY.
EXACTLY. AND HE WOULDN'T HAVE STOPPED THERE--HE HAD ENOUGH OF THAT SHIT STOCKPILED TO WIPE OUT HALF OF *CHICAGO.*
AND, ACCORDING TO HIS JOURNAL, EVERY INTENTION OF DOING JUST THAT.
BUT... *WHY?*
NO ONE KNOWS...IT *WASN'T* IN THE JOURNAL AND BINST ONLY SAID TWO WORDS AT HIS TRIAL:
NOT GUILTY.

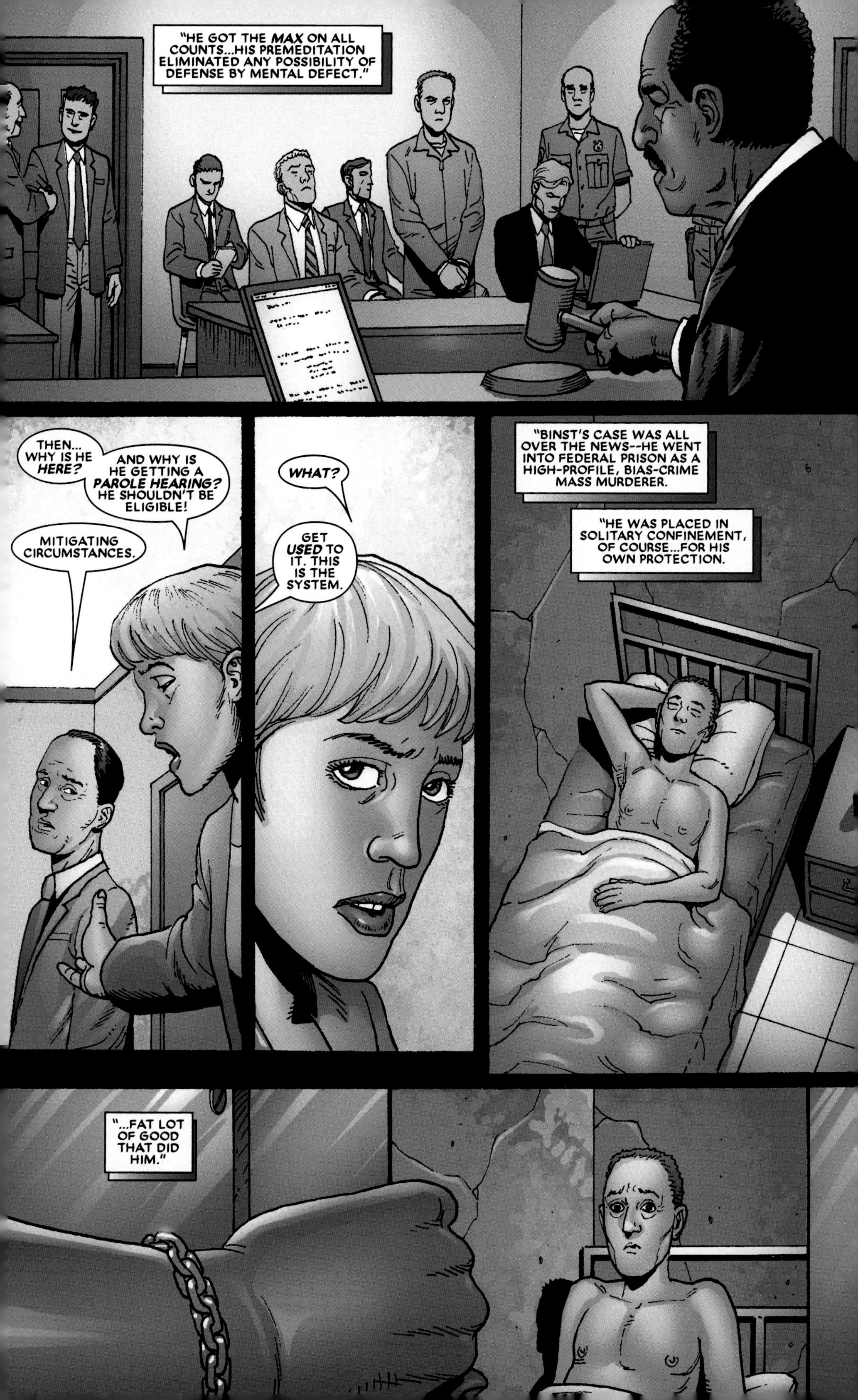
"HE GOT THE *MAX* ON ALL COUNTS...HIS PREMEDITATION ELIMINATED ANY POSSIBILITY OF DEFENSE BY MENTAL DEFECT."
THEN... WHY IS HE *HERE?*
AND WHY IS HE GETTING A *PAROLE HEARING?* HE SHOULDN'T BE ELIGIBLE!
MITIGATING CIRCUMSTANCES.
WHAT?
GET *USED* TO IT. THIS IS THE SYSTEM.
"BINST'S CASE WAS ALL OVER THE NEWS--HE WENT INTO FEDERAL PRISON AS A HIGH-PROFILE, BIAS-CRIME MASS MURDERER.
"HE WAS PLACED IN SOLITARY CONFINEMENT, OF COURSE...FOR HIS OWN PROTECTION.
"...FAT LOT OF GOOD THAT DID HIM."

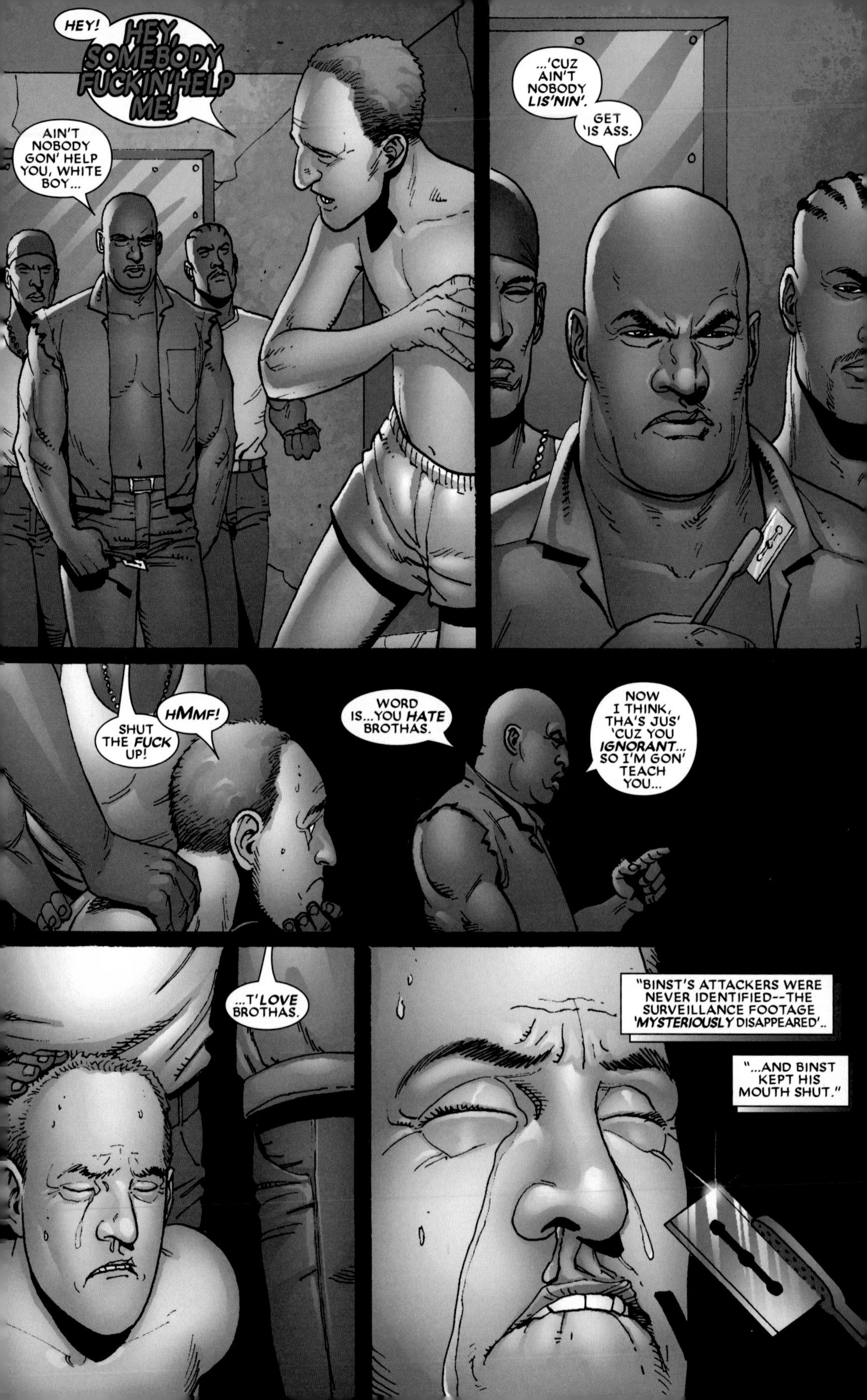
HEY!
HEY, SOMEBODY FUCKIN' HELP ME!
AIN'T NOBODY GON' HELP YOU, WHITE BOY...
...'CUZ AIN'T NOBODY LIS'NIN'.
GET 'IS ASS.
HMMF!
SHUT THE FUCK UP!
WORD IS...YOU HATE BROTHAS.
NOW I THINK, THA'S JUS' 'CUZ YOU IGNORANT... SO I'M GON' TEACH YOU...
...T'LOVE BROTHAS.
"BINST'S ATTACKERS WERE NEVER IDENTIFIED--THE SURVEILLANCE FOOTAGE 'MYSTERIOUSLY DISAPPEARED'..
"...AND BINST KEPT HIS MOUTH SHUT."

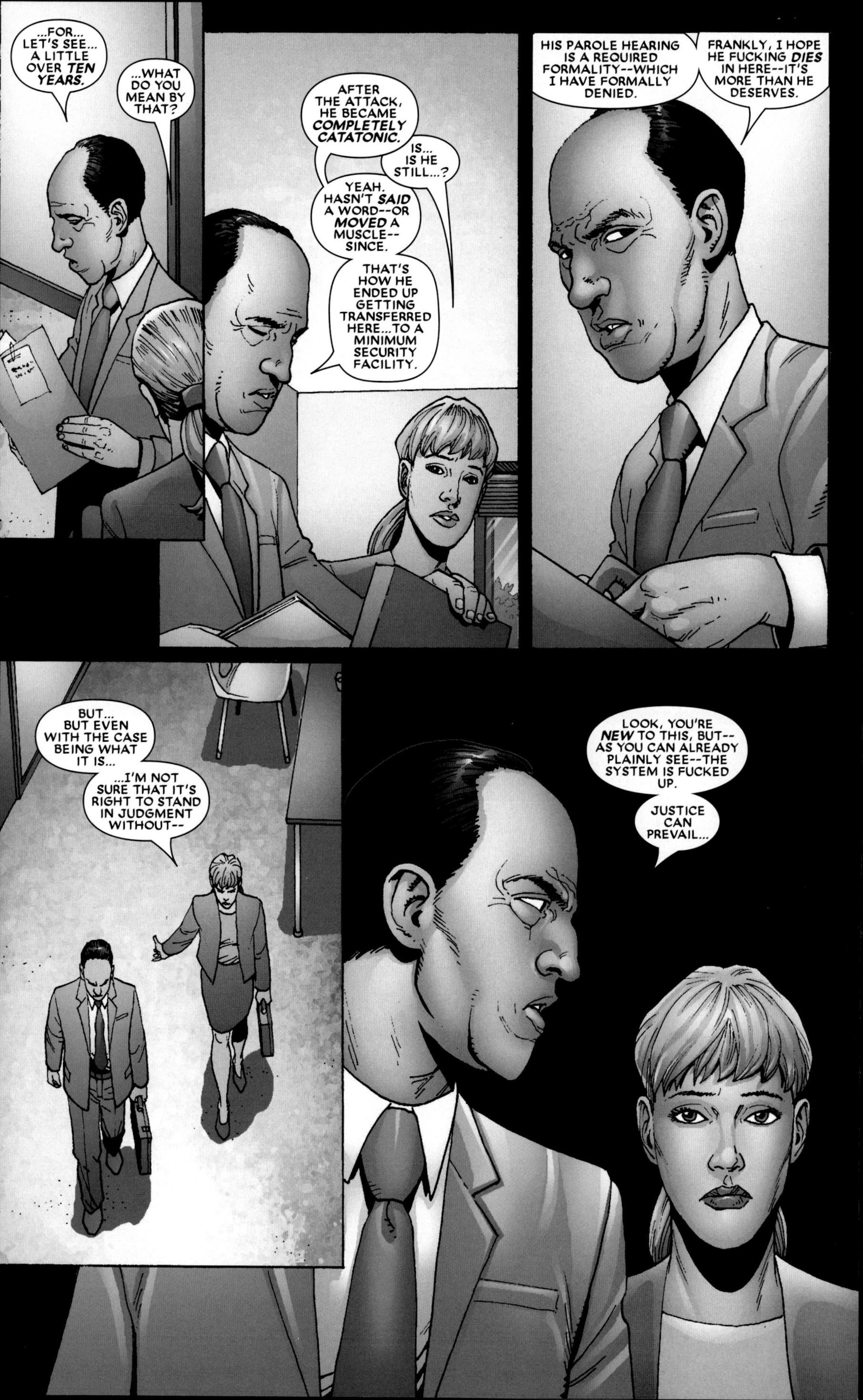
...FOR... LET'S SEE... A LITTLE OVER TEN YEARS.
...WHAT DO YOU MEAN BY THAT?
AFTER THE ATTACK, HE BECAME COMPLETELY CATATONIC.
IS... IS HE STILL...?
YEAH. HASN'T SAID A WORD--OR MOVED A MUSCLE--SINCE.
THAT'S HOW HE ENDED UP GETTING TRANSFERRED HERE...TO A MINIMUM SECURITY FACILITY.
HIS PAROLE HEARING IS A REQUIRED FORMALITY--WHICH I HAVE FORMALLY DENIED.
FRANKLY, I HOPE HE FUCKING DIES IN HERE--IT'S MORE THAN HE DESERVES.
BUT... BUT EVEN WITH THE CASE BEING WHAT IT IS...
...I'M NOT SURE THAT IT'S RIGHT TO STAND IN JUDGMENT WITHOUT--
LOOK, YOU'RE NEW TO THIS, BUT--AS YOU CAN ALREADY PLAINLY SEE--THE SYSTEM IS FUCKED UP.
JUSTICE CAN PREVAIL...

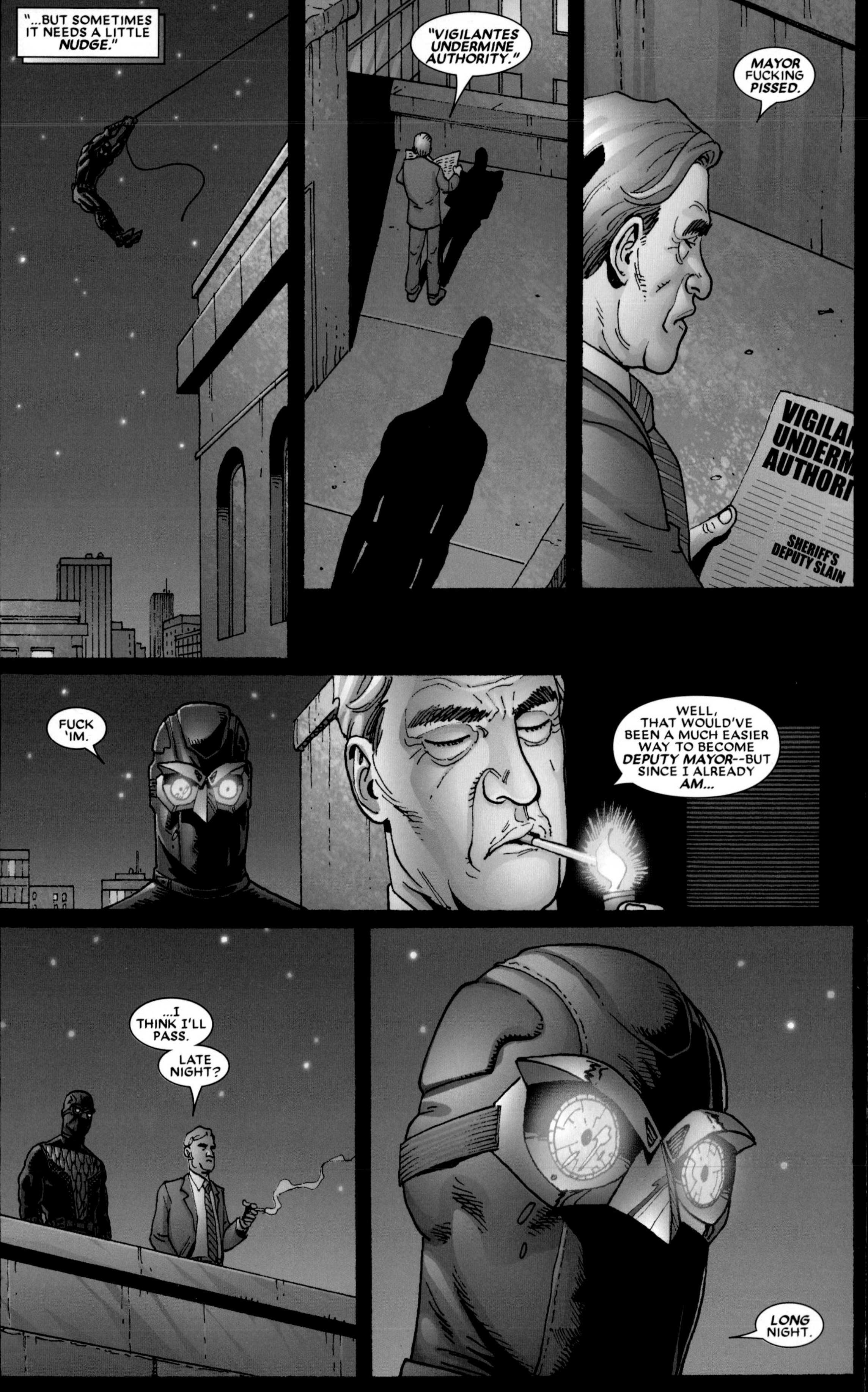
"...BUT SOMETIMES IT NEEDS A LITTLE NUDGE."
"VIGILANTES UNDERMINE AUTHORITY."
MAYOR FUCKING PISSED.
VIGILA UNDERM AUTHORI
SHERIFF'S DEPUTY SLAIN
FUCK 'IM.
WELL, THAT WOULD'VE BEEN A MUCH EASIER WAY TO BECOME DEPUTY MAYOR--BUT SINCE I ALREADY AM...
...I THINK I'LL PASS.
LATE NIGHT?
LONG NIGHT.

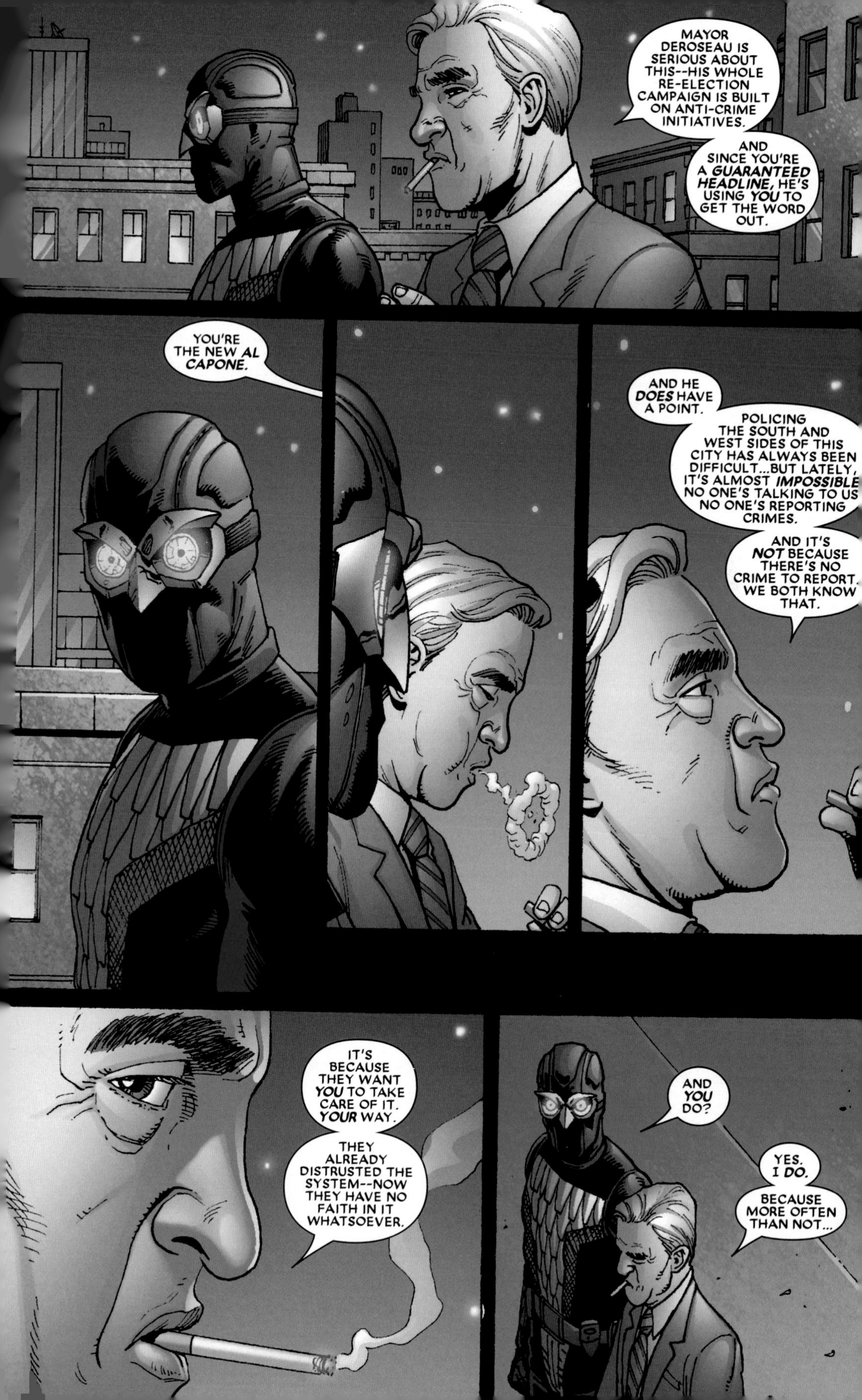
MAYOR DEROSEAU IS SERIOUS ABOUT THIS--HIS WHOLE RE-ELECTION CAMPAIGN IS BUILT ON ANTI-CRIME INITIATIVES.
AND SINCE YOU'RE A GUARANTEED HEADLINE, HE'S USING YOU TO GET THE WORD OUT.
YOU'RE THE NEW AL CAPONE.
AND HE DOES HAVE A POINT.
POLICING THE SOUTH AND WEST SIDES OF THIS CITY HAS ALWAYS BEEN DIFFICULT...BUT LATELY, IT'S ALMOST IMPOSSIBLE NO ONE'S TALKING TO US NO ONE'S REPORTING CRIMES.
AND IT'S NOT BECAUSE THERE'S NO CRIME TO REPORT. WE BOTH KNOW THAT.
IT'S BECAUSE THEY WANT YOU TO TAKE CARE OF IT. YOUR WAY.
THEY ALREADY DISTRUSTED THE SYSTEM--NOW THEY HAVE NO FAITH IN IT WHATSOEVER.
AND YOU DO?
YES. I DO.
BECAUSE MORE OFTEN THAN NOT...

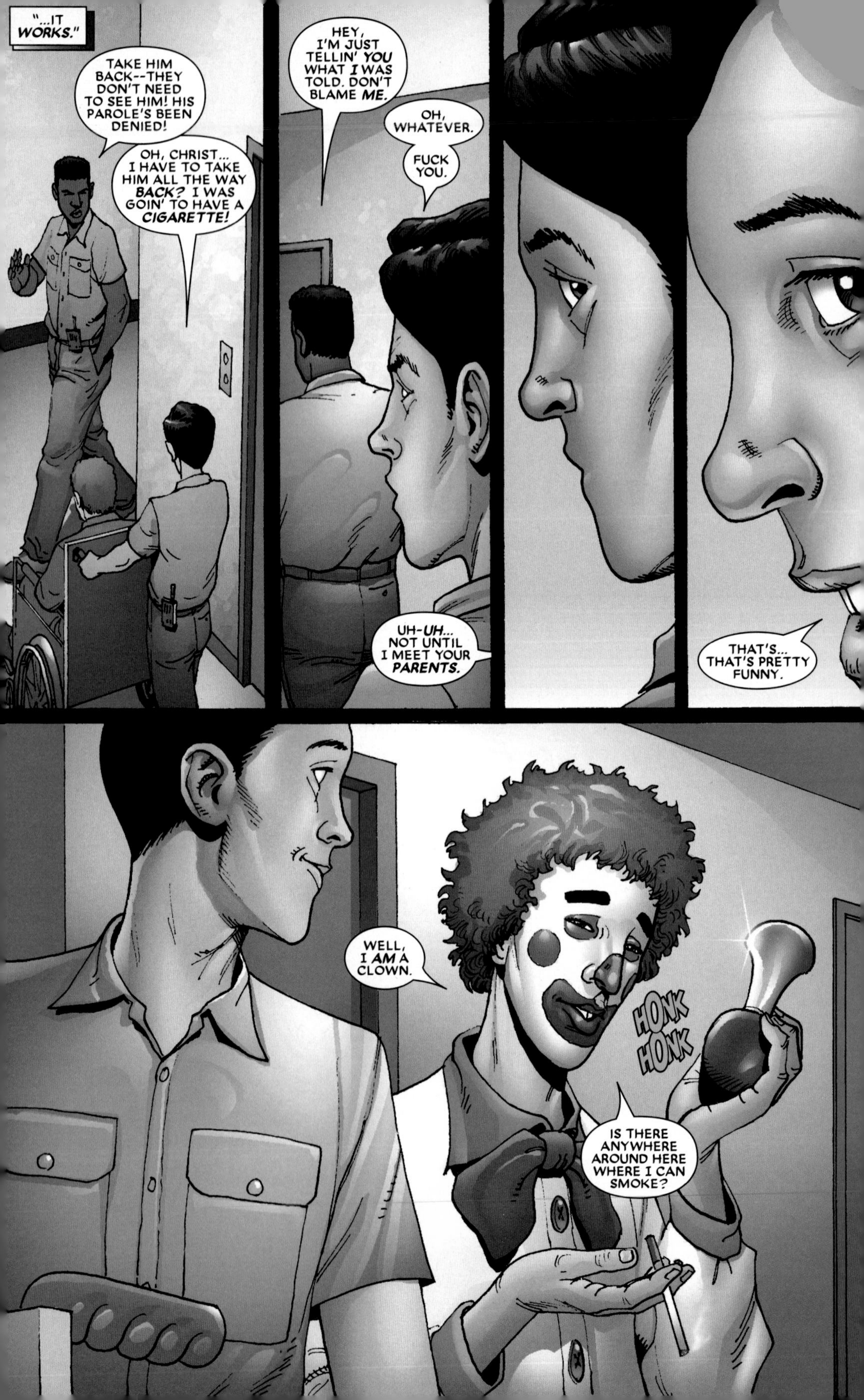
"...IT WORKS."
TAKE HIM BACK--THEY DON'T NEED TO SEE HIM! HIS PAROLE'S BEEN DENIED!
OH, CHRIST... I HAVE TO TAKE HIM ALL THE WAY BACK? I WAS GOIN' TO HAVE A CIGARETTE!
HEY, I'M JUST TELLIN' YOU WHAT I WAS TOLD. DON'T BLAME ME.
OH, WHATEVER.
FUCK YOU.
UH-UH... NOT UNTIL I MEET YOUR PARENTS.
THAT'S... THAT'S PRETTY FUNNY.
WELL, I AM A CLOWN.
HONK HONK
IS THERE ANYWHERE AROUND HERE WHERE I CAN SMOKE?

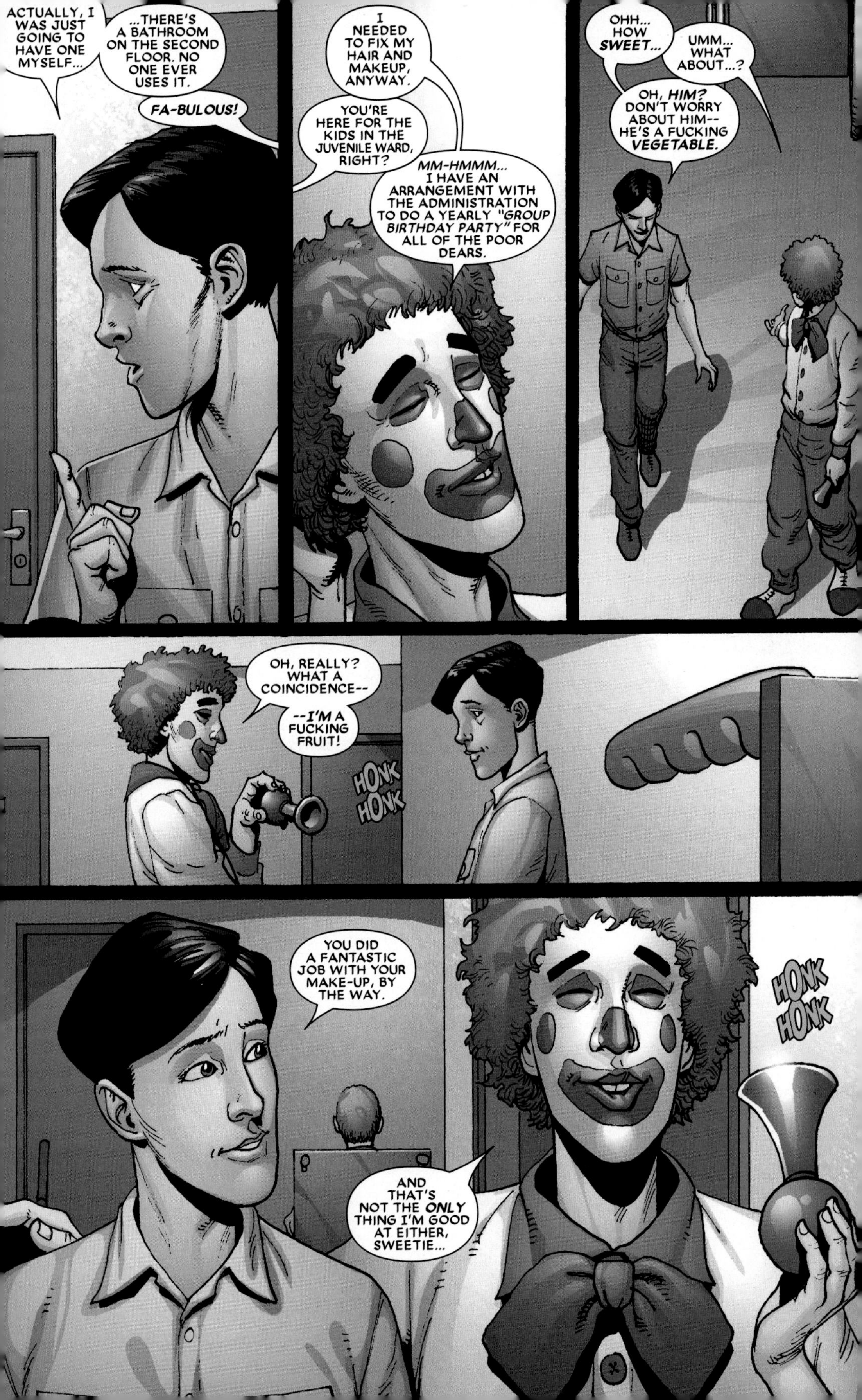
ACTUALLY, I WAS JUST GOING TO HAVE ONE MYSELF...
...THERE'S A BATHROOM ON THE SECOND FLOOR. NO ONE EVER USES IT.
FA-BULOUS!
I NEEDED TO FIX MY HAIR AND MAKEUP, ANYWAY.
YOU'RE HERE FOR THE KIDS IN THE JUVENILE WARD, RIGHT?
MM-HMMM... I HAVE AN ARRANGEMENT WITH THE ADMINISTRATION TO DO A YEARLY "GROUP BIRTHDAY PARTY" FOR ALL OF THE POOR DEARS.
OHH... HOW SWEET...
UMM... WHAT ABOUT...?
OH, HIM? DON'T WORRY ABOUT HIM-- HE'S A FUCKING VEGETABLE.
OH, REALLY? WHAT A COINCIDENCE--
--I'M A FUCKING FRUIT!
HONK HONK
YOU DID A FANTASTIC JOB WITH YOUR MAKE-UP, BY THE WAY.
AND THAT'S NOT THE ONLY THING I'M GOOD AT EITHER, SWEETIE...
HONK HONK

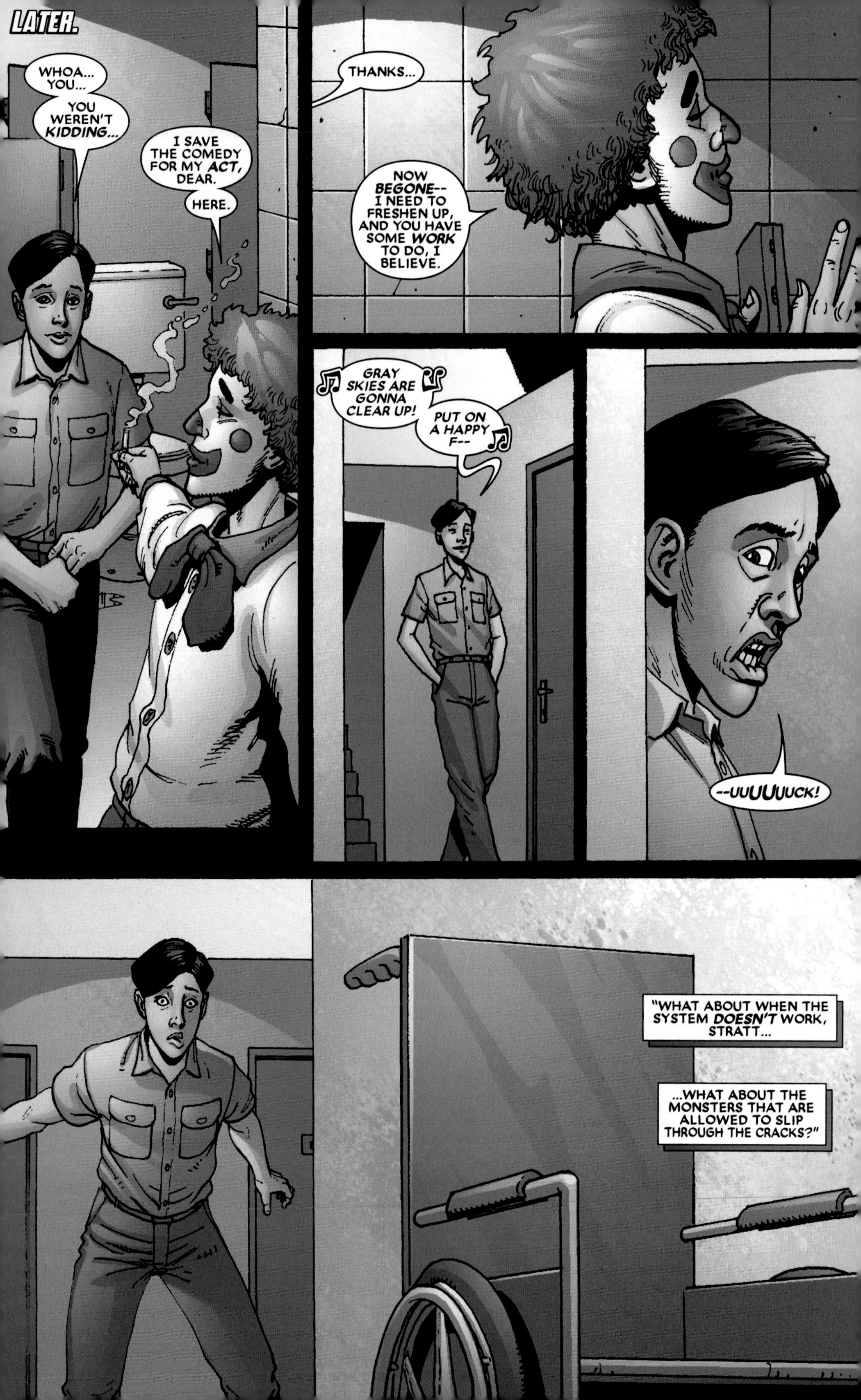
LATER.
WHOA... YOU...
YOU WEREN'T KIDDING...
I SAVE THE COMEDY FOR MY ACT, DEAR.
HERE.
THANKS...
NOW BEGONE-- I NEED TO FRESHEN UP, AND YOU HAVE SOME WORK TO DO, I BELIEVE.
GRAY SKIES ARE GONNA CLEAR UP!
PUT ON A HAPPY F--
--UUUUUUCK!
"WHAT ABOUT WHEN THE SYSTEM DOESN'T WORK, STRATT...
...WHAT ABOUT THE MONSTERS THAT ARE ALLOWED TO SLIP THROUGH THE CRACKS?"

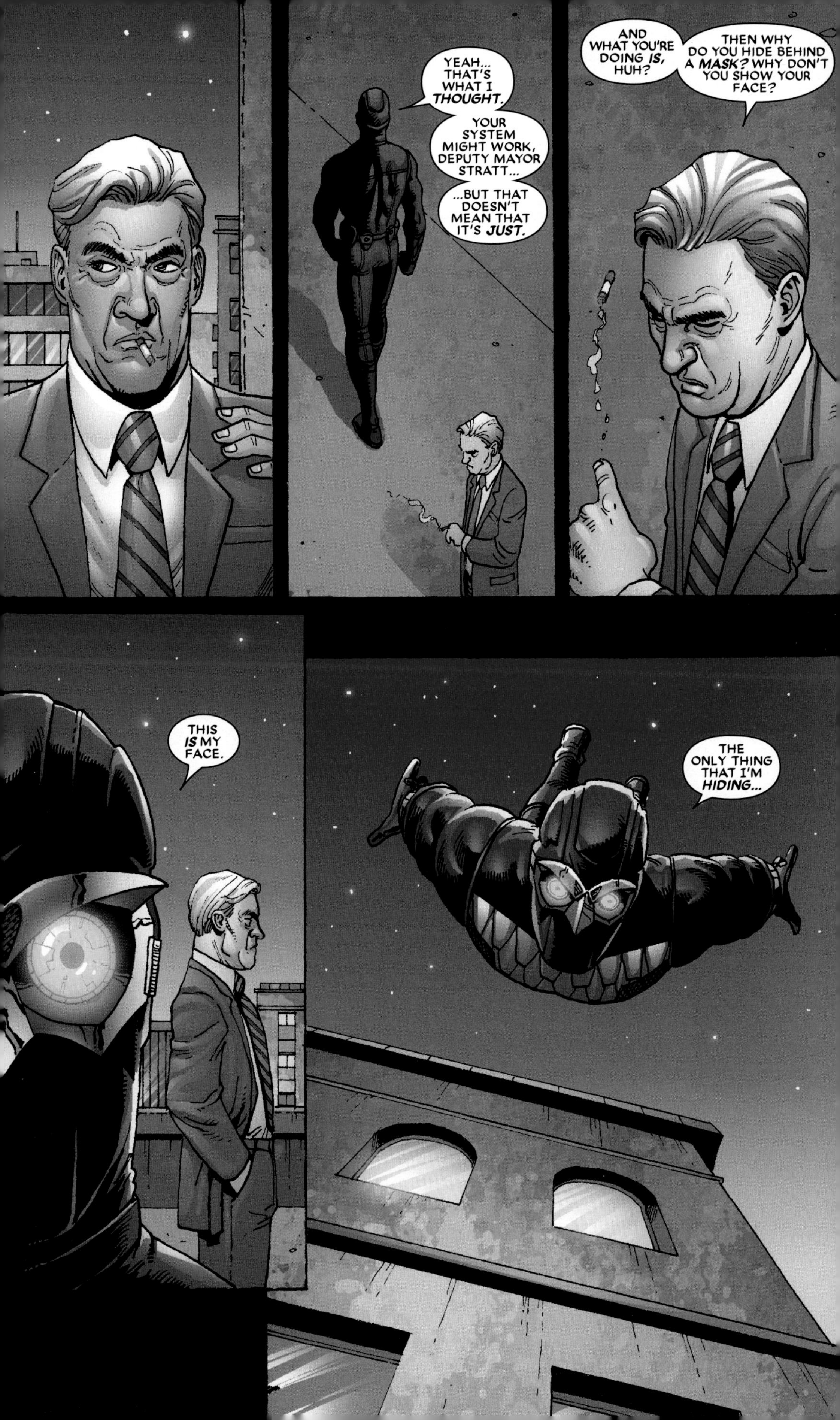

YEAH... THAT'S WHAT I *THOUGHT.*
YOUR SYSTEM MIGHT WORK, DEPUTY MAYOR STRATT...
...BUT THAT DOESN'T MEAN THAT IT'S *JUST.*
AND WHAT YOU'RE DOING *IS,* HUH?
THEN WHY DO YOU HIDE BEHIND A *MASK?* WHY DON'T YOU SHOW YOUR FACE?
THIS *IS* MY FACE.
THE ONLY THING THAT I'M *HIDING...*

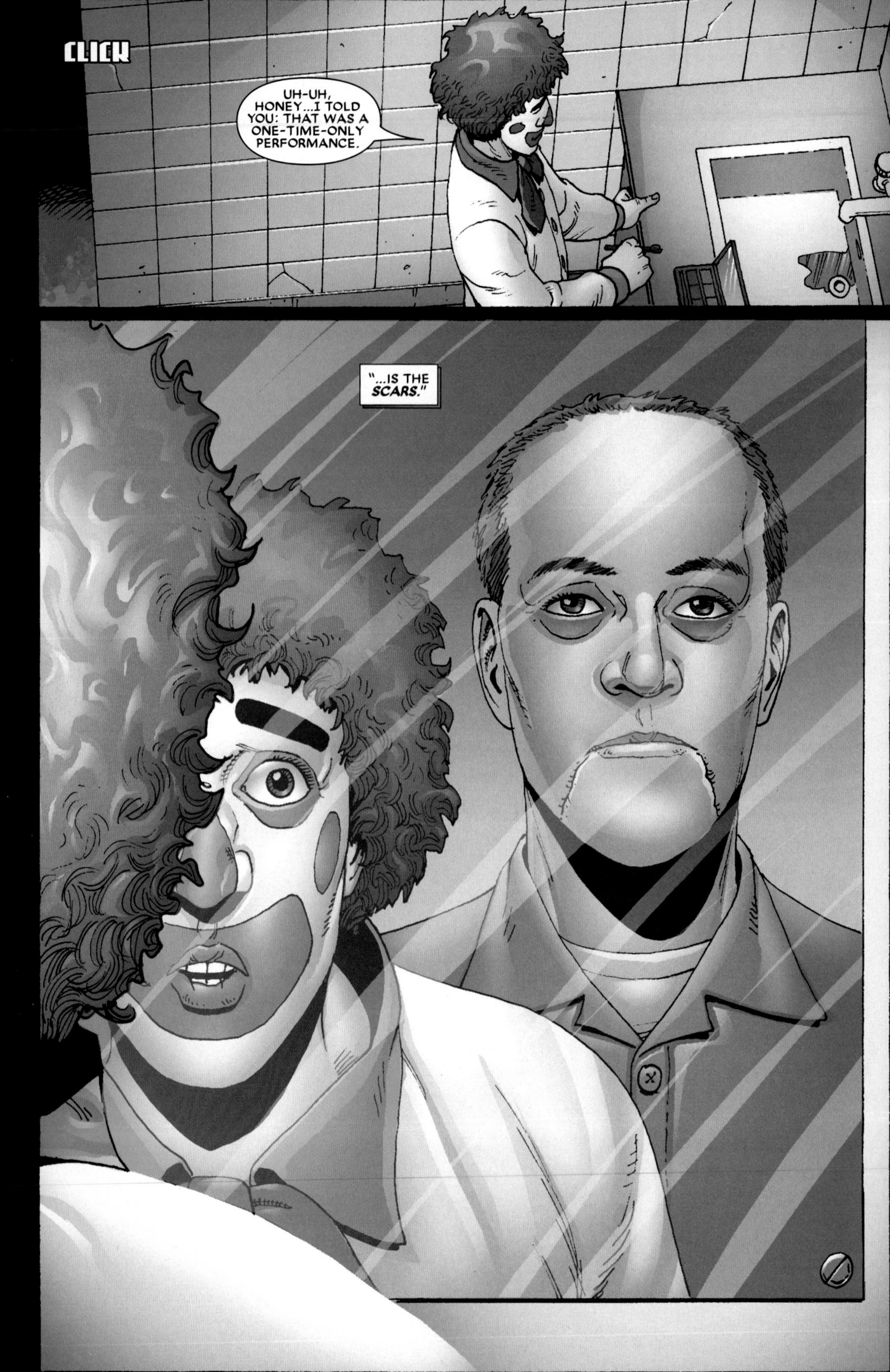
CLICK
UH-UH, HONEY...I TOLD YOU: THAT WAS A ONE-TIME-ONLY PERFORMANCE.
"...IS THE *SCARS.*"

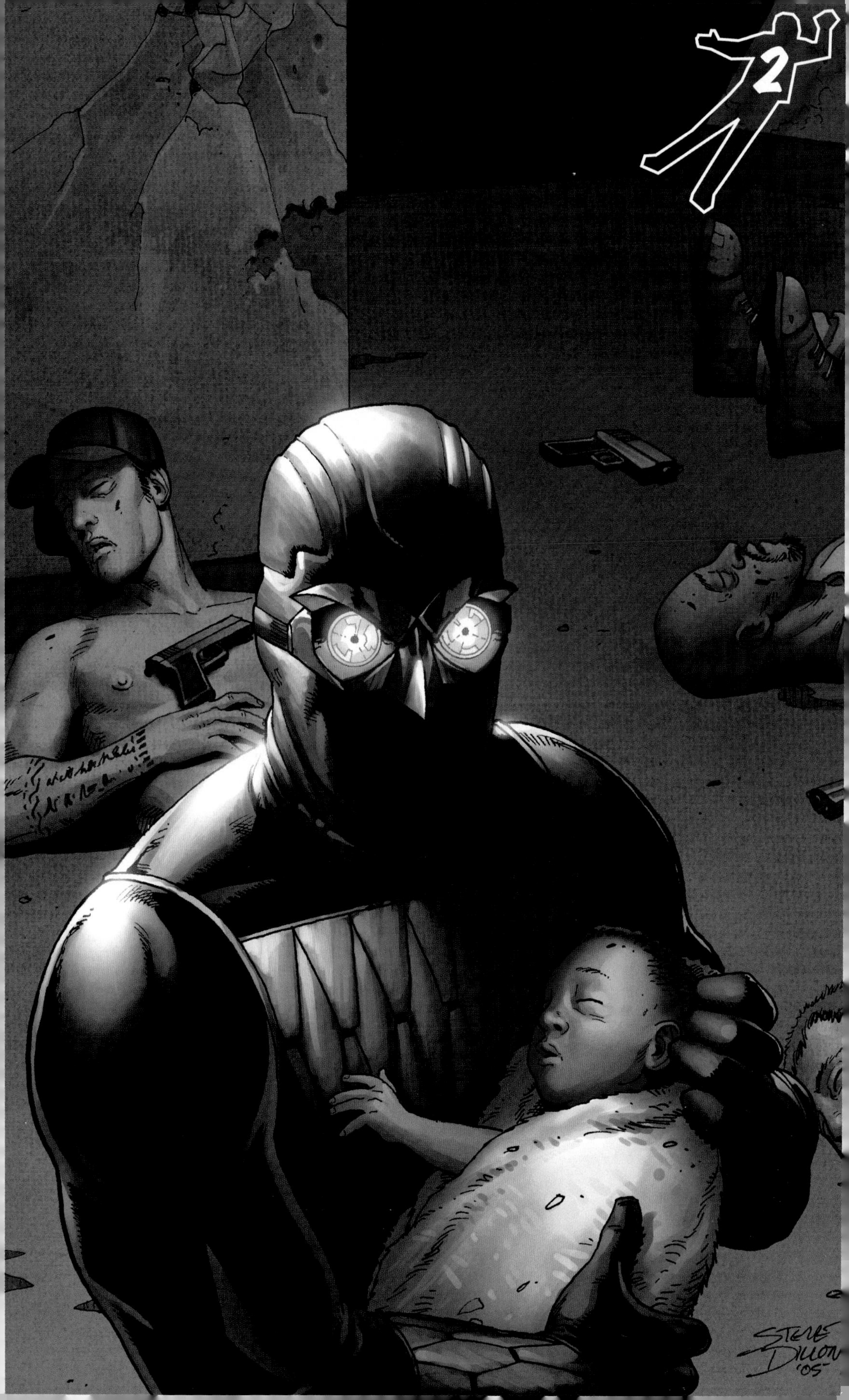
2
STEVE DILLON '05

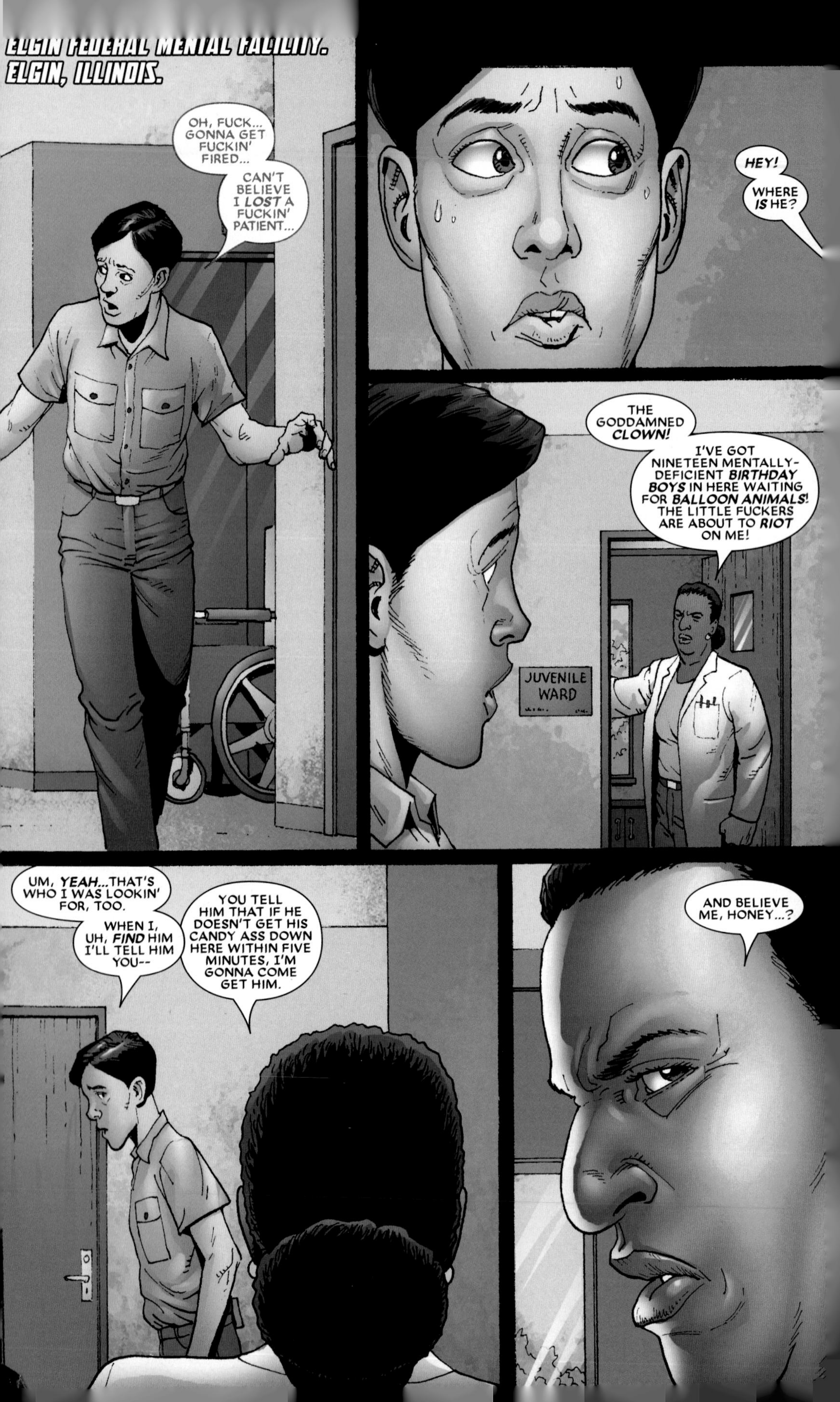
ELGIN FEDERAL MENTAL FACILITY. ELGIN, ILLINOIS.
OH, FUCK... GONNA GET FUCKIN' FIRED...
CAN'T BELIEVE I LOST A FUCKIN' PATIENT...
HEY!
WHERE IS HE?
THE GODDAMNED CLOWN!
I'VE GOT NINETEEN MENTALLY-DEFICIENT BIRTHDAY BOYS IN HERE WAITING FOR BALLOON ANIMALS! THE LITTLE FUCKERS ARE ABOUT TO RIOT ON ME!
JUVENILE WARD
UM, YEAH...THAT'S WHO I WAS LOOKIN' FOR, TOO.
WHEN I, UH, FIND HIM I'LL TELL HIM YOU--
YOU TELL HIM THAT IF HE DOESN'T GET HIS CANDY ASS DOWN HERE WITHIN FIVE MINUTES, I'M GONNA COME GET HIM.
AND BELIEVE ME, HONEY...?

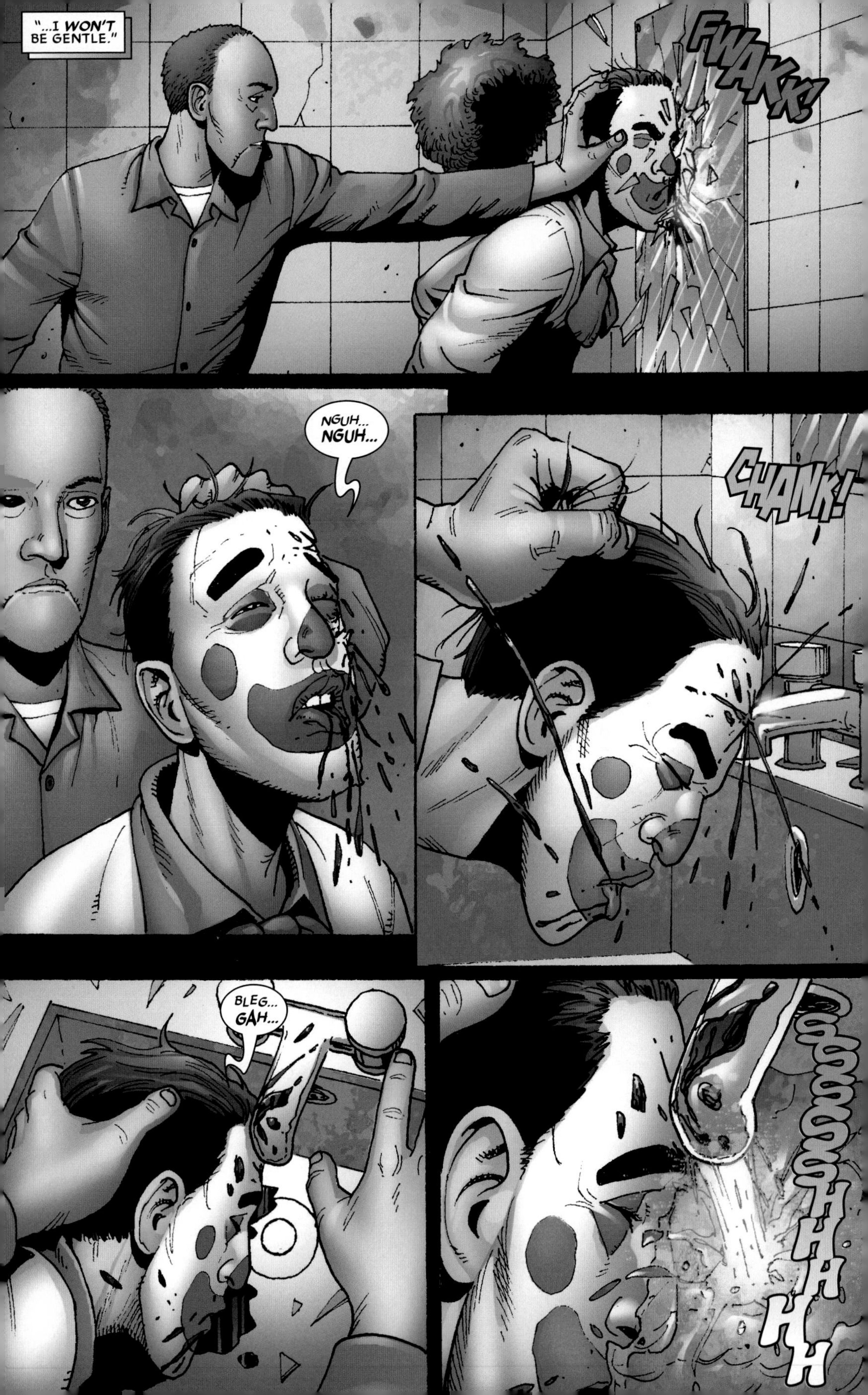
"...I WON'T BE GENTLE."
FWAKK!
NGUH... NGUH...
CHANK!
BLEG... GAH...
GSSSSSSHHHHHH

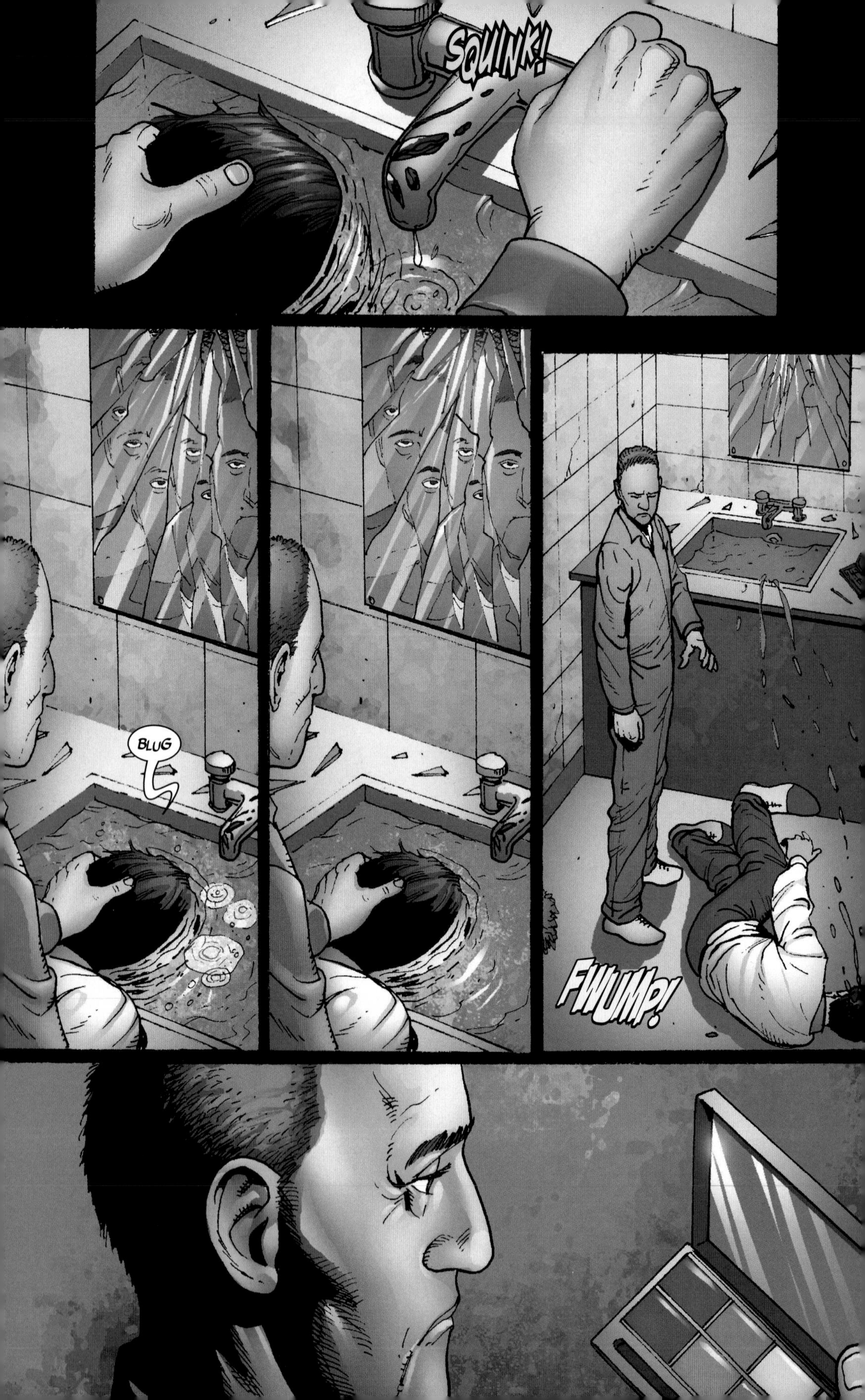
SQUINK!
BLUG
FWUMP!

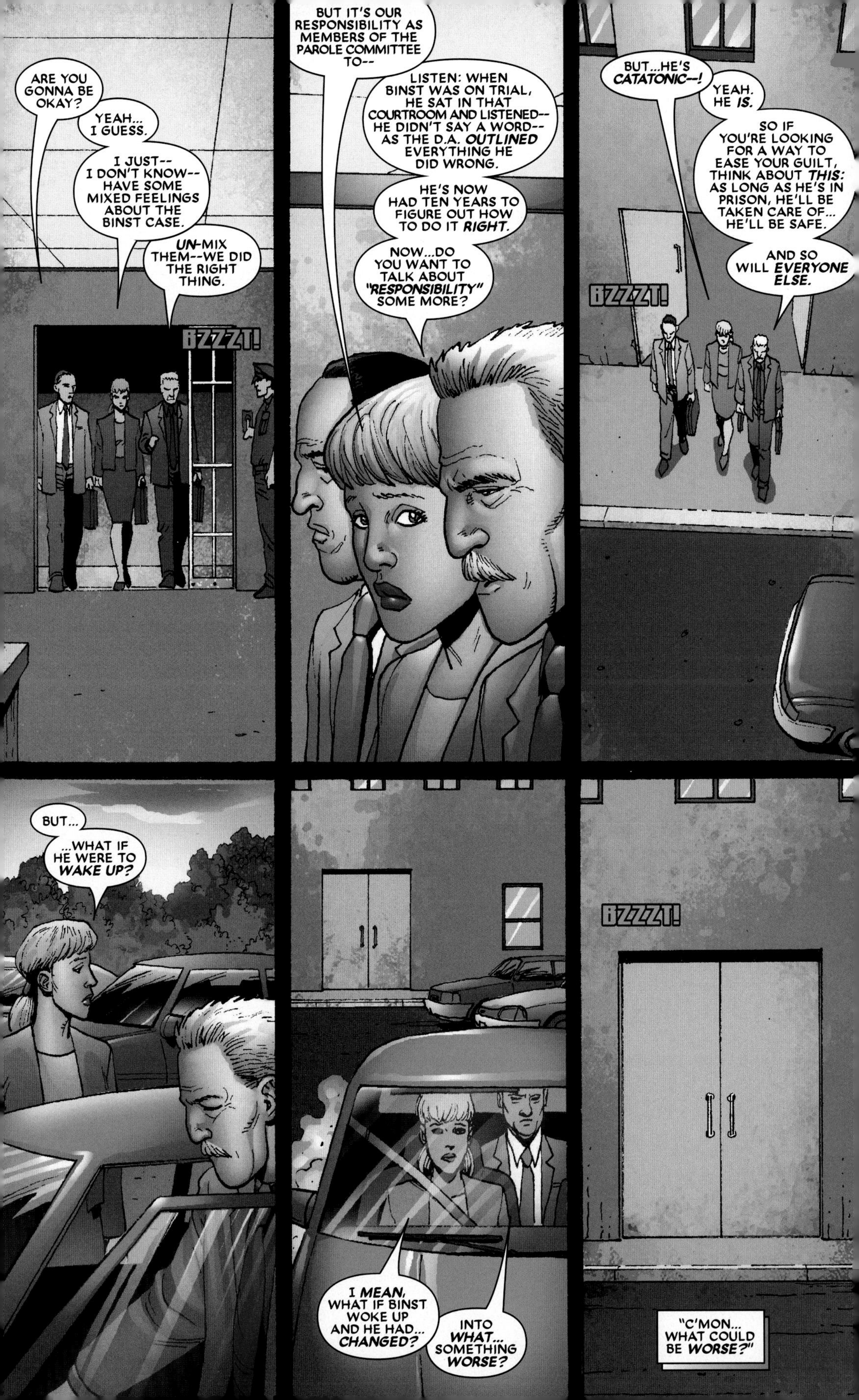

ARE YOU GONNA BE OKAY?
YEAH... I GUESS.
I JUST-- I DON'T KNOW-- HAVE SOME MIXED FEELINGS ABOUT THE BINST CASE.
UN-MIX THEM--WE DID THE RIGHT THING.
BZZZT!
BUT IT'S OUR RESPONSIBILITY AS MEMBERS OF THE PAROLE COMMITTEE TO--
LISTEN: WHEN BINST WAS ON TRIAL, HE SAT IN THAT COURTROOM AND LISTENED-- HE DIDN'T SAY A WORD-- AS THE D.A. OUTLINED EVERYTHING HE DID WRONG.
HE'S NOW HAD TEN YEARS TO FIGURE OUT HOW TO DO IT RIGHT.
NOW...DO YOU WANT TO TALK ABOUT "RESPONSIBILITY" SOME MORE?
BUT...HE'S CATATONIC--!
YEAH. HE IS.
SO IF YOU'RE LOOKING FOR A WAY TO EASE YOUR GUILT, THINK ABOUT THIS: AS LONG AS HE'S IN PRISON, HE'LL BE TAKEN CARE OF... HE'LL BE SAFE.
AND SO WILL EVERYONE ELSE.
BZZZT!
BUT...
...WHAT IF HE WERE TO WAKE UP?
I MEAN, WHAT IF BINST WOKE UP AND HE HAD... CHANGED?
INTO WHAT... SOMETHING WORSE?
BZZZT!
"C'MON... WHAT COULD BE WORSE?"

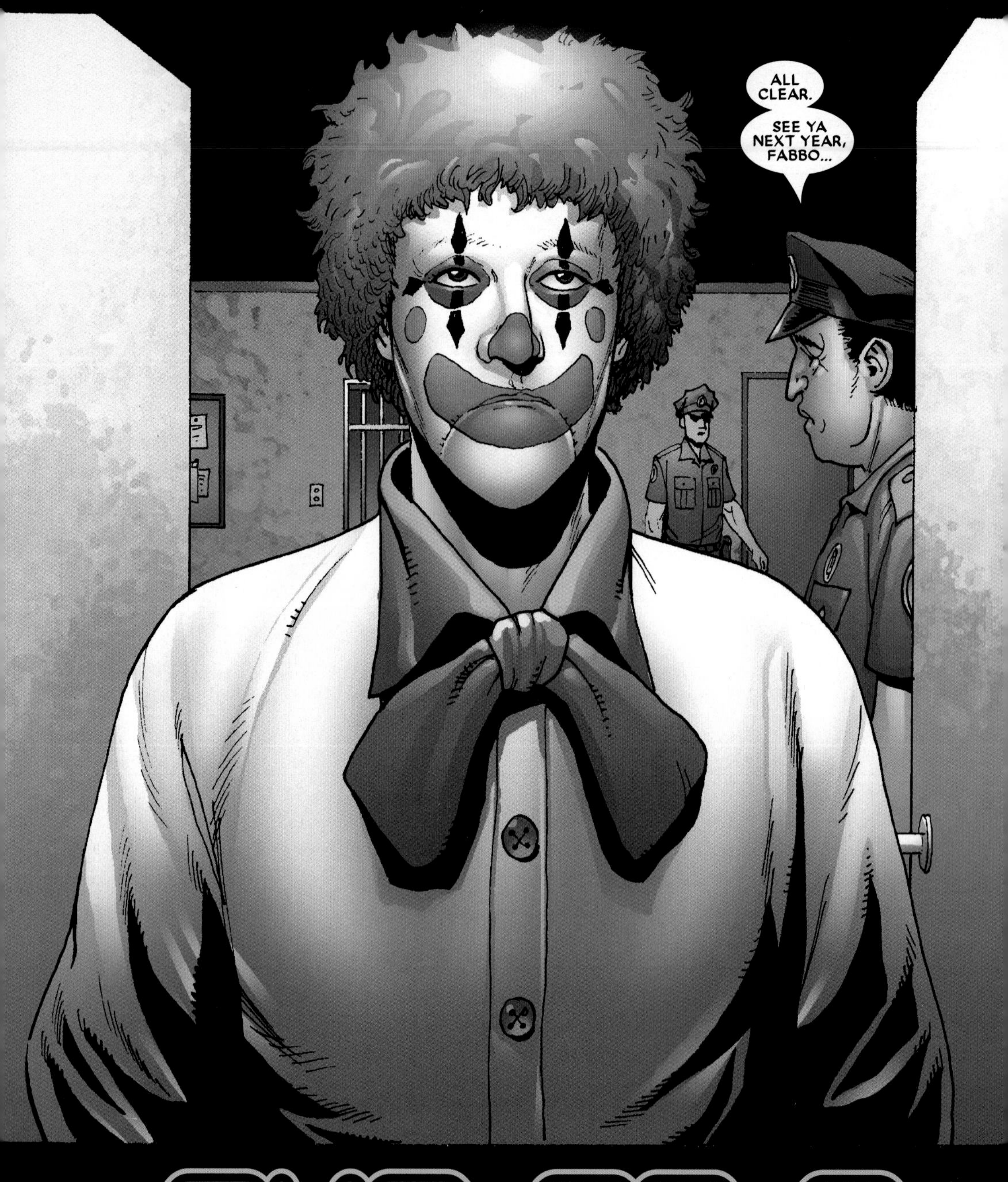
ALL CLEAR.
SEE YA NEXT YEAR, FABBO...

PUT ON A HAPPY FACE

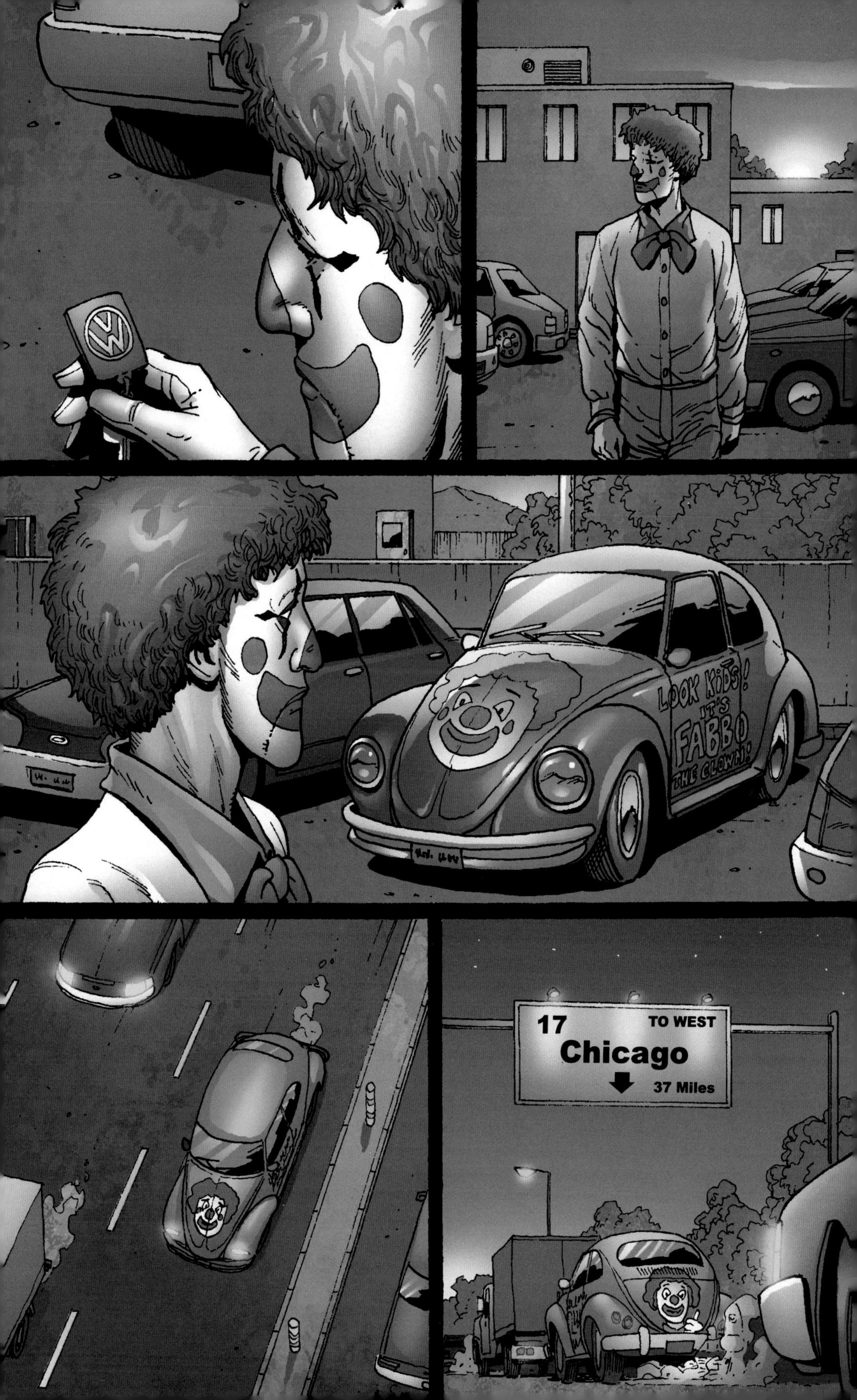
LOOK KIDS! IT'S FABBO THE CLOWN!
17 TO WEST
Chicago
37 Miles

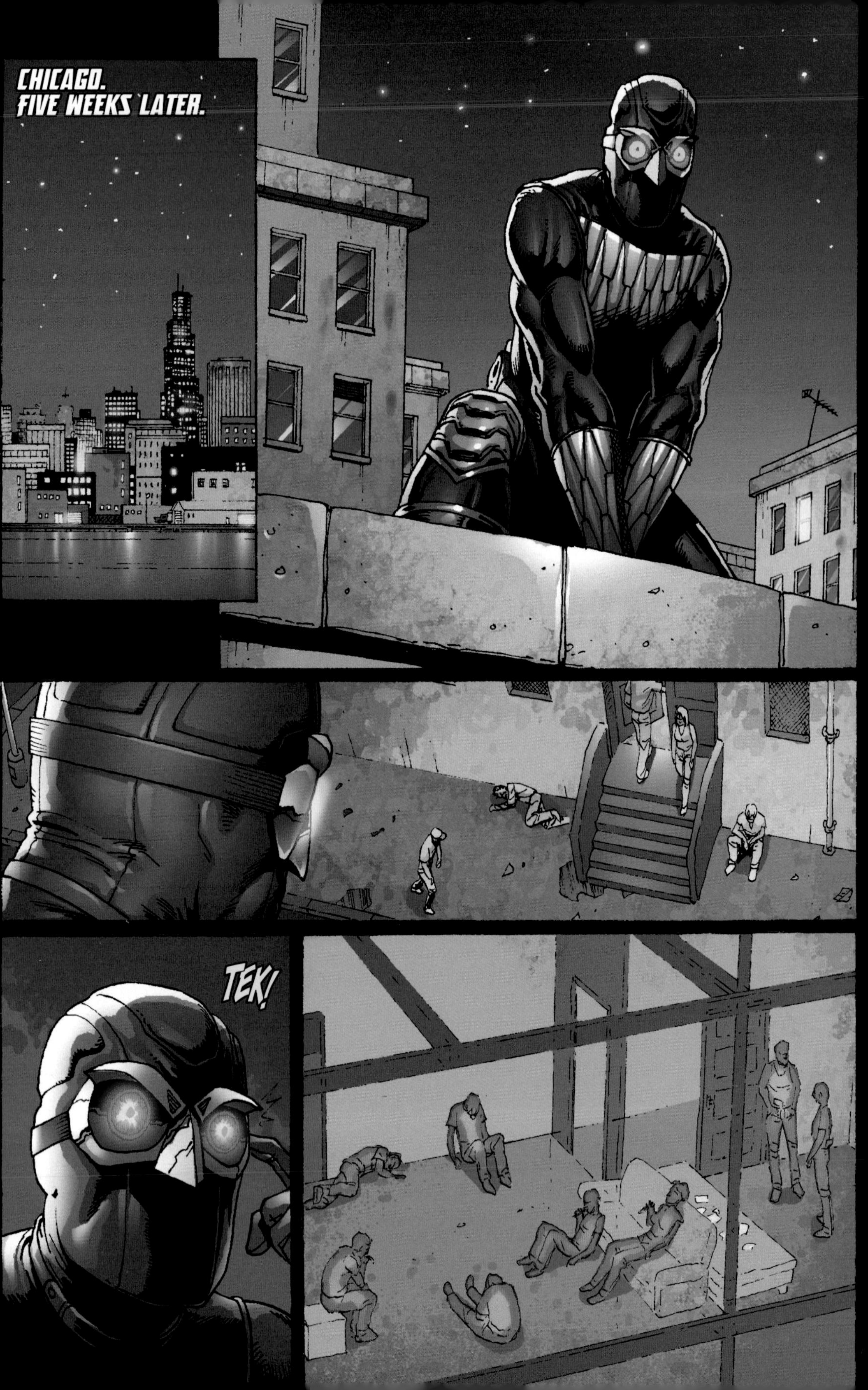
CHICAGO.
FIVE WEEKS LATER.
TEK!

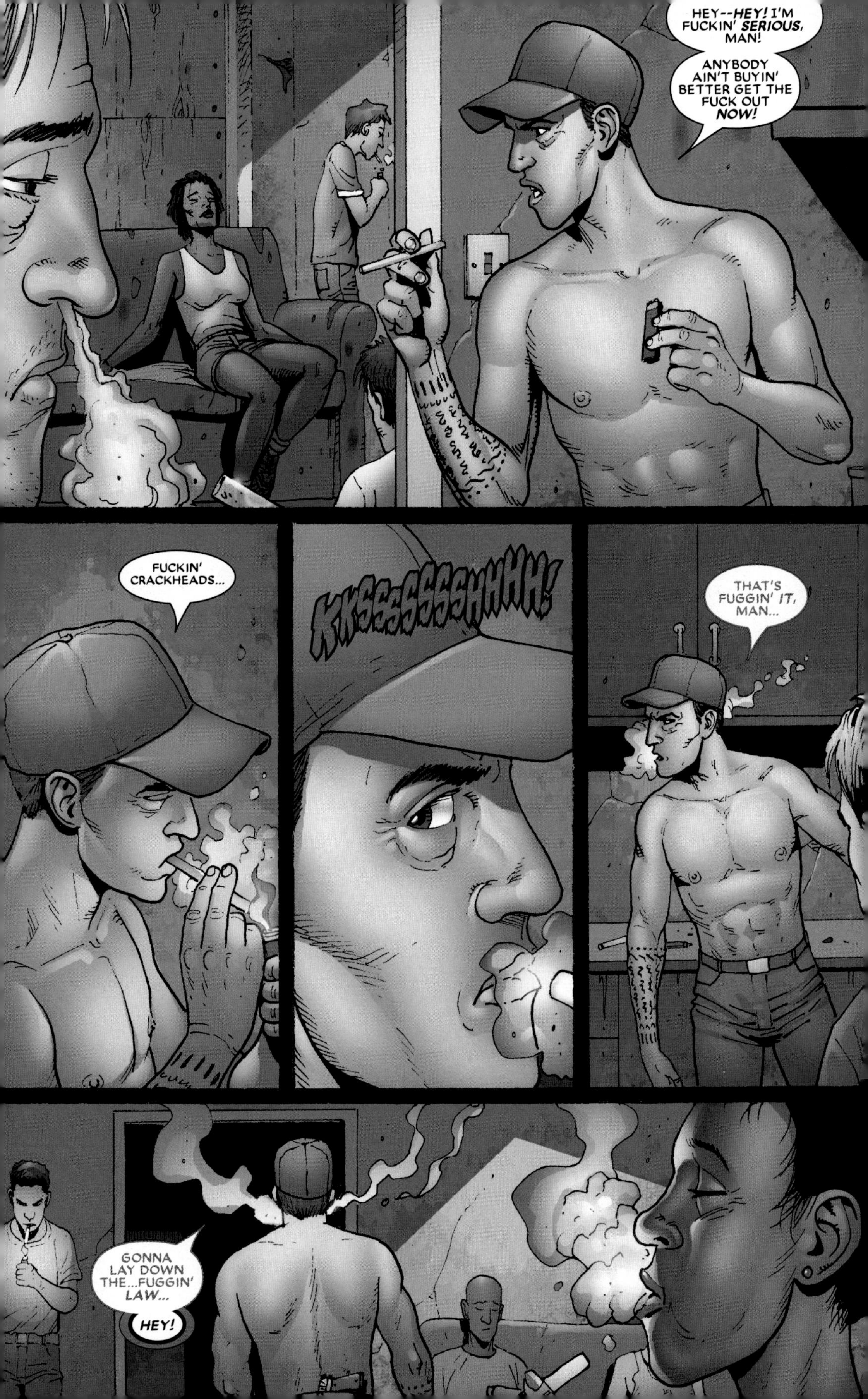
HEY--*HEY!* I'M FUCKIN' *SERIOUS*, MAN!
ANYBODY AIN'T BUYIN' BETTER GET THE FUCK OUT *NOW!*
FUCKIN' CRACKHEADS...
KKSSSSSSSHHHH!
THAT'S FUGGIN' *IT*, MAN...
GONNA LAY DOWN THE...FUGGIN' *LAW*...
HEY!

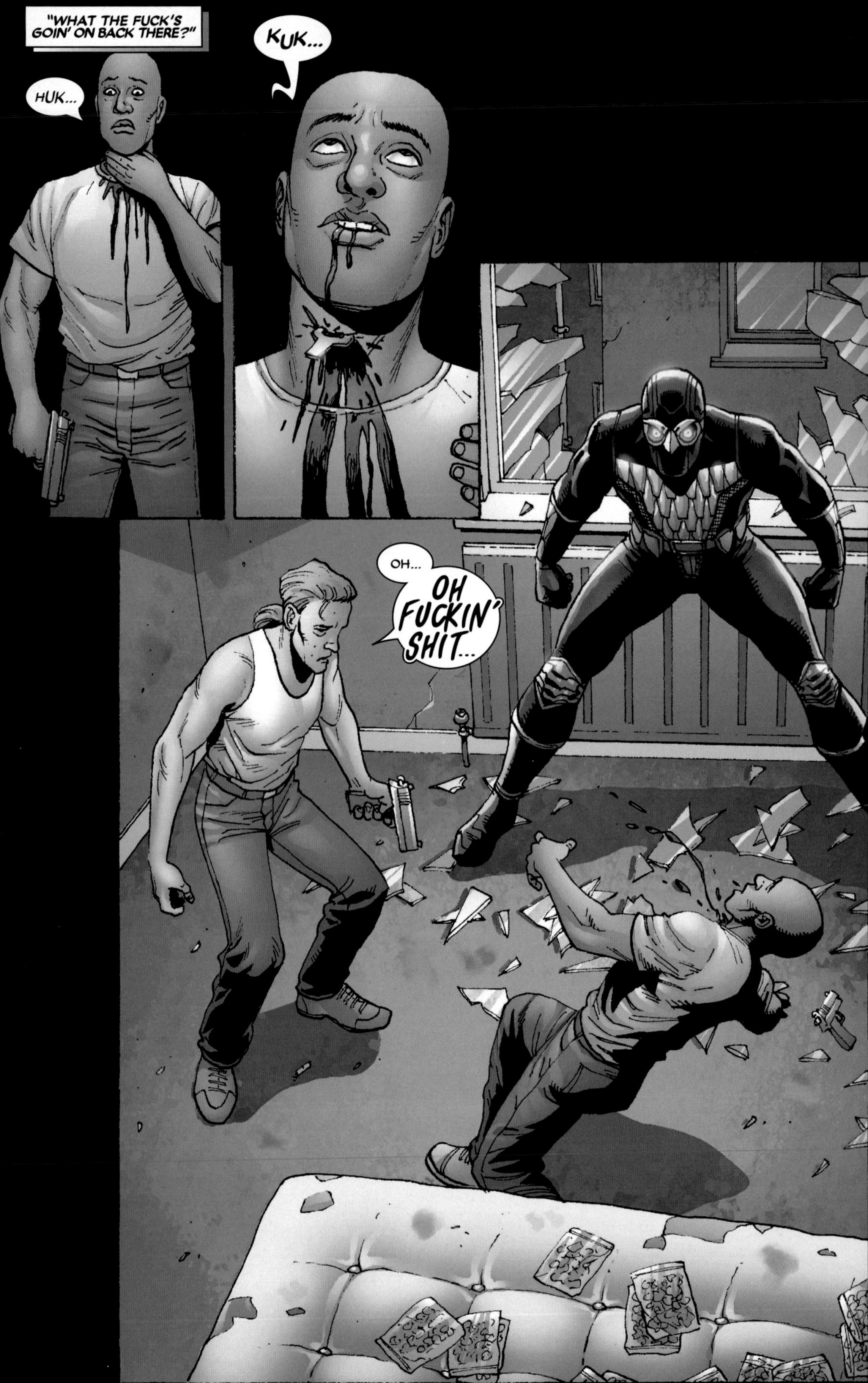
"WHAT THE FUCK'S GOIN' ON BACK THERE?"
HUK...
KUK...
OH...
OH FUCKIN' SHIT...

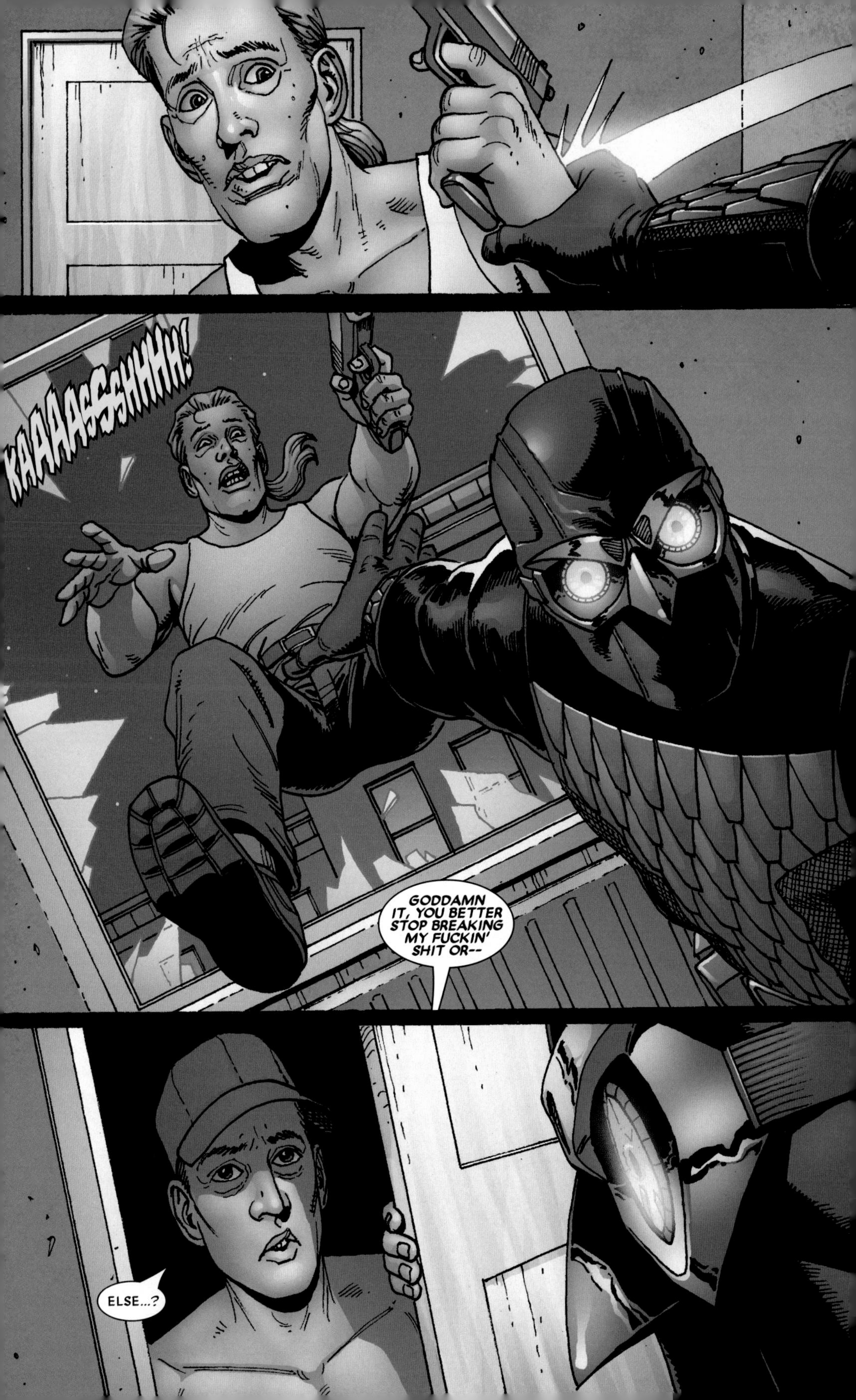
KAAAASSSHHHH!
GODDAMN IT, YOU BETTER STOP BREAKING MY FUCKIN' SHIT OR--
ELSE...?

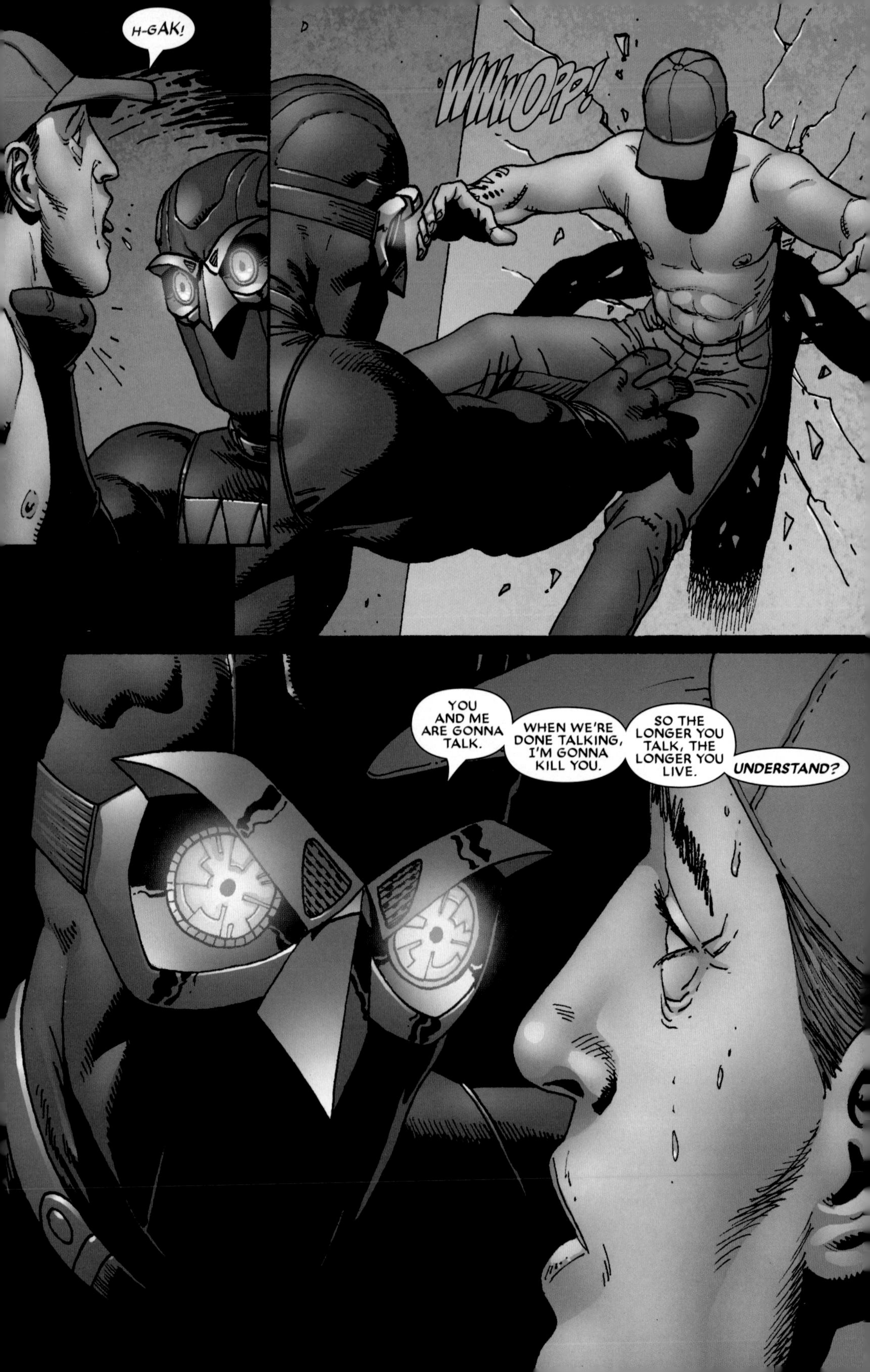
H-GAK!
WWWOPP!
YOU AND ME ARE GONNA TALK.
WHEN WE'RE DONE TALKING, I'M GONNA KILL YOU.
SO THE LONGER YOU TALK, THE LONGER YOU LIVE.
UNDERSTAND?

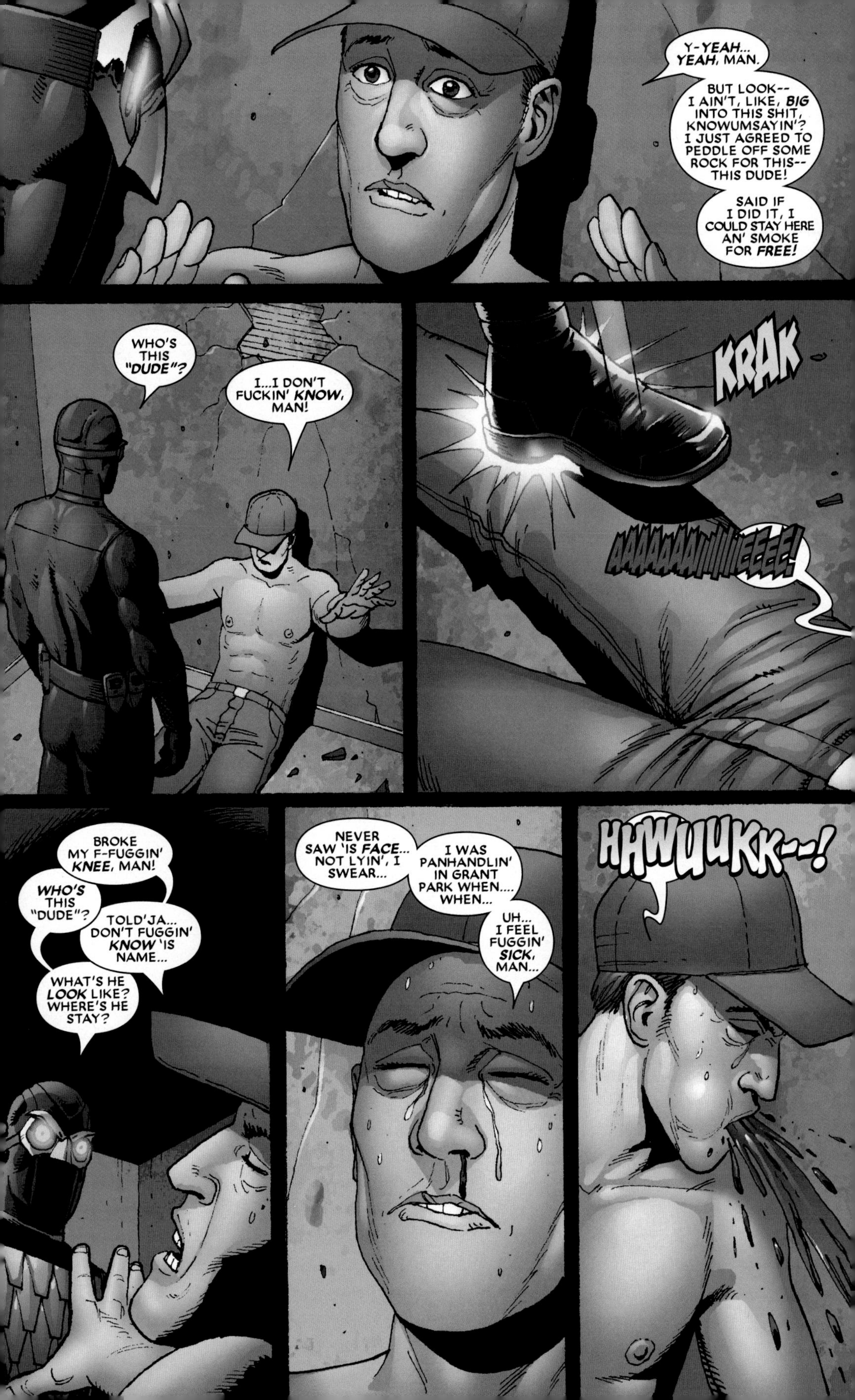

Y-YEAH... YEAH, MAN.
BUT LOOK-- I AIN'T, LIKE, BIG INTO THIS SHIT, KNOWUMSAYIN'? I JUST AGREED TO PEDDLE OFF SOME ROCK FOR THIS-- THIS DUDE!
SAID IF I DID IT, I COULD STAY HERE AN' SMOKE FOR FREE!
WHO'S THIS "DUDE"?
I...I DON'T FUCKIN' KNOW, MAN!
KRAK
AAAAAAAIIIIIIIEEEE!
BROKE MY F-FUGGIN' KNEE, MAN!
WHO'S THIS "DUDE"?
TOLD'JA... DON'T FUGGIN' KNOW 'IS NAME...
WHAT'S HE LOOK LIKE? WHERE'S HE STAY?
NEVER SAW 'IS FACE... NOT LYIN', I SWEAR...
I WAS PANHANDLIN' IN GRANT PARK WHEN.... WHEN...
UH... I FEEL FUGGIN' SICK, MAN...
HHWUUKK--!

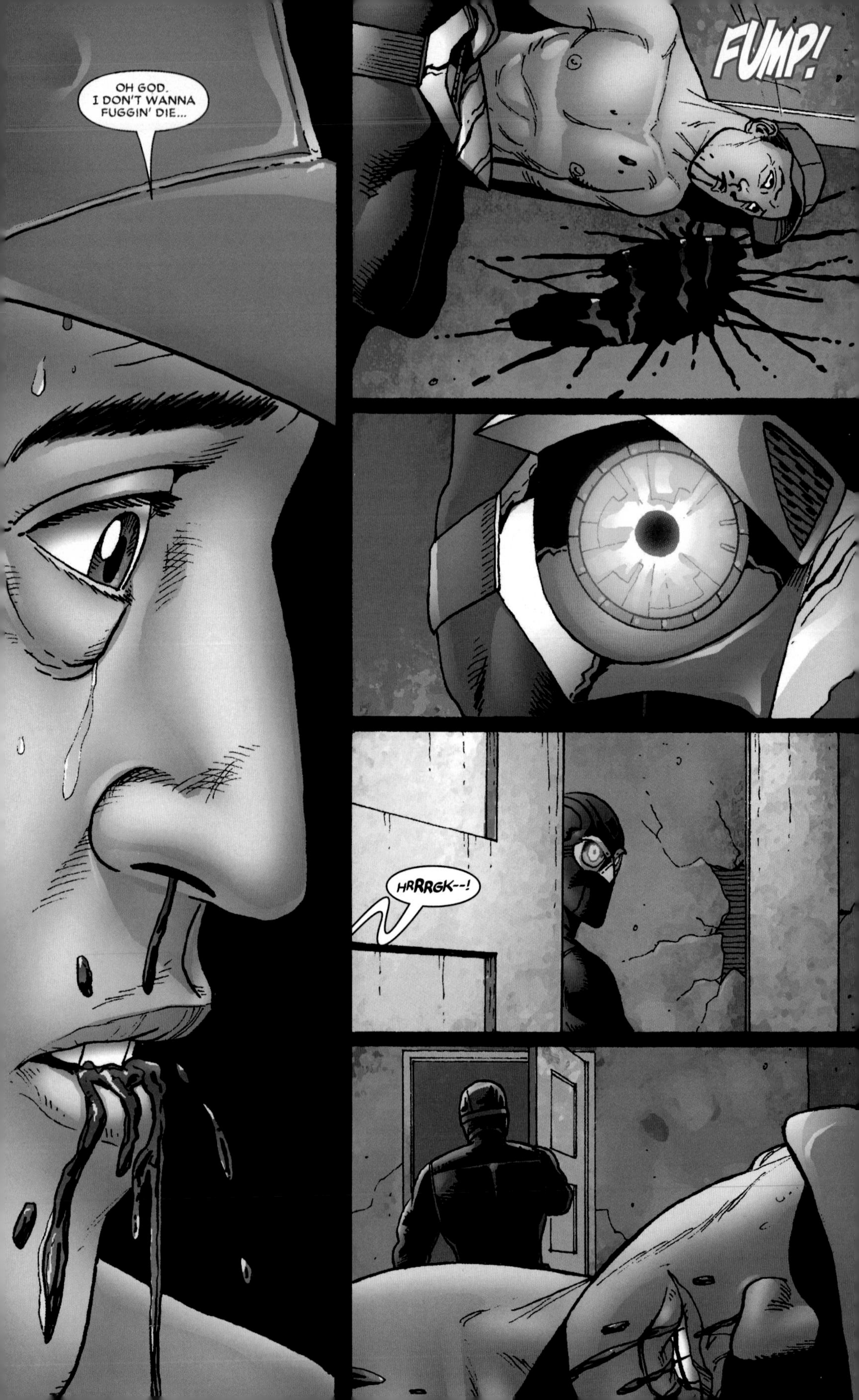

OH GOD. I DON'T WANNA FUGGIN' DIE...
FUMP!
HRRRGK--!

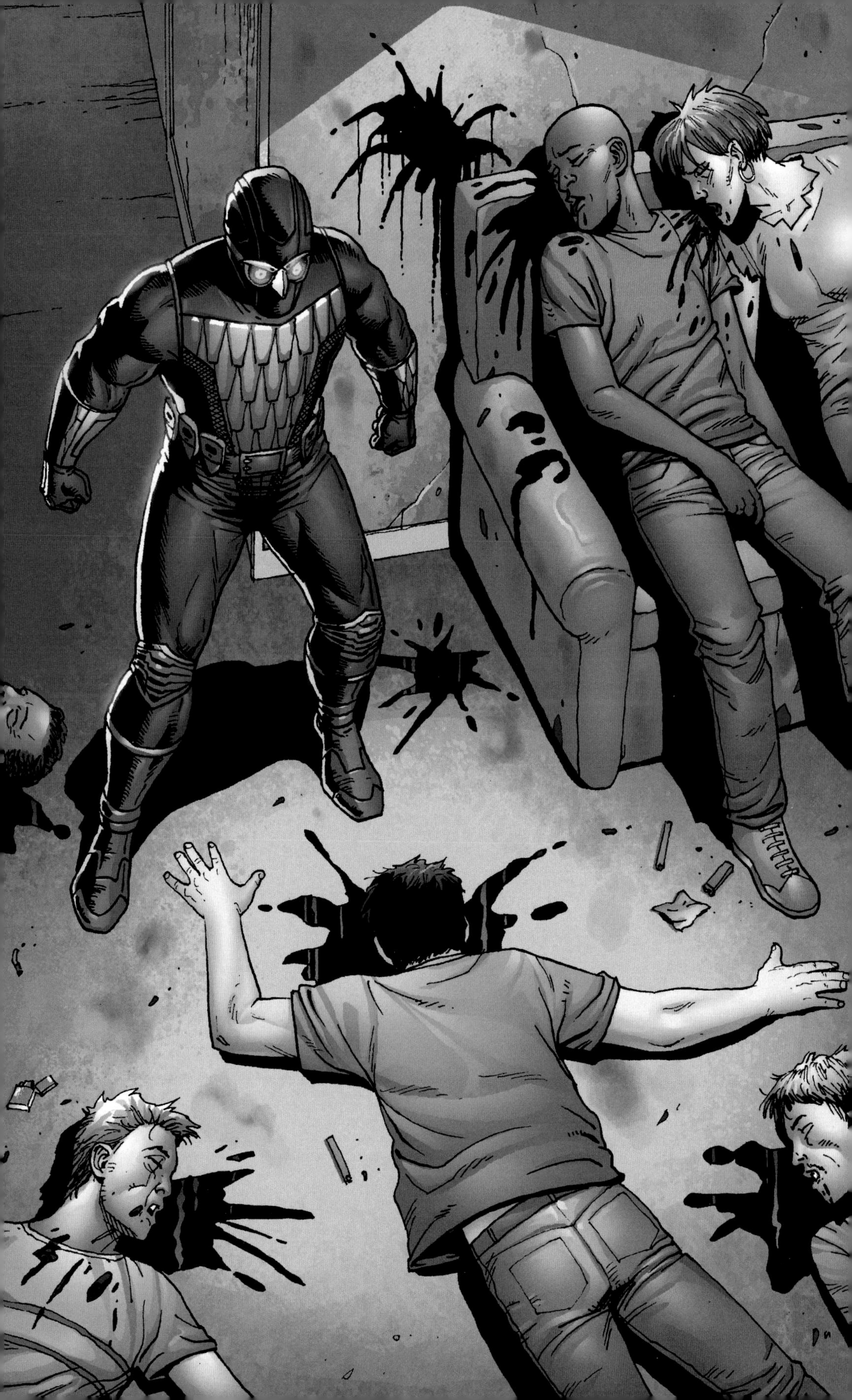

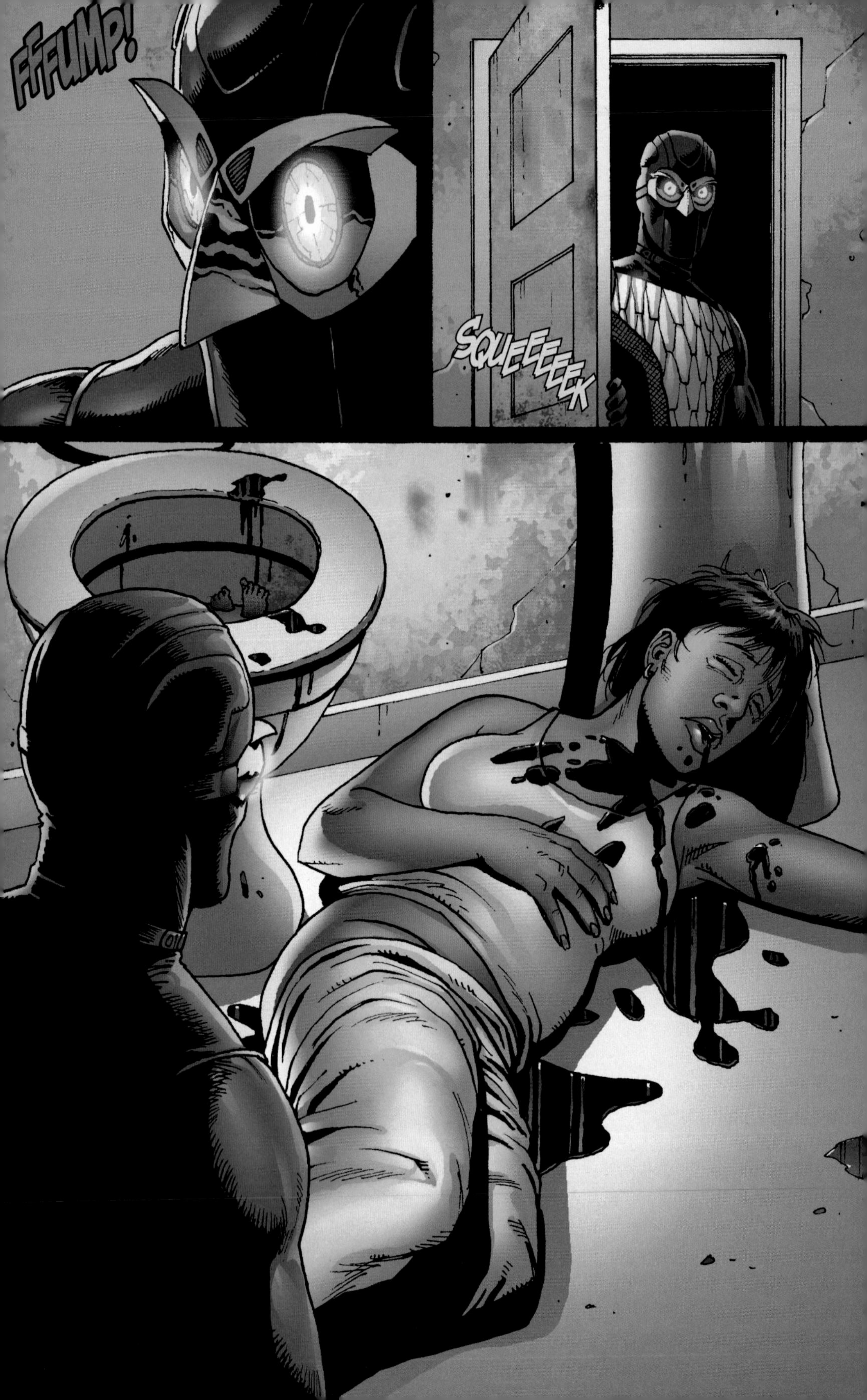
FFFUMP!
SQUEEEEEK

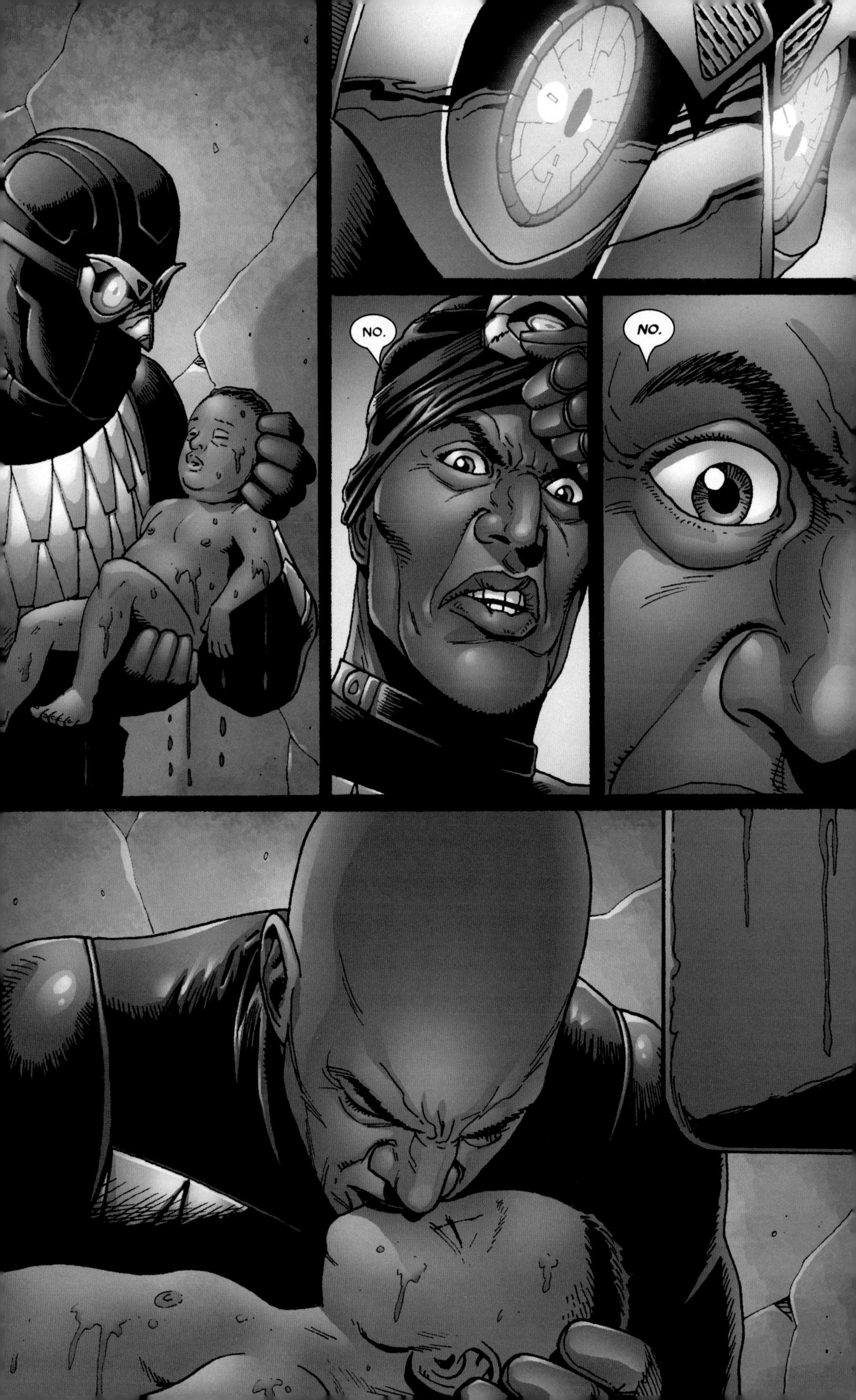
NO.
NO.

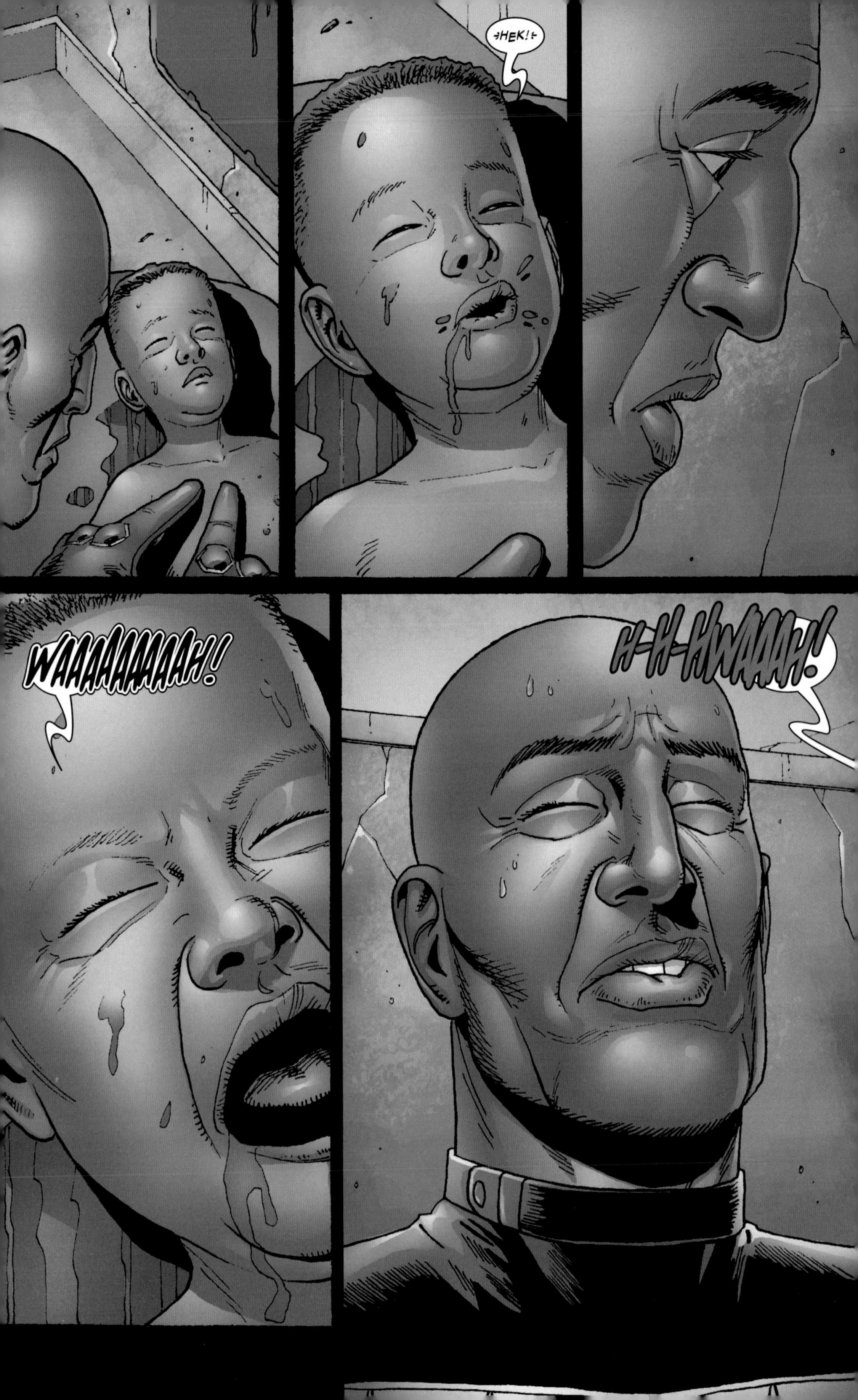
HEK!
WAAAAAAAAAH!
H-H-HWAAAH!

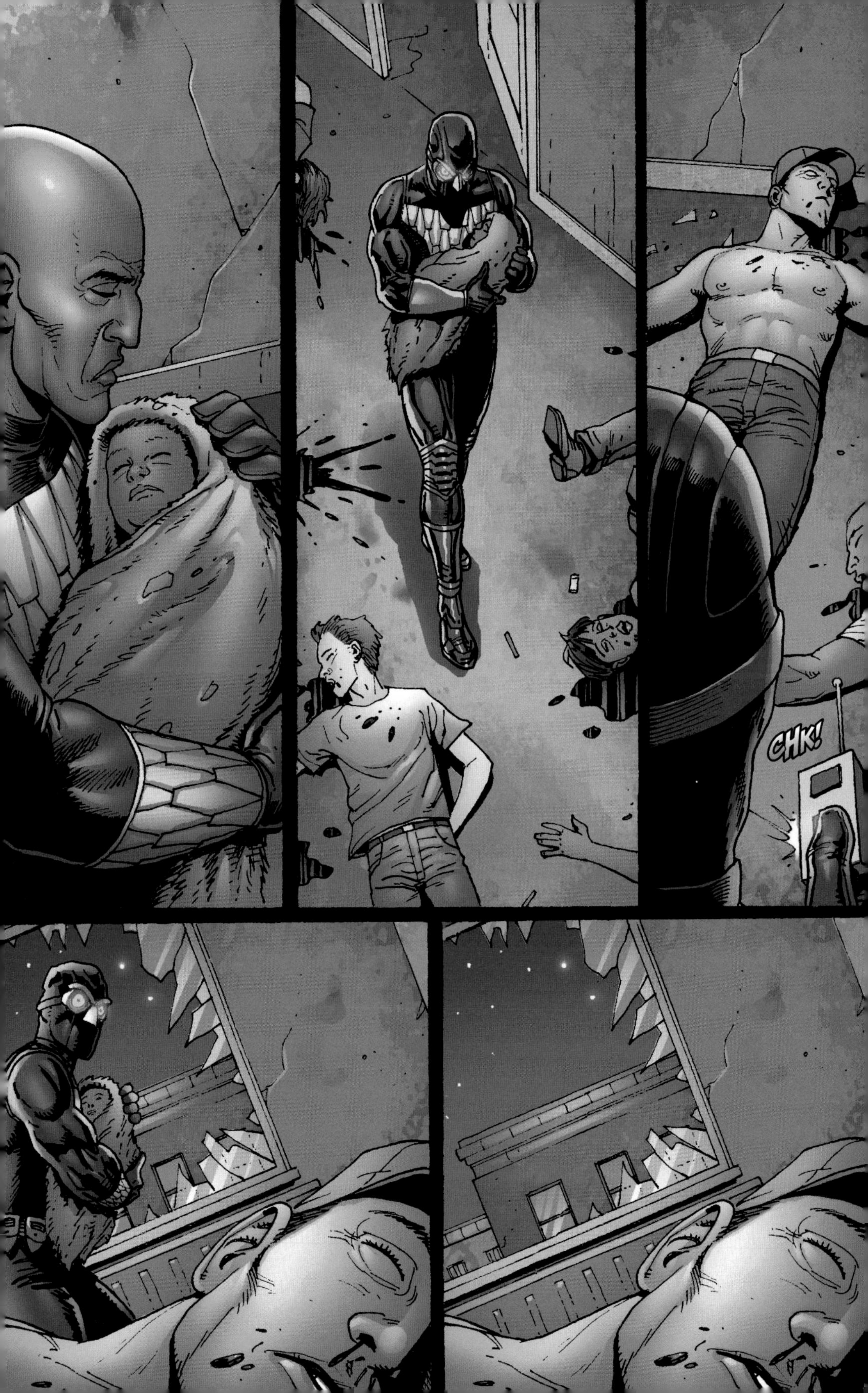
CHK!

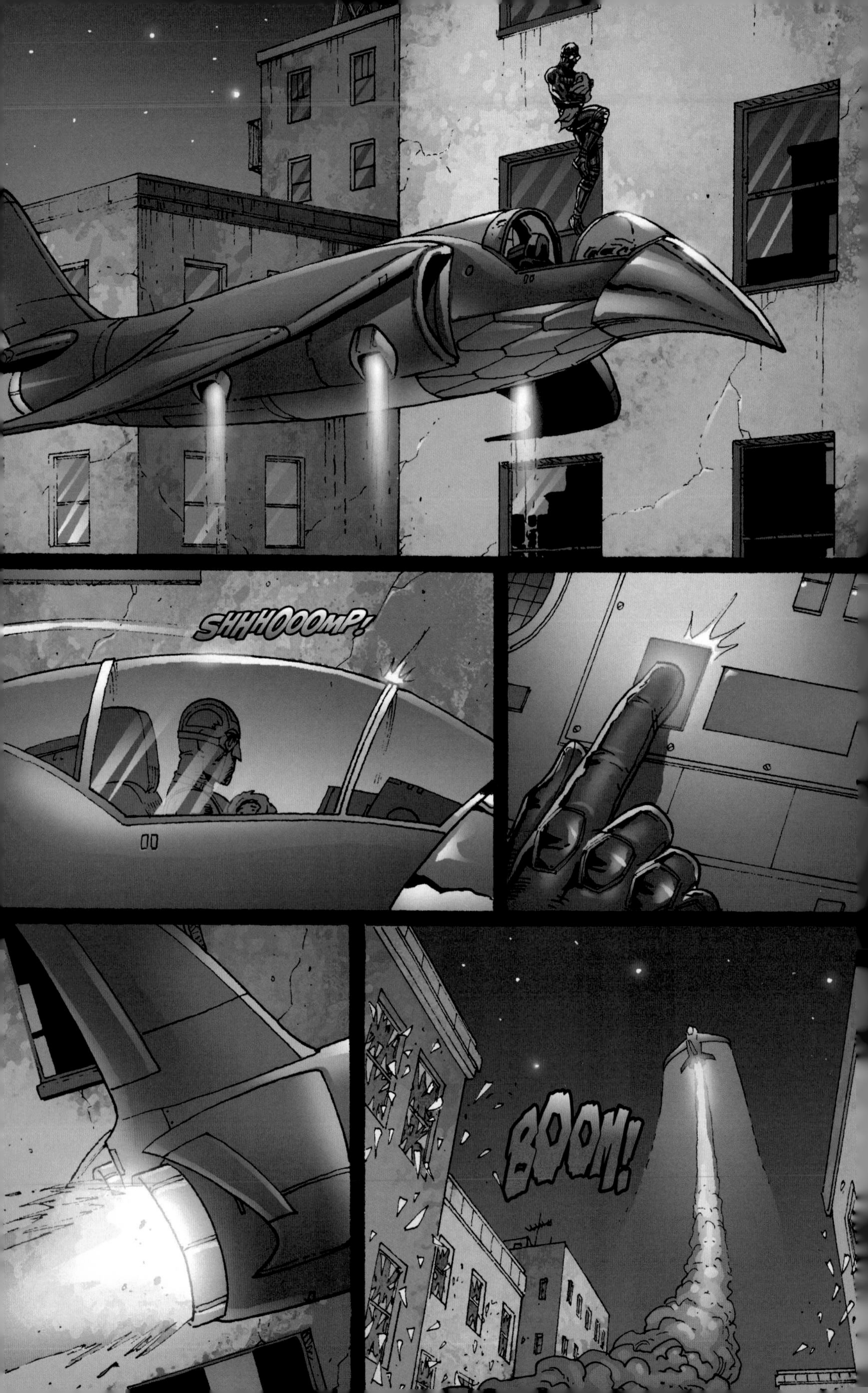
SHHHOOOMP!
BOOM!

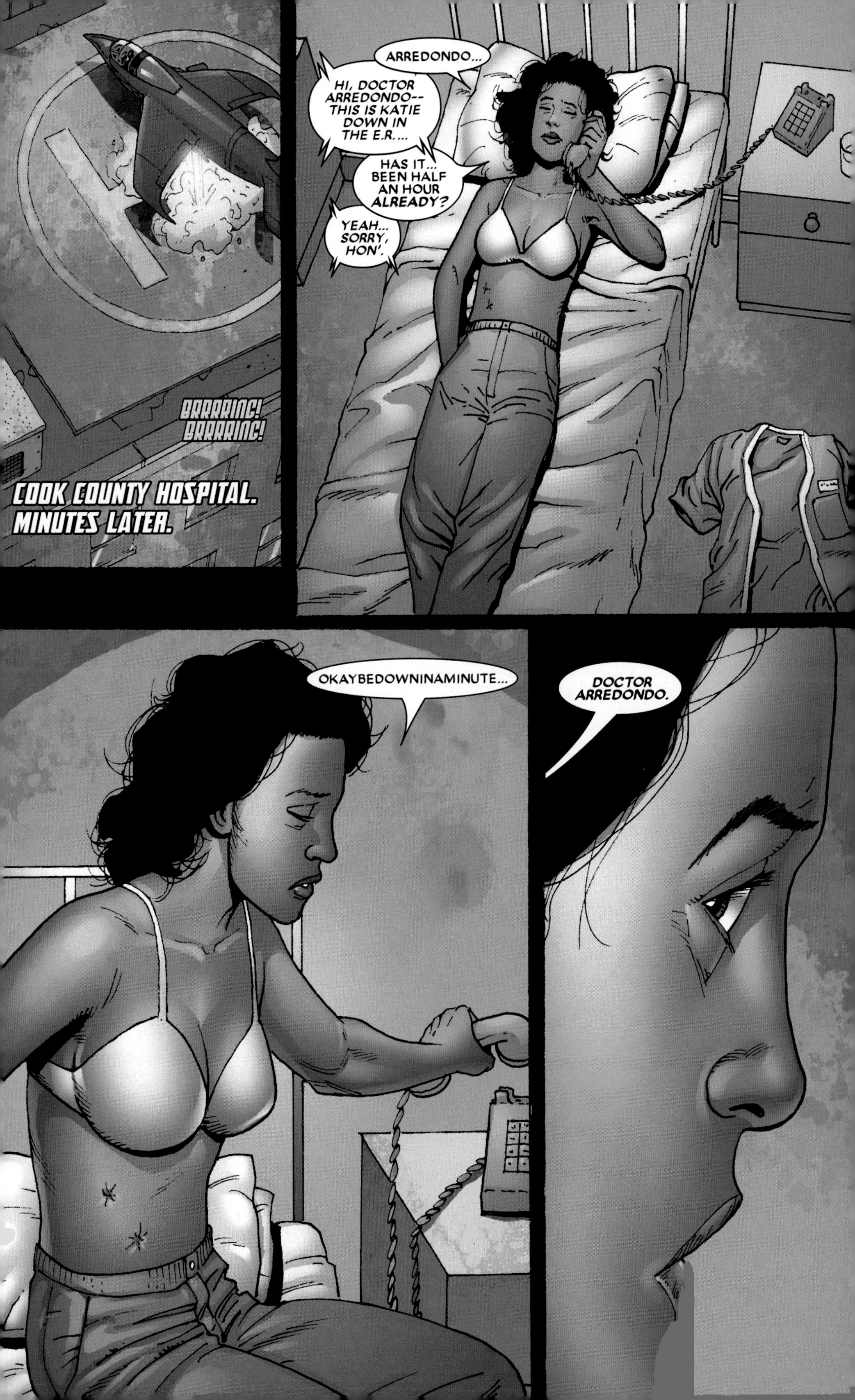
BRRRRING!
BRRRRING!
COOK COUNTY HOSPITAL. MINUTES LATER.
ARREDONDO...
HI, DOCTOR ARREDONDO-- THIS IS KATIE DOWN IN THE E.R....
HAS IT... BEEN HALF AN HOUR ALREADY?
YEAH... SORRY, HON'.
OKAYBEDOWNINAMINUTE...
DOCTOR ARREDONDO.

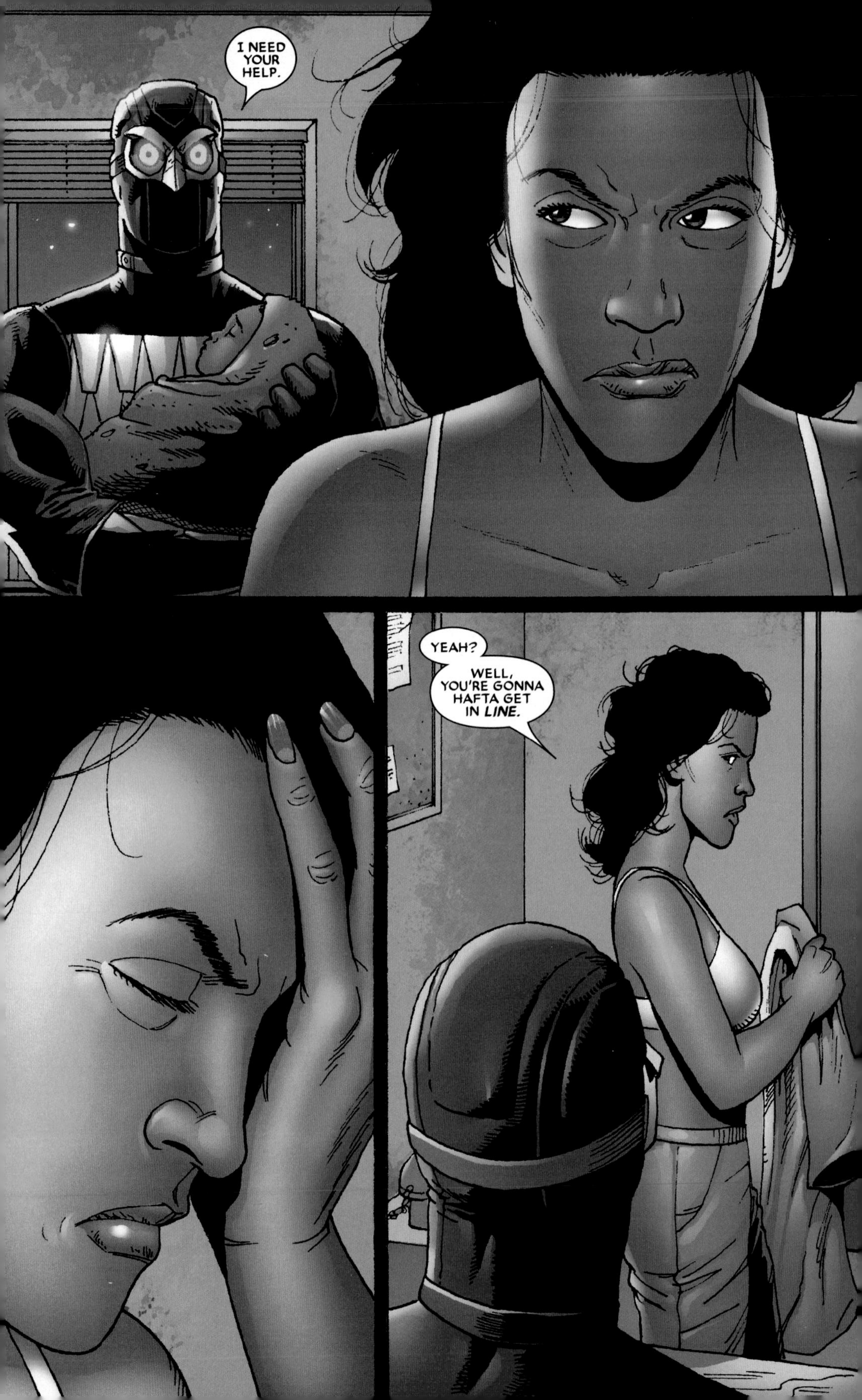
I NEED YOUR HELP.
YEAH?
WELL, YOU'RE GONNA HAFTA GET IN *LINE.*

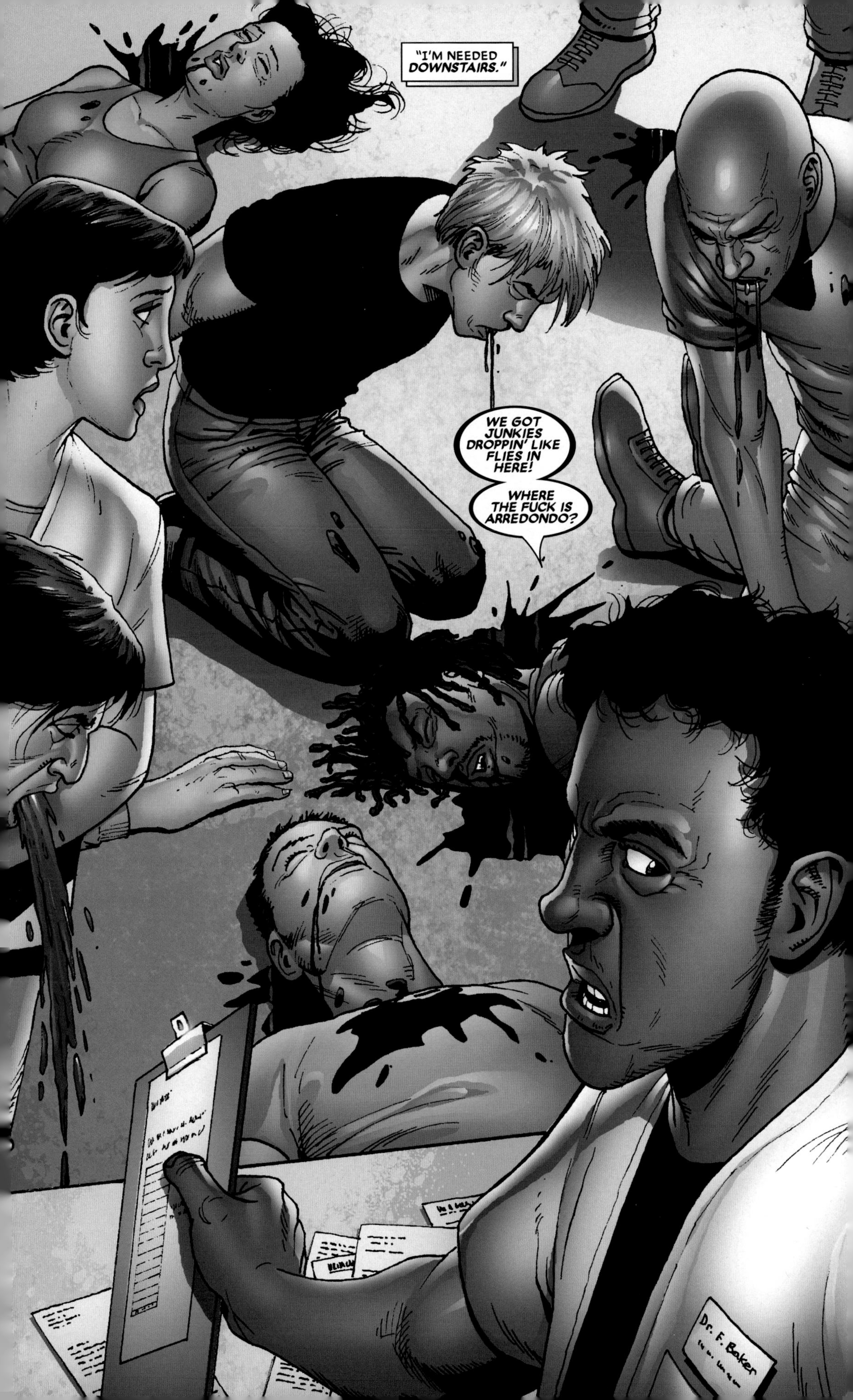
"I'M NEEDED DOWNSTAIRS."
WE GOT JUNKIES DROPPIN' LIKE FLIES IN HERE!
WHERE THE FUCK IS ARREDONDO?
Dr. F. Baker

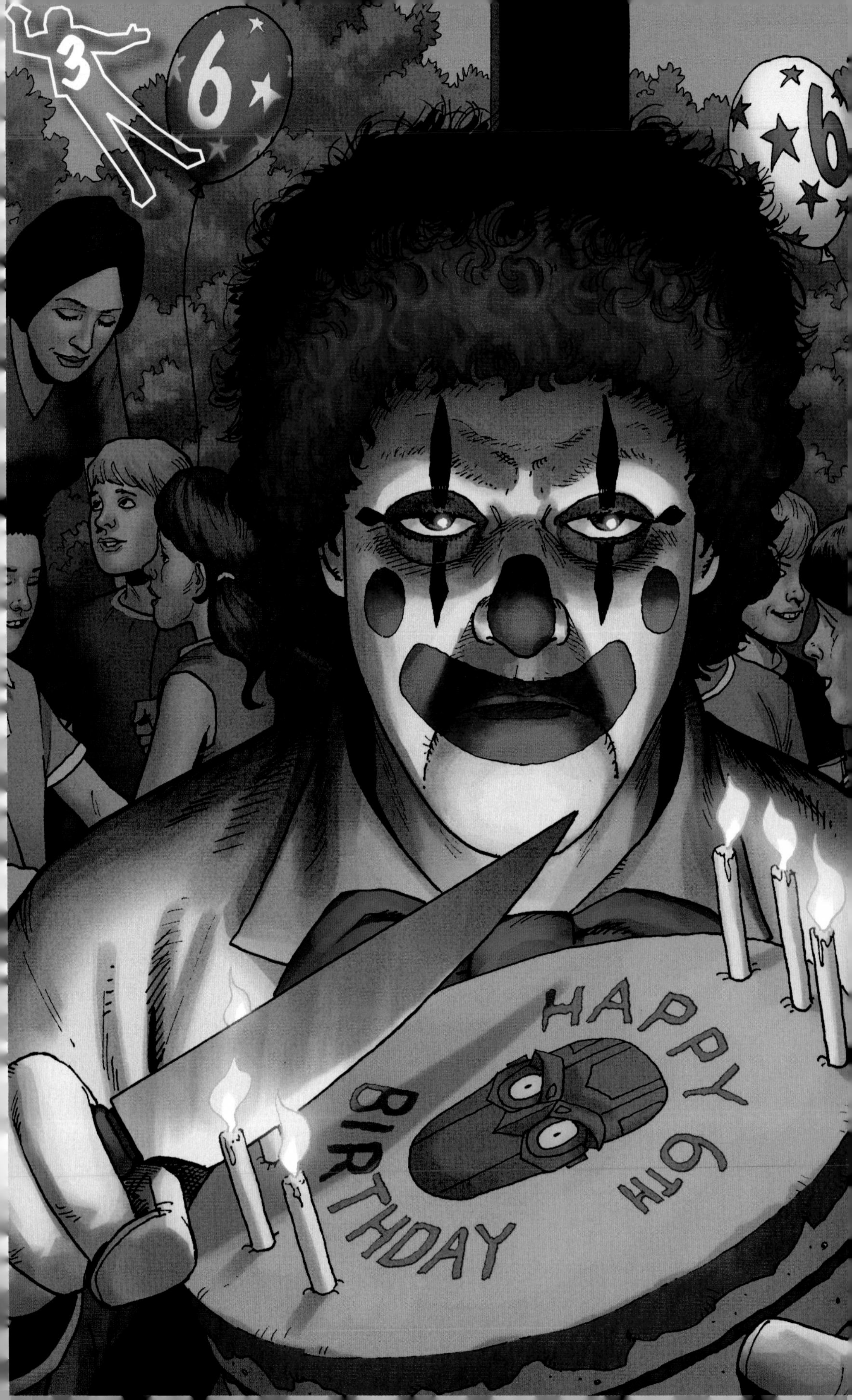
3
6
6
HAPPY
BIRTHDAY
6TH

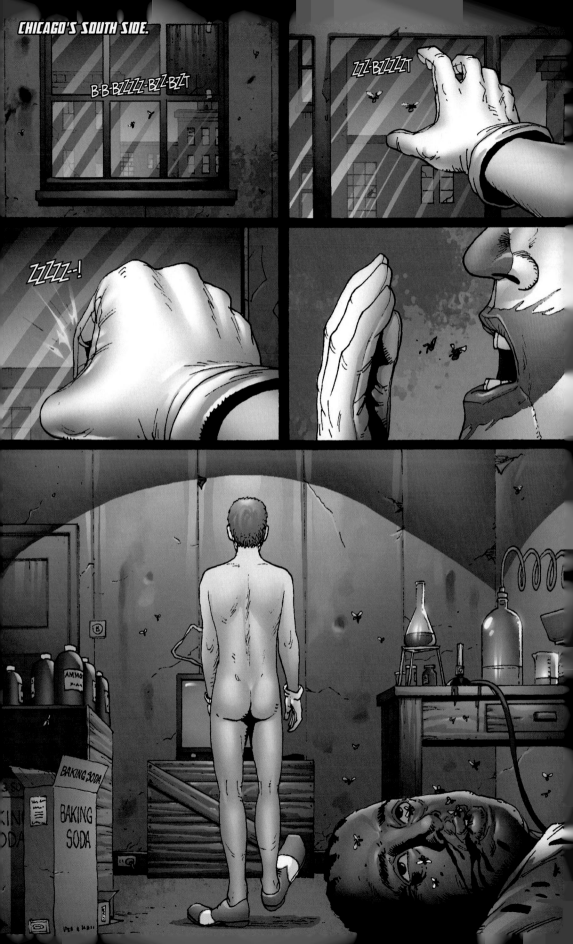

B-B-BZZZZ-BZZ-BZT

ZZZ-BZZZZT

ZZZZZ--!

BAKING SODA

BAKING SODA

AMMO

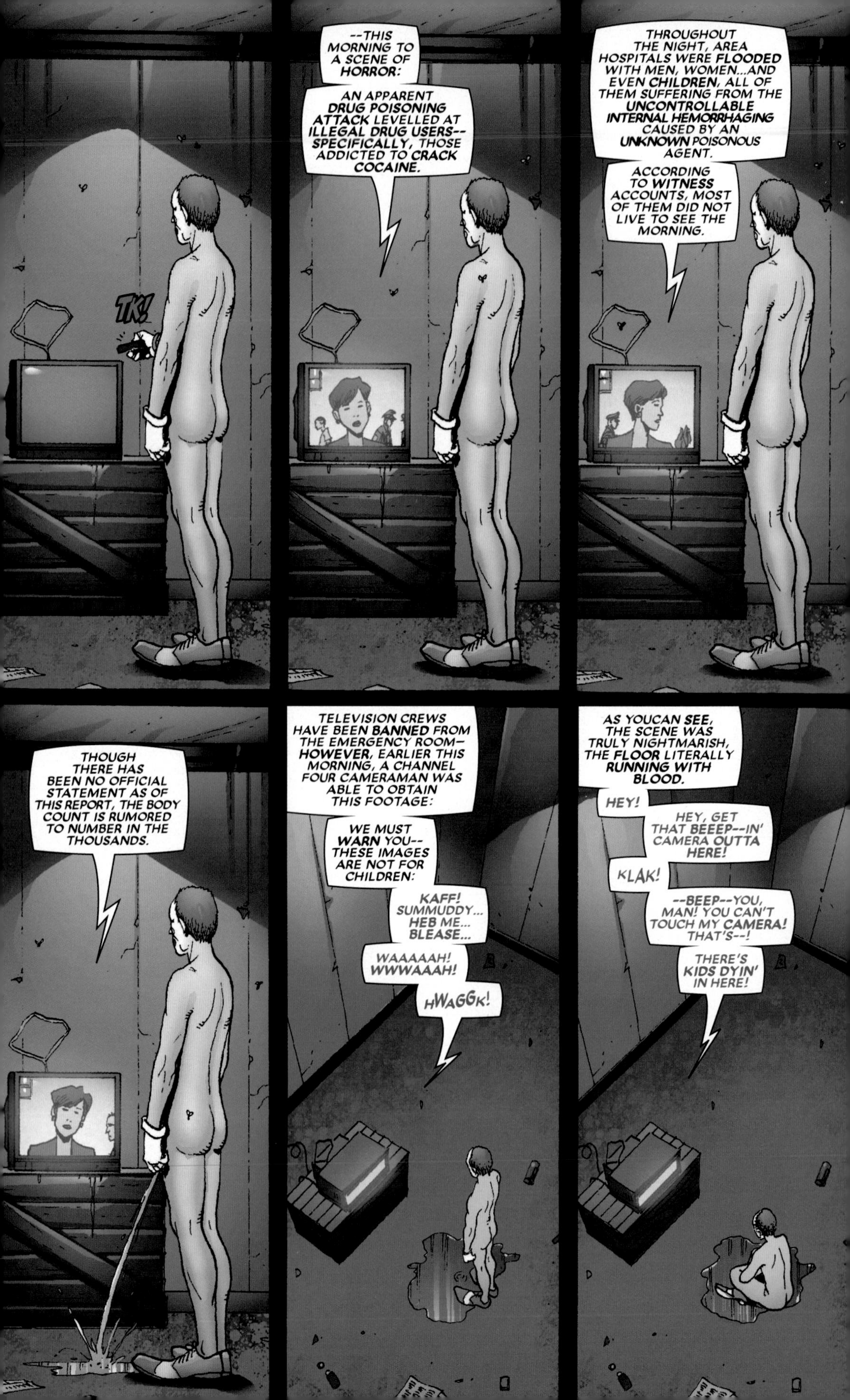
TK!
--THIS MORNING TO A SCENE OF HORROR:
AN APPARENT DRUG POISONING ATTACK LEVELLED AT ILLEGAL DRUG USERS-- SPECIFICALLY, THOSE ADDICTED TO CRACK COCAINE.
THROUGHOUT THE NIGHT, AREA HOSPITALS WERE FLOODED WITH MEN, WOMEN...AND EVEN CHILDREN, ALL OF THEM SUFFERING FROM THE UNCONTROLLABLE INTERNAL HEMORRHAGING CAUSED BY AN UNKNOWN POISONOUS AGENT.
ACCORDING TO WITNESS ACCOUNTS, MOST OF THEM DID NOT LIVE TO SEE THE MORNING.
THOUGH THERE HAS BEEN NO OFFICIAL STATEMENT AS OF THIS REPORT, THE BODY COUNT IS RUMORED TO NUMBER IN THE THOUSANDS.
TELEVISION CREWS HAVE BEEN BANNED FROM THE EMERGENCY ROOM— HOWEVER, EARLIER THIS MORNING, A CHANNEL FOUR CAMERAMAN WAS ABLE TO OBTAIN THIS FOOTAGE:
WE MUST WARN YOU-- THESE IMAGES ARE NOT FOR CHILDREN:
KAFF! SUMMUDDY... HEB ME... BLEASE...
WAAAAAH! WWWAAAH!
HWAGGK!
AS YOUCAN SEE, THE SCENE WAS TRULY NIGHTMARISH, THE FLOOR LITERALLY RUNNING WITH BLOOD.
HEY!
HEY, GET THAT BEEEP--IN' CAMERA OUTTA HERE!
KLAK!
--BEEP--YOU, MAN! YOU CAN'T TOUCH MY CAMERA! THAT'S--!
THERE'S KIDS DYIN' IN HERE!

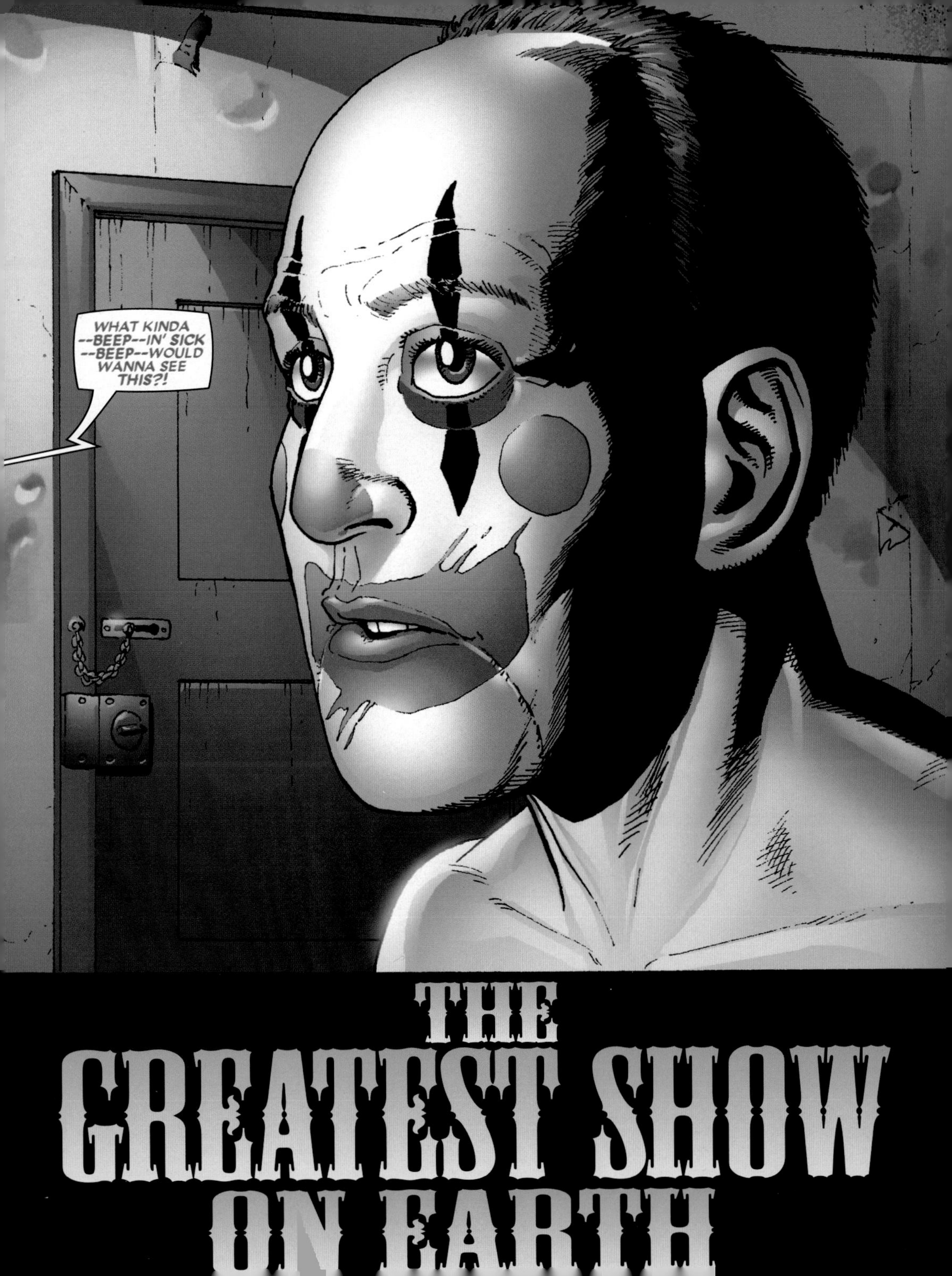
WHAT KINDA --BEEP--IN' SICK --BEEP--WOULD WANNA SEE THIS?!

THE GREATEST SHOW ON EARTH

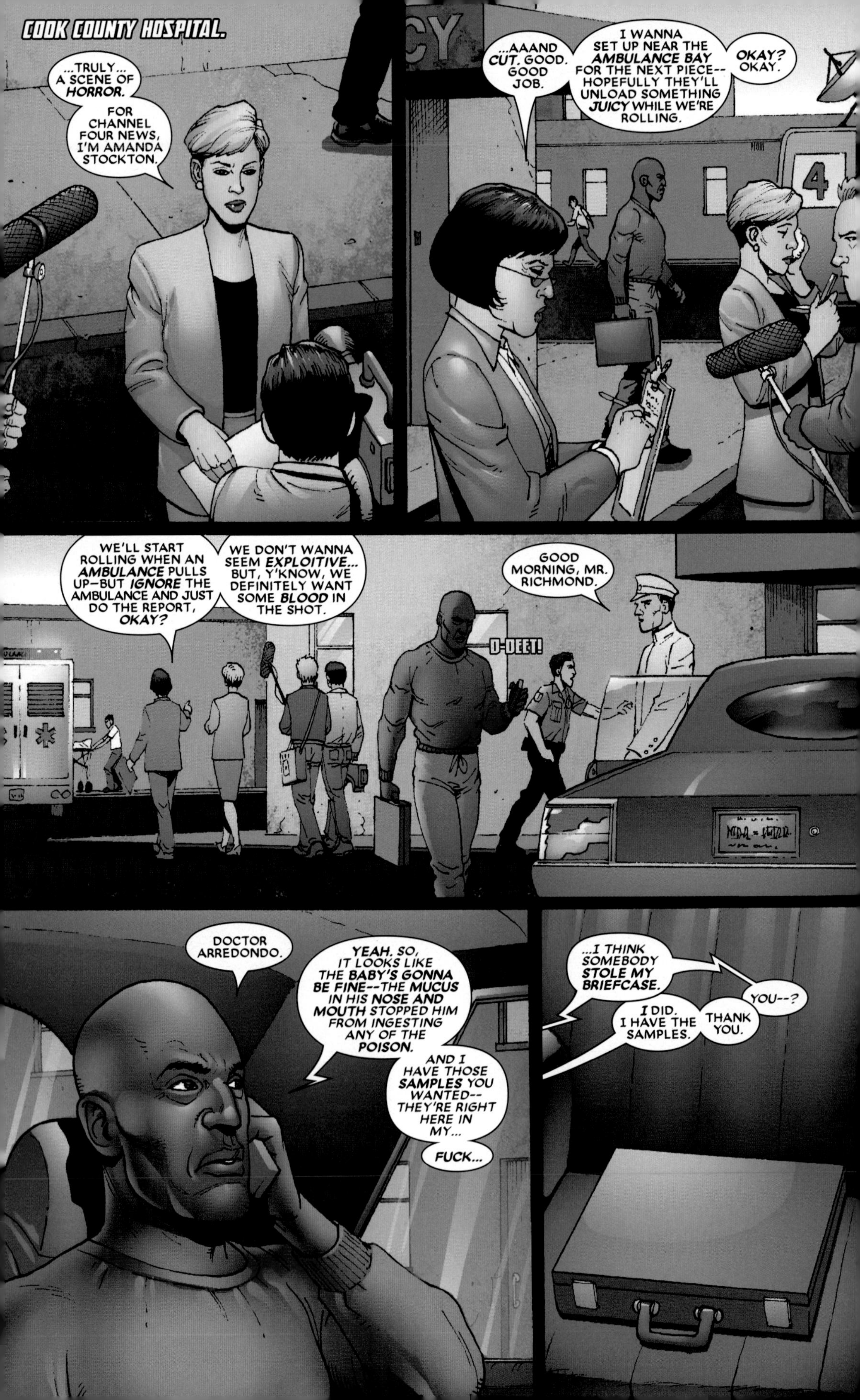
COOK COUNTY HOSPITAL.
...TRULY... A SCENE OF HORROR.
FOR CHANNEL FOUR NEWS, I'M AMANDA STOCKTON.
...AAAND CUT. GOOD. GOOD JOB.
I WANNA SET UP NEAR THE AMBULANCE BAY FOR THE NEXT PIECE-- HOPEFULLY THEY'LL UNLOAD SOMETHING JUICY WHILE WE'RE ROLLING.
OKAY? OKAY.
WE'LL START ROLLING WHEN AN AMBULANCE PULLS UP—BUT IGNORE THE AMBULANCE AND JUST DO THE REPORT, OKAY?
WE DON'T WANNA SEEM EXPLOITIVE... BUT, Y'KNOW, WE DEFINITELY WANT SOME BLOOD IN THE SHOT.
GOOD MORNING, MR. RICHMOND.
D-DEET!
DOCTOR ARREDONDO.
YEAH. SO, IT LOOKS LIKE THE BABY'S GONNA BE FINE--THE MUCUS IN HIS NOSE AND MOUTH STOPPED HIM FROM INGESTING ANY OF THE POISON.
AND I HAVE THOSE SAMPLES YOU WANTED-- THEY'RE RIGHT HERE IN MY...
FUCK...
...I THINK SOMEBODY STOLE MY BRIEFCASE.
YOU--?
I DID. I HAVE THE SAMPLES.
THANK YOU.

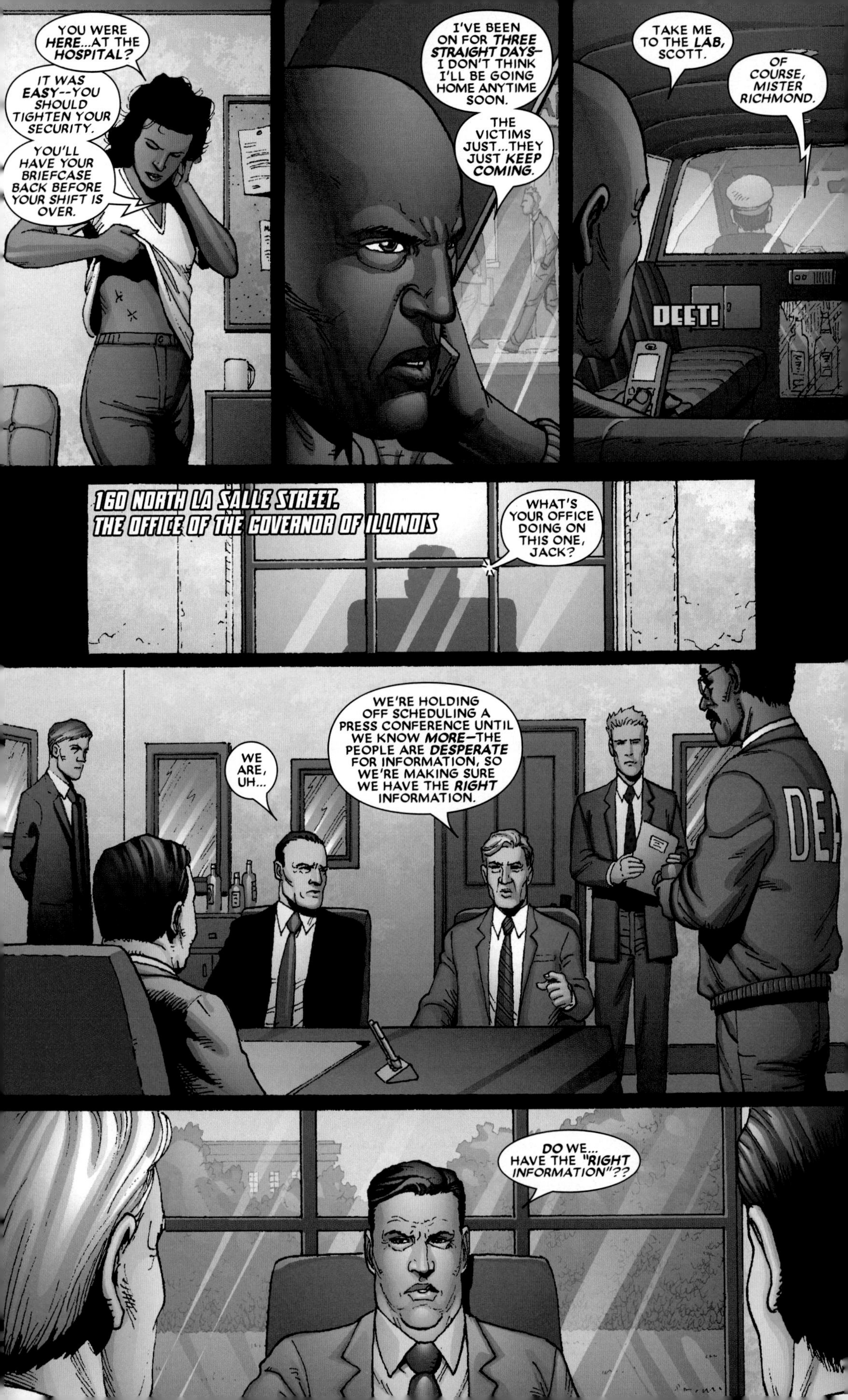
YOU WERE HERE...AT THE HOSPITAL?
IT WAS EASY--YOU SHOULD TIGHTEN YOUR SECURITY.
YOU'LL HAVE YOUR BRIEFCASE BACK BEFORE YOUR SHIFT IS OVER.
I'VE BEEN ON FOR THREE STRAIGHT DAYS-- I DON'T THINK I'LL BE GOING HOME ANYTIME SOON.
THE VICTIMS JUST...THEY JUST KEEP COMING.
TAKE ME TO THE LAB, SCOTT.
OF COURSE, MISTER RICHMOND.
DEET!
160 NORTH LA SALLE STREET.
THE OFFICE OF THE GOVERNOR OF ILLINOIS
WHAT'S YOUR OFFICE DOING ON THIS ONE, JACK?
WE ARE, UH...
WE'RE HOLDING OFF SCHEDULING A PRESS CONFERENCE UNTIL WE KNOW MORE--THE PEOPLE ARE DESPERATE FOR INFORMATION, SO WE'RE MAKING SURE WE HAVE THE RIGHT INFORMATION.
DEA
DO WE... HAVE THE "RIGHT INFORMATION"??

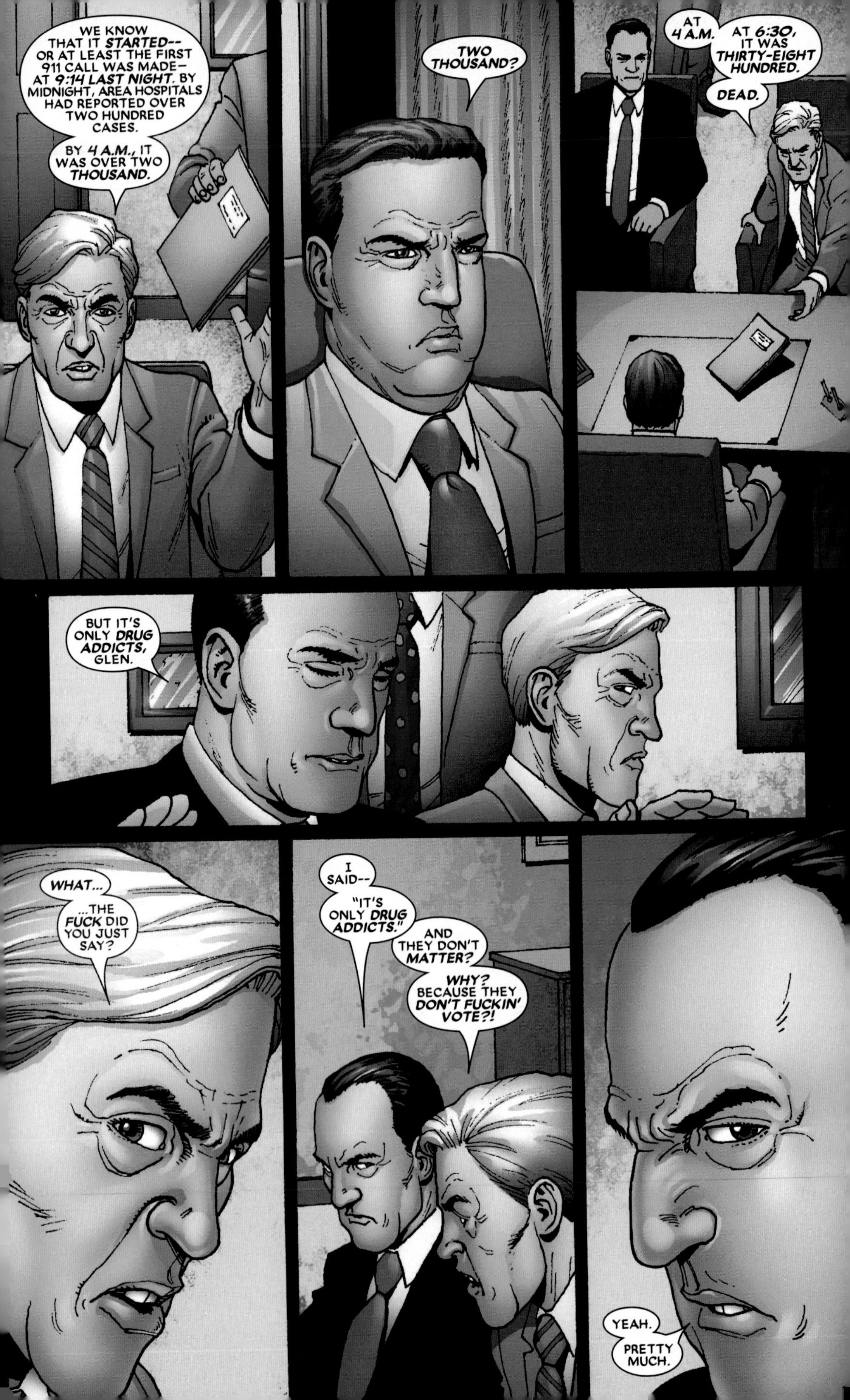
WE KNOW THAT IT STARTED-- OR AT LEAST THE FIRST 911 CALL WAS MADE-- AT 9:14 LAST NIGHT. BY MIDNIGHT, AREA HOSPITALS HAD REPORTED OVER TWO HUNDRED CASES.
BY 4 A.M., IT WAS OVER TWO THOUSAND.
TWO THOUSAND?
AT 4 A.M.
AT 6:30, IT WAS THIRTY-EIGHT HUNDRED.
DEAD.
BUT IT'S ONLY DRUG ADDICTS, GLEN.
WHAT...
...THE FUCK DID YOU JUST SAY?
I SAID--
"IT'S ONLY DRUG ADDICTS."
AND THEY DON'T MATTER?
WHY? BECAUSE THEY DON'T FUCKIN' VOTE?!
YEAH.
PRETTY MUCH.

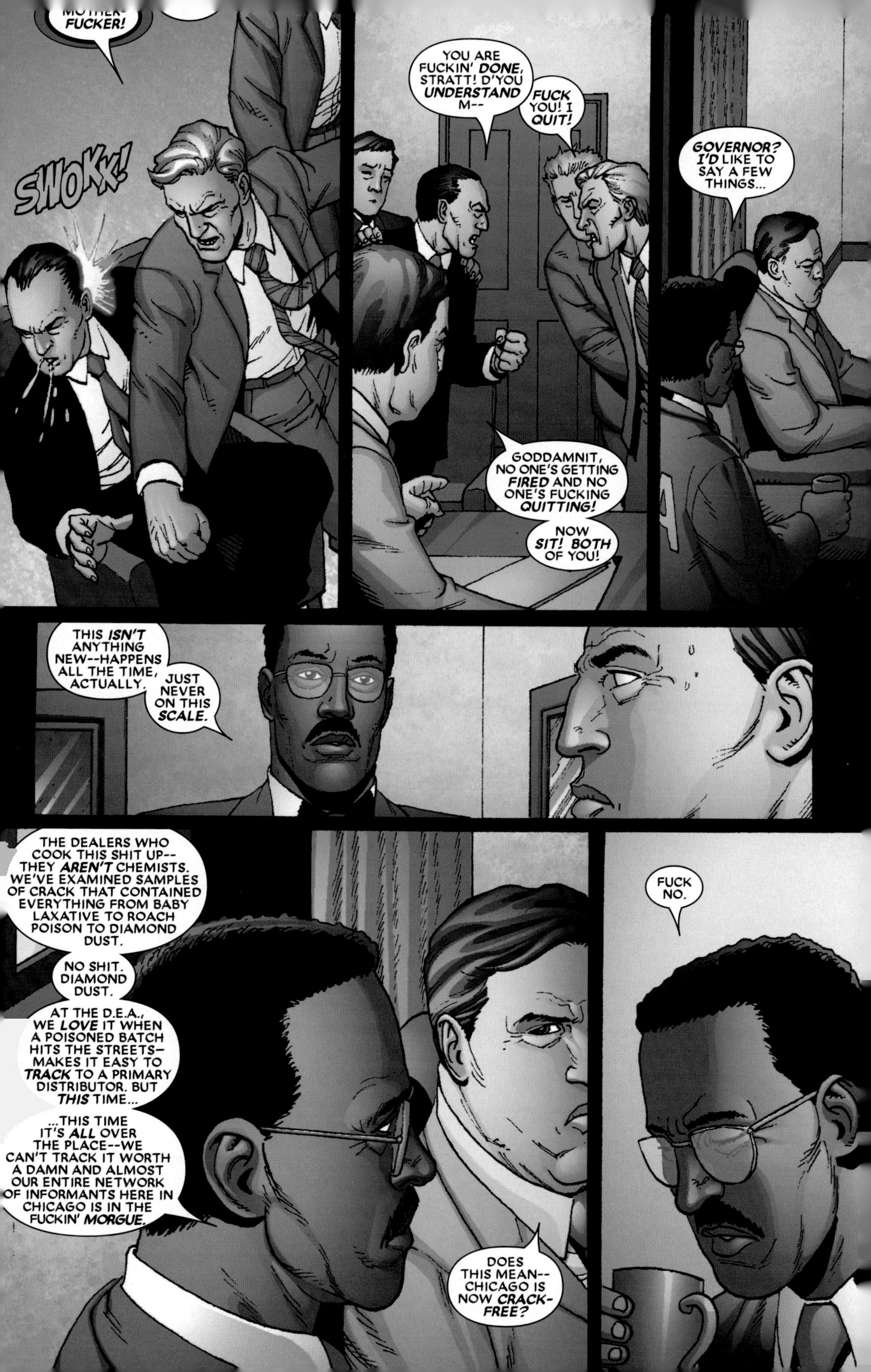
MOTHER-FUCKER!
SWOKK!
YOU ARE FUCKIN' DONE, STRATT! D'YOU UNDERSTAND M--
FUCK YOU! I QUIT!
GODDAMNIT, NO ONE'S GETTING FIRED AND NO ONE'S FUCKING QUITTING!
NOW SIT! BOTH OF YOU!
GOVERNOR? I'D LIKE TO SAY A FEW THINGS...
THIS ISN'T ANYTHING NEW--HAPPENS ALL THE TIME, ACTUALLY.
JUST NEVER ON THIS SCALE.
THE DEALERS WHO COOK THIS SHIT UP-- THEY AREN'T CHEMISTS. WE'VE EXAMINED SAMPLES OF CRACK THAT CONTAINED EVERYTHING FROM BABY LAXATIVE TO ROACH POISON TO DIAMOND DUST.
NO SHIT. DIAMOND DUST.
AT THE D.E.A., WE LOVE IT WHEN A POISONED BATCH HITS THE STREETS-MAKES IT EASY TO TRACK TO A PRIMARY DISTRIBUTOR. BUT THIS TIME...
...THIS TIME IT'S ALL OVER THE PLACE--WE CAN'T TRACK IT WORTH A DAMN AND ALMOST OUR ENTIRE NETWORK OF INFORMANTS HERE IN CHICAGO IS IN THE FUCKIN' MORGUE.
DOES THIS MEAN-- CHICAGO IS NOW CRACK-FREE?
FUCK NO.

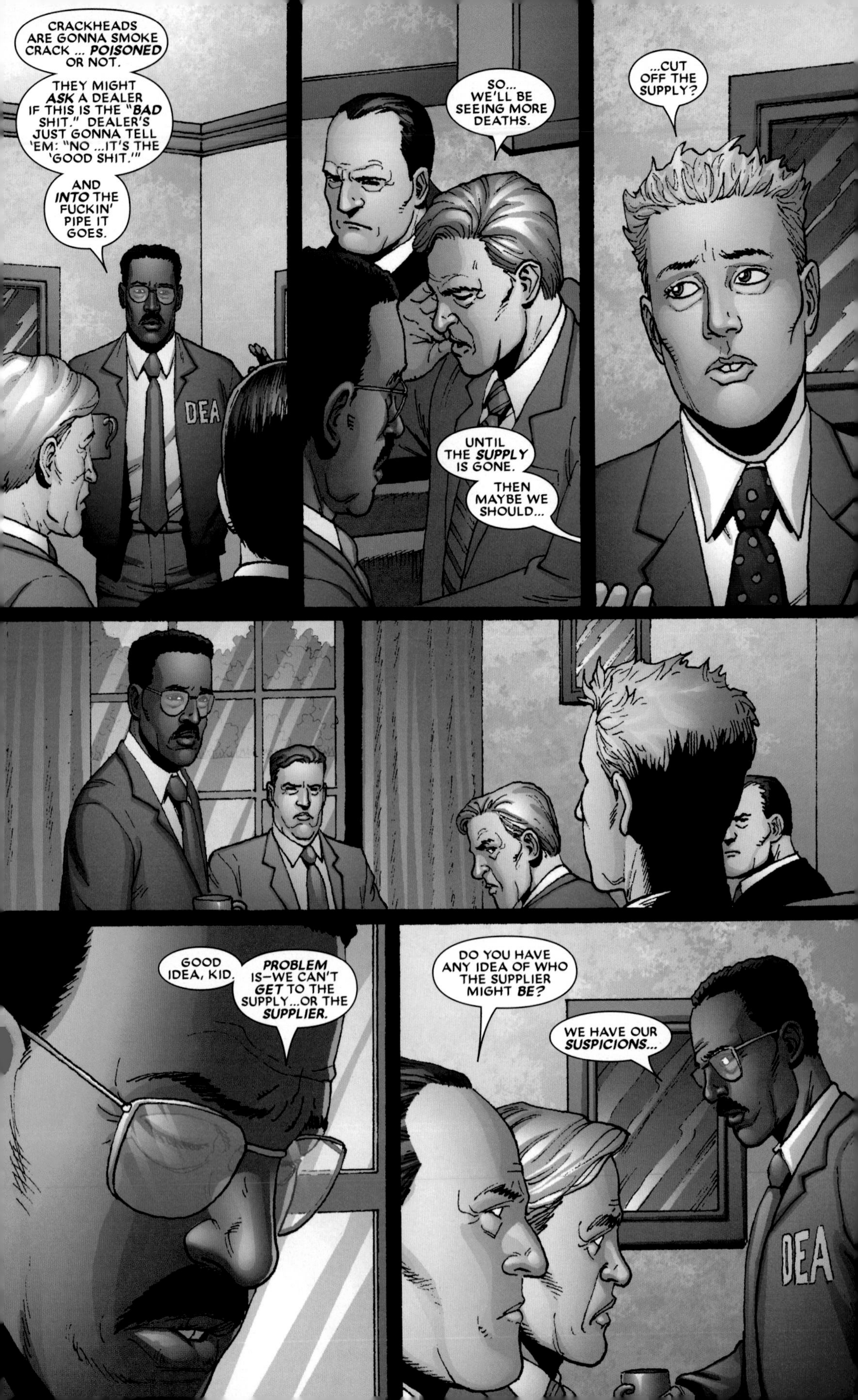
CRACKHEADS ARE GONNA SMOKE CRACK ... POISONED OR NOT.
THEY MIGHT ASK A DEALER IF THIS IS THE "BAD SHIT." DEALER'S JUST GONNA TELL 'EM: "NO ...IT'S THE 'GOOD SHIT.'"
AND INTO THE FUCKIN' PIPE IT GOES.
SO... WE'LL BE SEEING MORE DEATHS.
UNTIL THE SUPPLY IS GONE.
THEN MAYBE WE SHOULD...
...CUT OFF THE SUPPLY?
DEA
GOOD IDEA, KID.
PROBLEM IS—WE CAN'T GET TO THE SUPPLY...OR THE SUPPLIER.
DO YOU HAVE ANY IDEA OF WHO THE SUPPLIER MIGHT BE?
WE HAVE OUR SUSPICIONS...
DEA

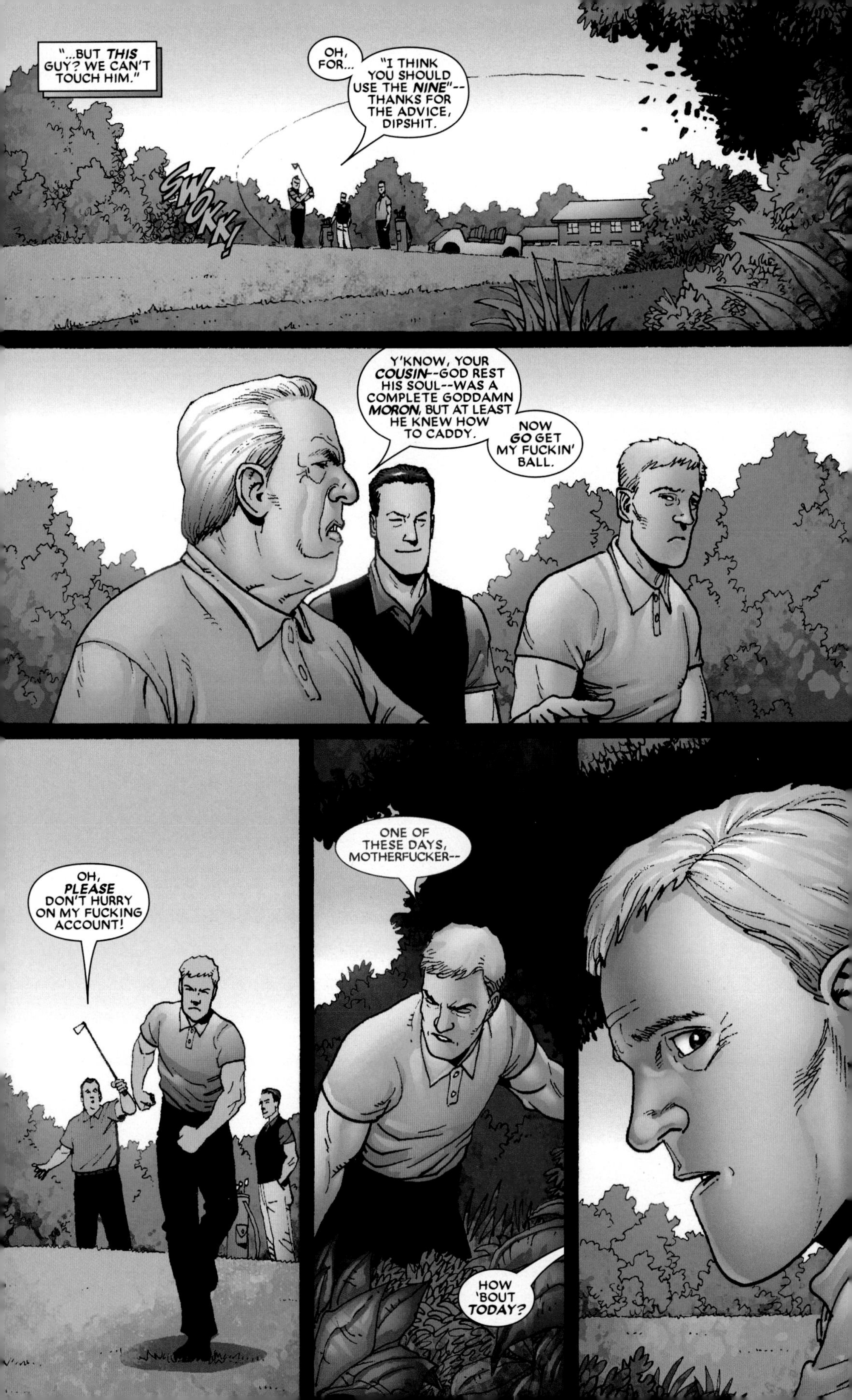

"...BUT *THIS* GUY? WE CAN'T TOUCH HIM."
OH, FOR... "I THINK YOU SHOULD USE THE *NINE*"-- THANKS FOR THE ADVICE, DIPSHIT.
SWOKK!
Y'KNOW, YOUR *COUSIN*--GOD REST HIS SOUL--WAS A COMPLETE GODDAMN *MORON*, BUT AT LEAST HE KNEW HOW TO CADDY.
NOW *GO* GET MY FUCKIN' BALL.
OH, *PLEASE* DON'T HURRY ON MY FUCKING ACCOUNT!
ONE OF THESE DAYS, MOTHERFUCKER--
HOW 'BOUT *TODAY*?

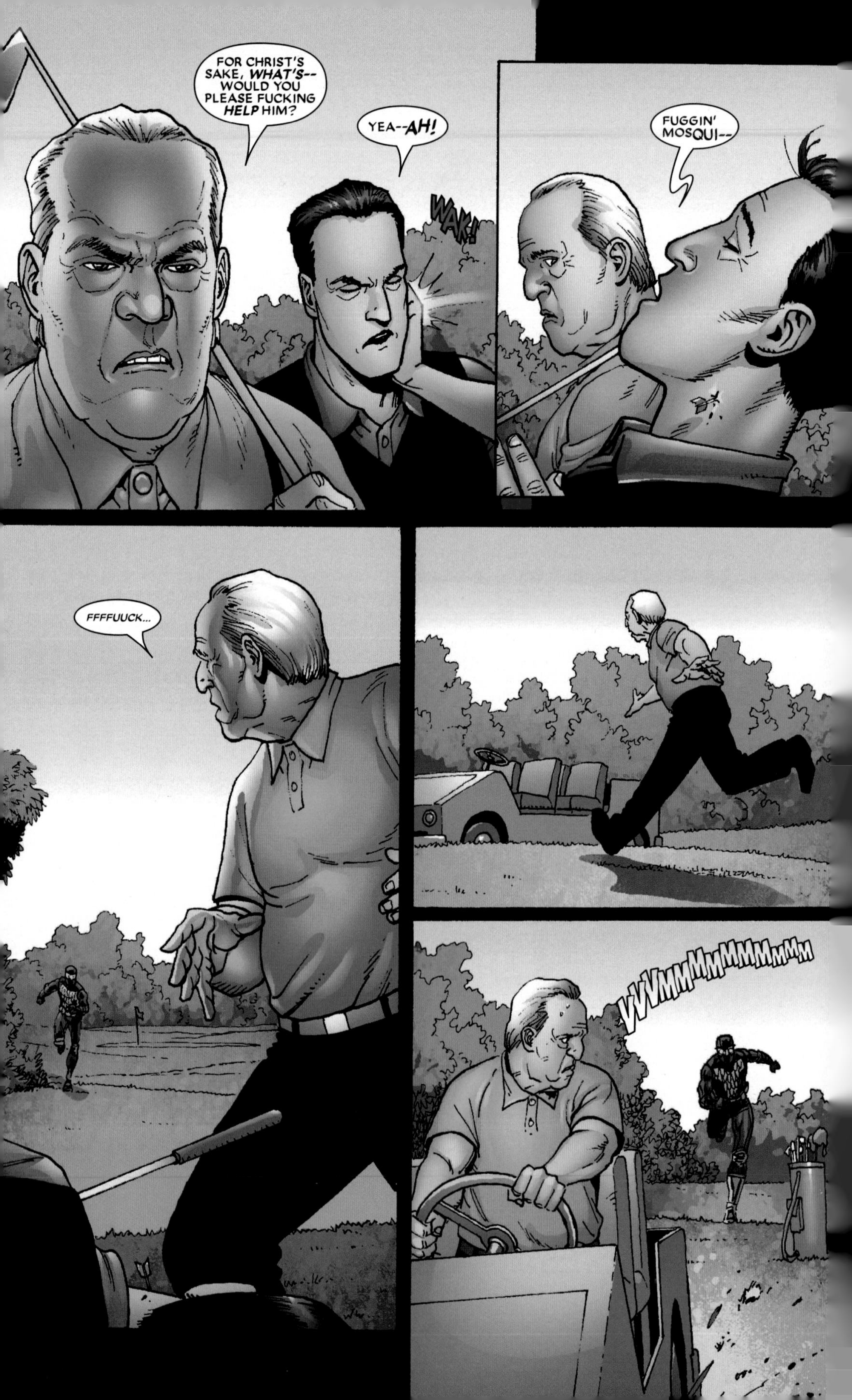
FOR CHRIST'S SAKE, WHAT'S-- WOULD YOU PLEASE FUCKING HELP HIM?
YEA--AH!
WAK!
FUGGIN' MOSQUI--
FFFFUUCK...
VVVMMMMMMMMMMMM

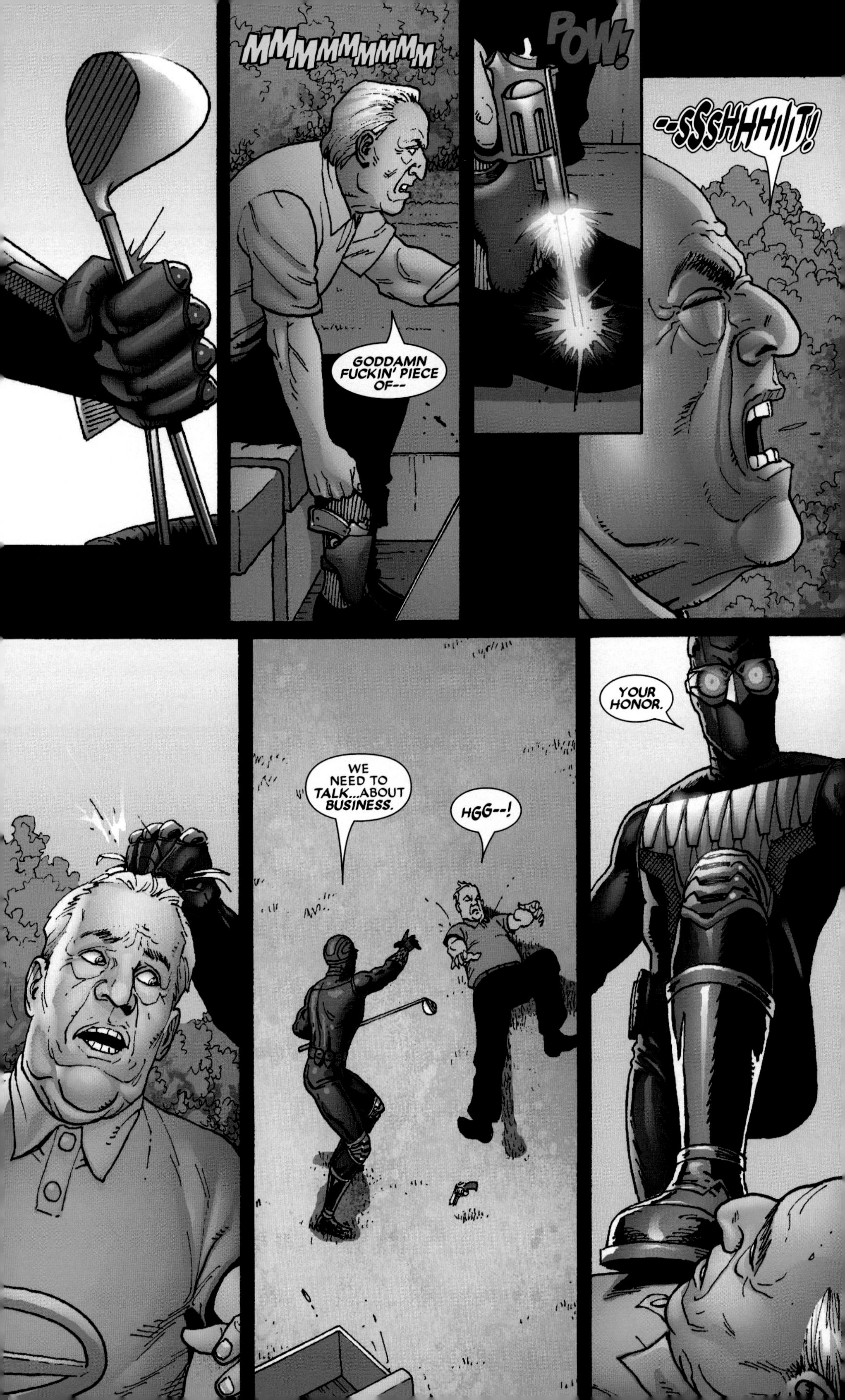
MMMMMMMMMM
GODDAMN FUCKIN' PIECE OF--
POW!
--SSSHHHIIIT!
WE NEED TO TALK...ABOUT BUSINESS.
HGG--!
YOUR HONOR.

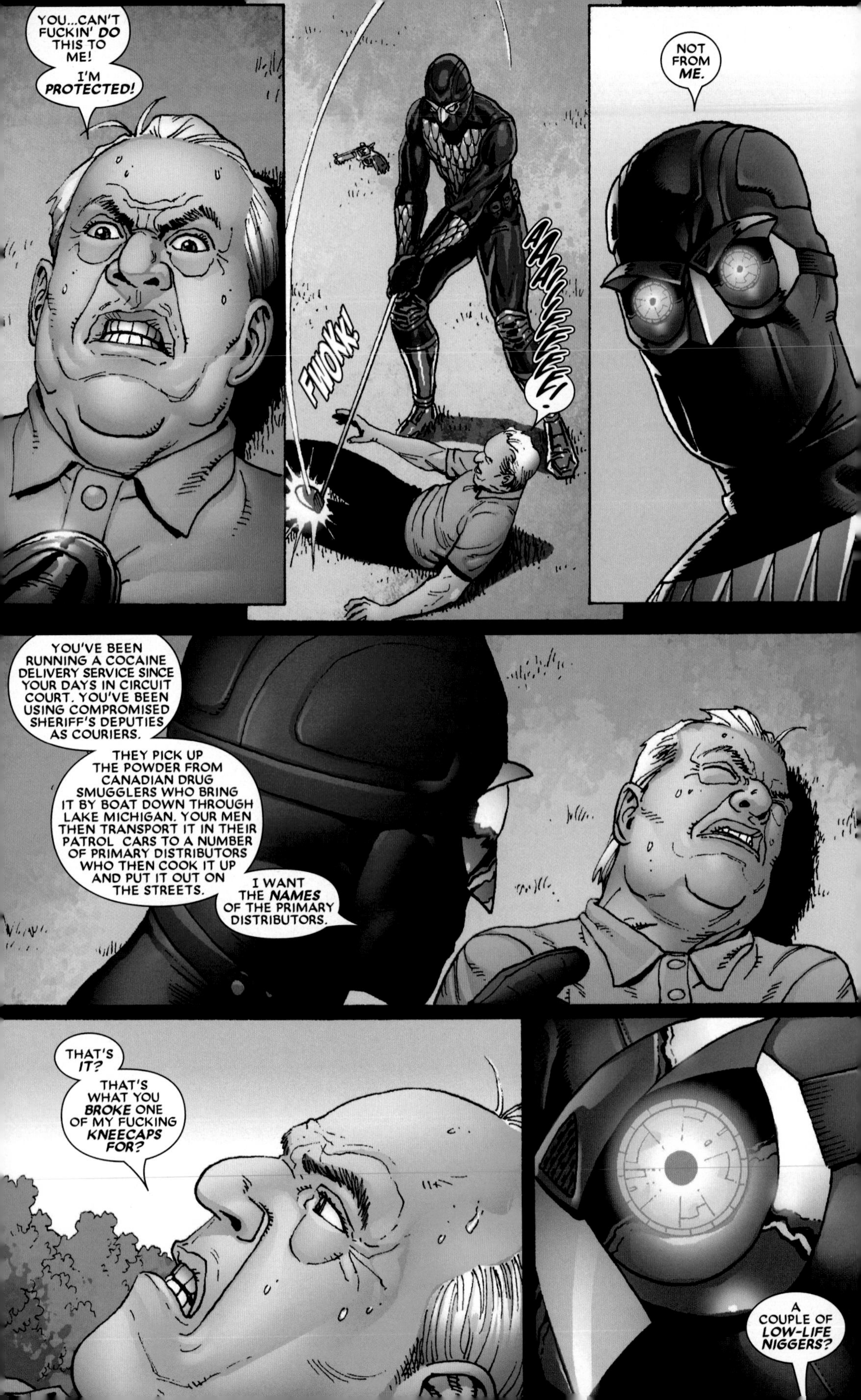
YOU...CAN'T FUCKIN' *DO* THIS TO ME!
I'M *PROTECTED!*
FWOKK!
AAAIIIEEEEE!
NOT FROM *ME.*
YOU'VE BEEN RUNNING A COCAINE DELIVERY SERVICE SINCE YOUR DAYS IN CIRCUIT COURT. YOU'VE BEEN USING COMPROMISED SHERIFF'S DEPUTIES AS COURIERS.
THEY PICK UP THE POWDER FROM CANADIAN DRUG SMUGGLERS WHO BRING IT BY BOAT DOWN THROUGH LAKE MICHIGAN. YOUR MEN THEN TRANSPORT IT IN THEIR PATROL CARS TO A NUMBER OF PRIMARY DISTRIBUTORS WHO THEN COOK IT UP AND PUT IT OUT ON THE STREETS.
I WANT THE *NAMES* OF THE PRIMARY DISTRIBUTORS.
THAT'S *IT?*
THAT'S WHAT YOU *BROKE* ONE OF MY FUCKING *KNEECAPS FOR?*
A COUPLE OF *LOW-LIFE NIGGERS?*

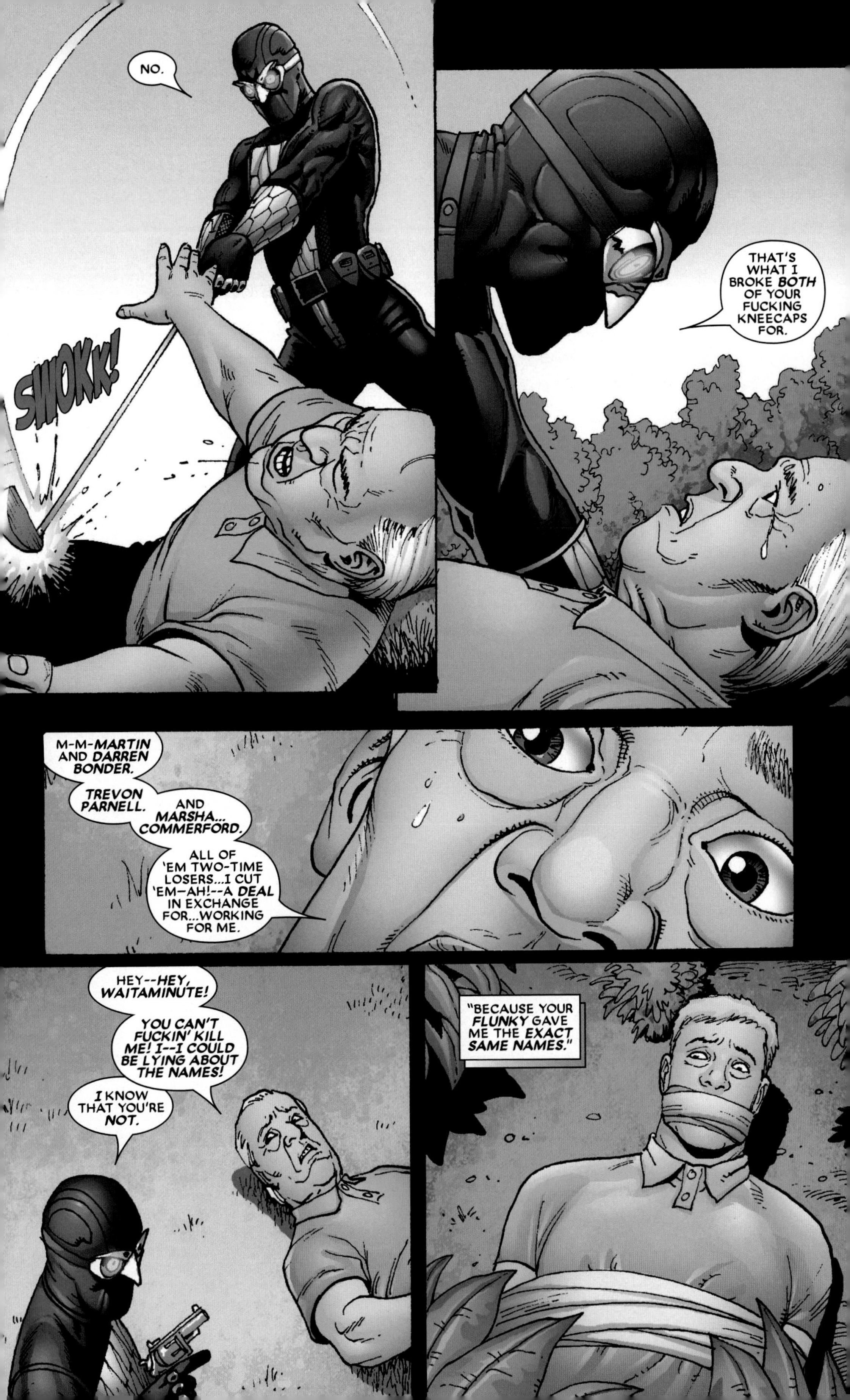
NO.
SWOKK!
THAT'S WHAT I BROKE BOTH OF YOUR FUCKING KNEECAPS FOR.
M-M-MARTIN AND DARREN BONDER.
TREVON PARNELL.
AND MARSHA... COMMERFORD.
ALL OF 'EM TWO-TIME LOSERS...I CUT 'EM--AH!--A DEAL IN EXCHANGE FOR...WORKING FOR ME.
HEY--HEY, WAITAMINUTE!
YOU CAN'T FUCKIN' KILL ME! I--I COULD BE LYING ABOUT THE NAMES!
I KNOW THAT YOU'RE NOT.
"BECAUSE YOUR FLUNKY GAVE ME THE EXACT SAME NAMES."

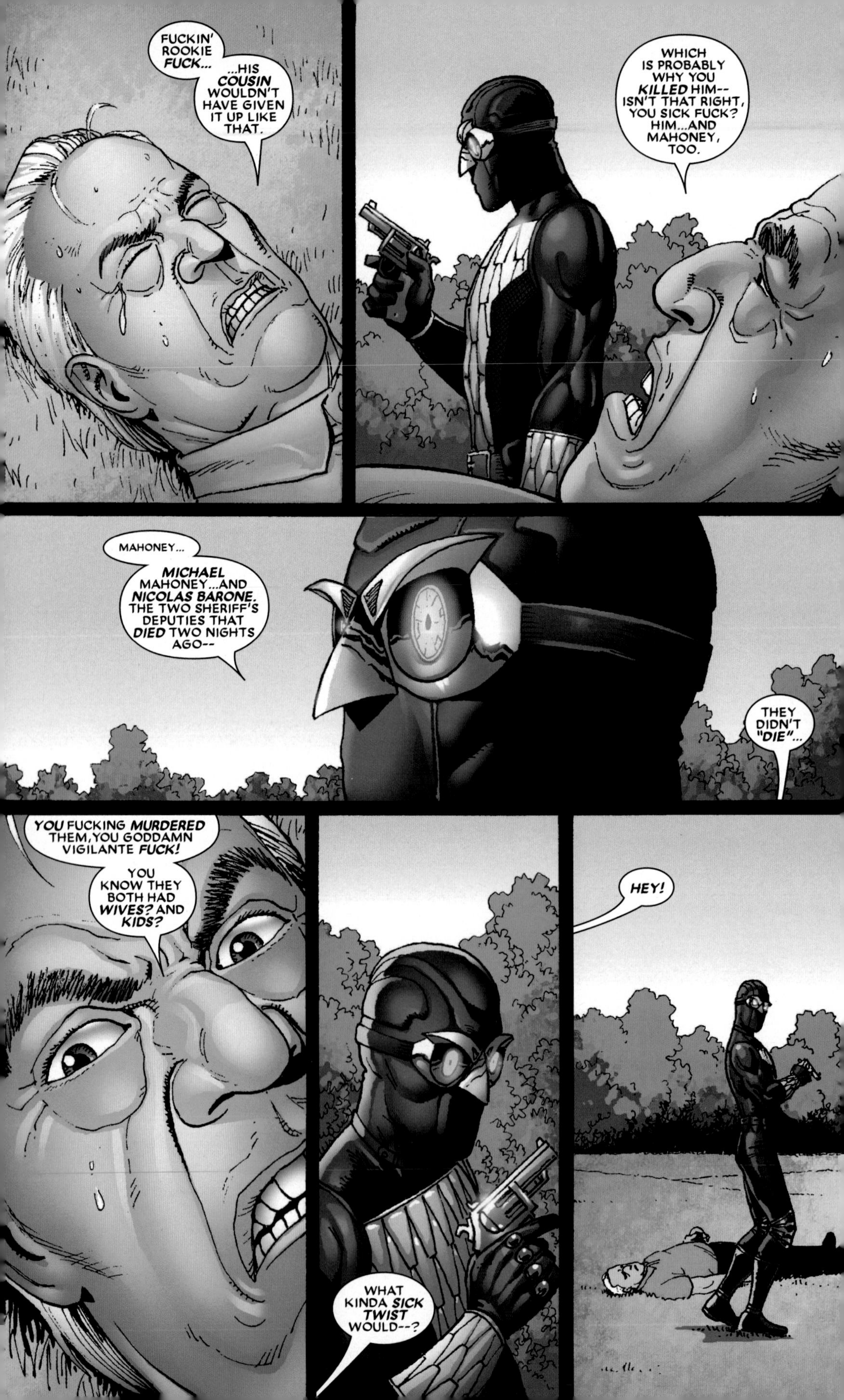
FUCKIN' ROOKIE FUCK...
...HIS COUSIN WOULDN'T HAVE GIVEN IT UP LIKE THAT.
WHICH IS PROBABLY WHY YOU KILLED HIM-- ISN'T THAT RIGHT, YOU SICK FUCK? HIM...AND MAHONEY, TOO.
MAHONEY...
MICHAEL MAHONEY...AND NICOLAS BARONE. THE TWO SHERIFF'S DEPUTIES THAT DIED TWO NIGHTS AGO--
THEY DIDN'T "DIE"...
YOU FUCKING MURDERED THEM, YOU GODDAMN VIGILANTE FUCK!
YOU KNOW THEY BOTH HAD WIVES? AND KIDS?
WHAT KINDA SICK TWIST WOULD--?
HEY!

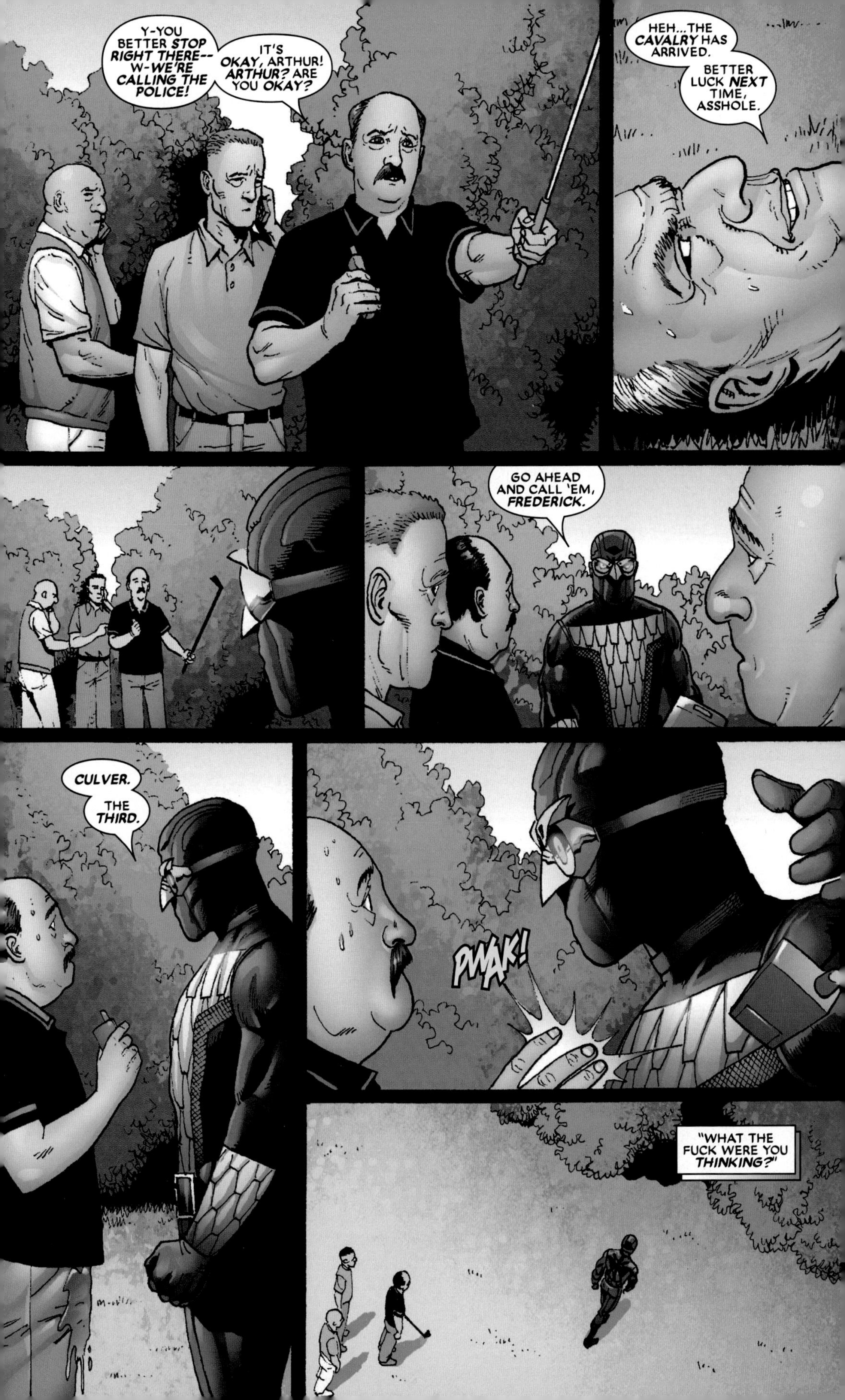
Y-YOU BETTER STOP RIGHT THERE-- W-WE'RE CALLING THE POLICE!
IT'S OKAY, ARTHUR! ARTHUR? ARE YOU OKAY?
HEH...THE CAVALRY HAS ARRIVED.
BETTER LUCK NEXT TIME, ASSHOLE.
GO AHEAD AND CALL 'EM, FREDERICK.
CULVER.
THE THIRD.
PWAK!
"WHAT THE FUCK WERE YOU THINKING?"

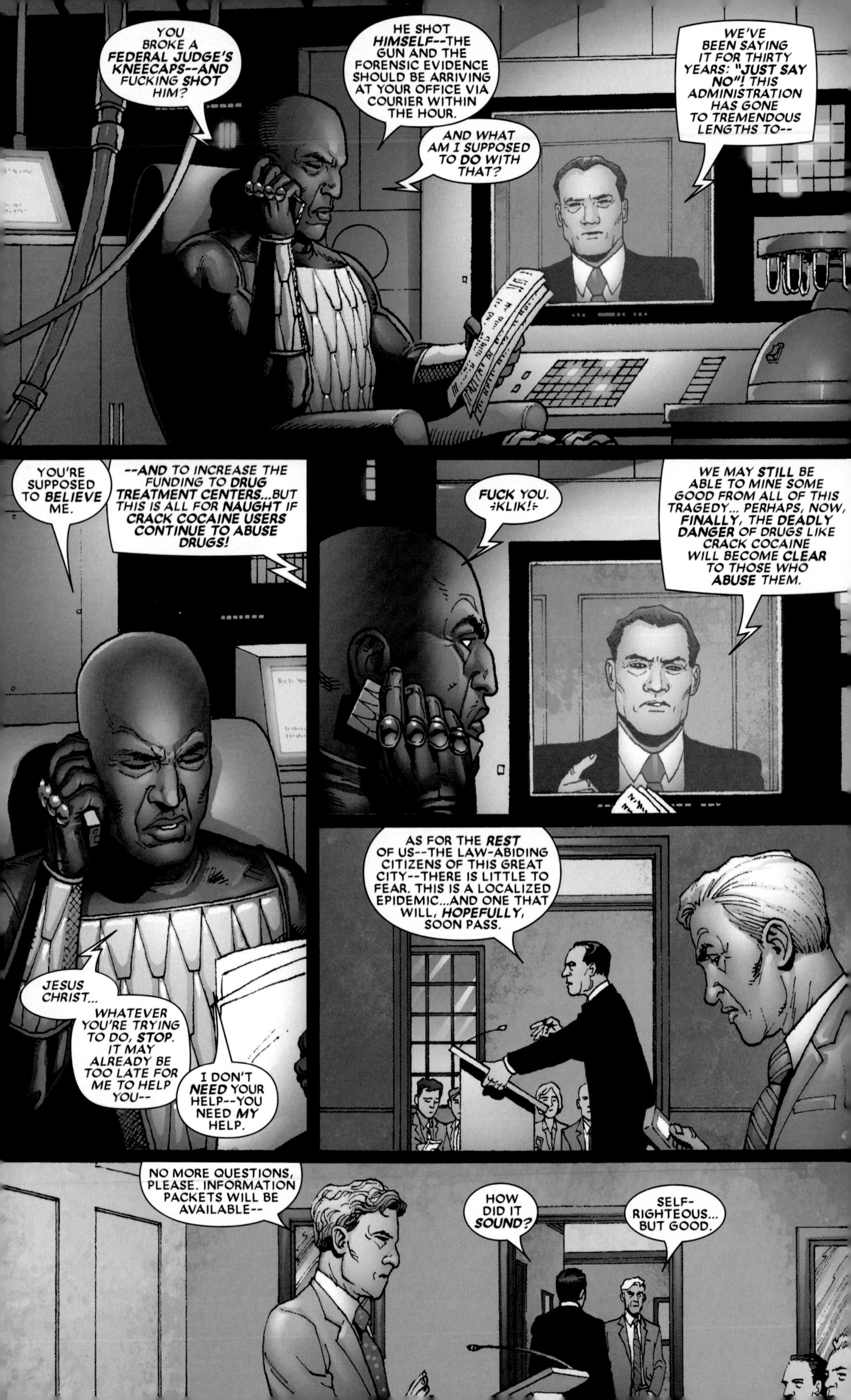
YOU BROKE A FEDERAL JUDGE'S KNEECAPS--AND FUCKING SHOT HIM?
HE SHOT HIMSELF--THE GUN AND THE FORENSIC EVIDENCE SHOULD BE ARRIVING AT YOUR OFFICE VIA COURIER WITHIN THE HOUR.
AND WHAT AM I SUPPOSED TO DO WITH THAT?
WE'VE BEEN SAYING IT FOR THIRTY YEARS: "JUST SAY NO"! THIS ADMINISTRATION HAS GONE TO TREMENDOUS LENGTHS TO--
YOU'RE SUPPOSED TO BELIEVE ME.
--AND TO INCREASE THE FUNDING TO DRUG TREATMENT CENTERS...BUT THIS IS ALL FOR NAUGHT IF CRACK COCAINE USERS CONTINUE TO ABUSE DRUGS!
JESUS CHRIST...
WHATEVER YOU'RE TRYING TO DO, STOP. IT MAY ALREADY BE TOO LATE FOR ME TO HELP YOU--
I DON'T NEED YOUR HELP--YOU NEED MY HELP.
FUCK YOU. ≠KLIK!≠
WE MAY STILL BE ABLE TO MINE SOME GOOD FROM ALL OF THIS TRAGEDY... PERHAPS, NOW, FINALLY, THE DEADLY DANGER OF DRUGS LIKE CRACK COCAINE WILL BECOME CLEAR TO THOSE WHO ABUSE THEM.
AS FOR THE REST OF US--THE LAW-ABIDING CITIZENS OF THIS GREAT CITY--THERE IS LITTLE TO FEAR. THIS IS A LOCALIZED EPIDEMIC...AND ONE THAT WILL, HOPEFULLY, SOON PASS.
NO MORE QUESTIONS, PLEASE. INFORMATION PACKETS WILL BE AVAILABLE--
HOW DID IT SOUND?
SELF-RIGHTEOUS... BUT GOOD.

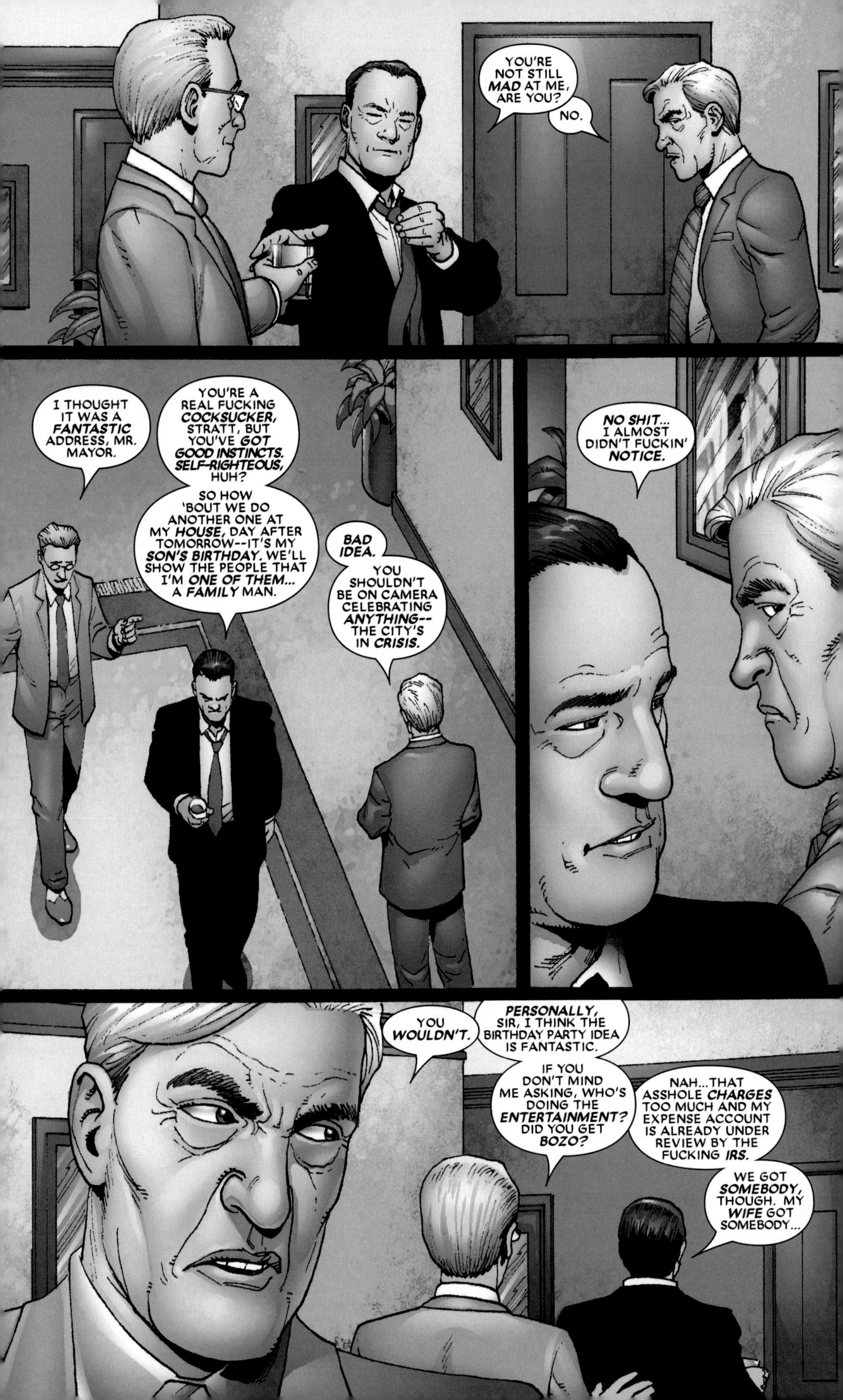
YOU'RE NOT STILL MAD AT ME, ARE YOU?
NO.
I THOUGHT IT WAS A FANTASTIC ADDRESS, MR. MAYOR.
YOU'RE A REAL FUCKING COCKSUCKER, STRATT, BUT YOU'VE GOT GOOD INSTINCTS. SELF-RIGHTEOUS, HUH?
SO HOW 'BOUT WE DO ANOTHER ONE AT MY HOUSE, DAY AFTER TOMORROW--IT'S MY SON'S BIRTHDAY. WE'LL SHOW THE PEOPLE THAT I'M ONE OF THEM... A FAMILY MAN.
BAD IDEA.
YOU SHOULDN'T BE ON CAMERA CELEBRATING ANYTHING-- THE CITY'S IN CRISIS.
NO SHIT... I ALMOST DIDN'T FUCKIN' NOTICE.
YOU WOULDN'T.
PERSONALLY, SIR, I THINK THE BIRTHDAY PARTY IDEA IS FANTASTIC.
IF YOU DON'T MIND ME ASKING, WHO'S DOING THE ENTERTAINMENT? DID YOU GET BOZO?
NAH...THAT ASSHOLE CHARGES TOO MUCH AND MY EXPENSE ACCOUNT IS ALREADY UNDER REVIEW BY THE FUCKING IRS.
WE GOT SOMEBODY, THOUGH. MY WIFE GOT SOMEBODY...

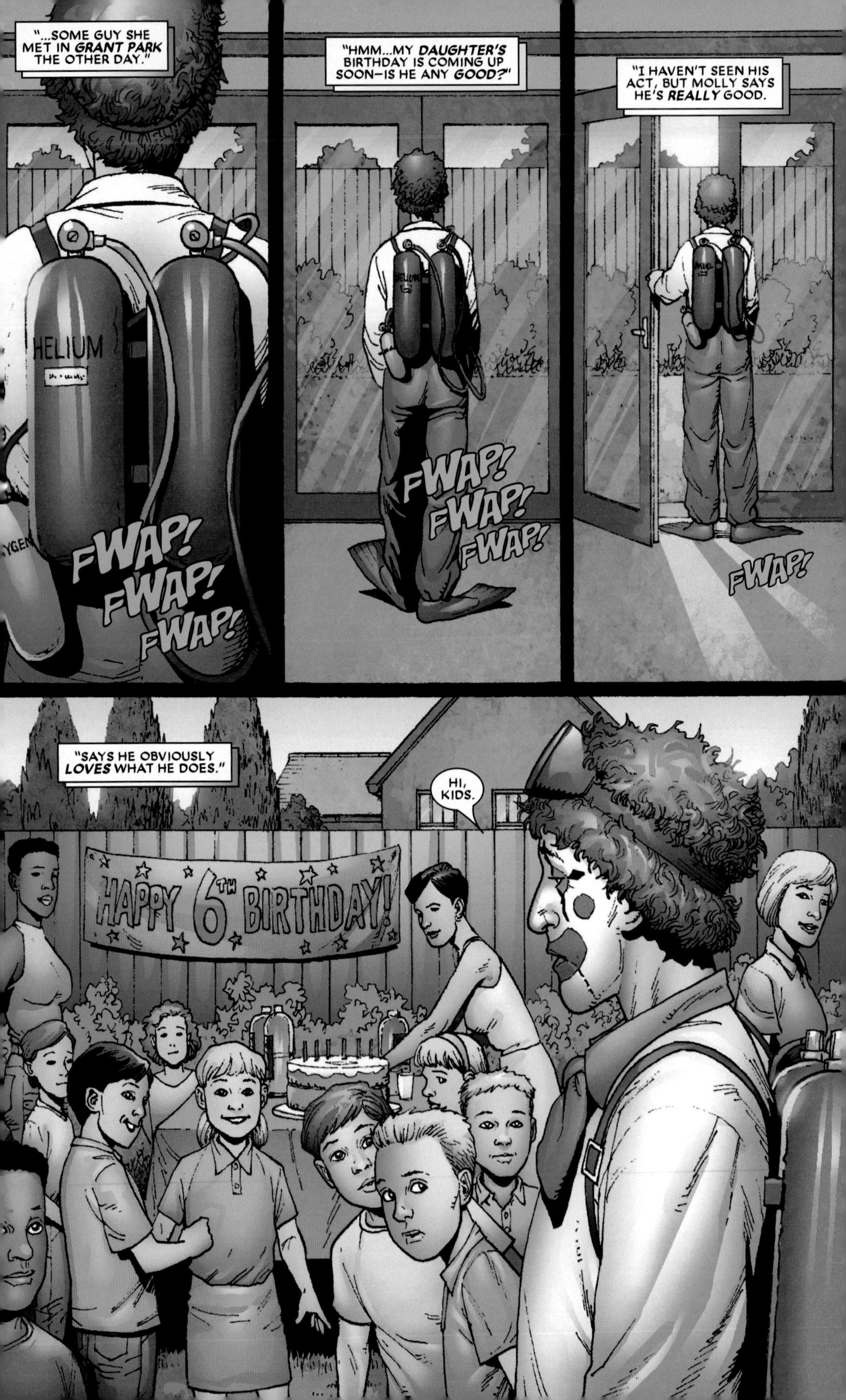
"...SOME GUY SHE MET IN GRANT PARK THE OTHER DAY."
HELIUM
FWAP! FWAP! FWAP!
"HMM...MY DAUGHTER'S BIRTHDAY IS COMING UP SOON—IS HE ANY GOOD?"
HELIUM
FWAP! FWAP! FWAP!
"I HAVEN'T SEEN HIS ACT, BUT MOLLY SAYS HE'S REALLY GOOD.
FWAP!
"SAYS HE OBVIOUSLY LOVES WHAT HE DOES."
HI, KIDS.
HAPPY 6TH BIRTHDAY!

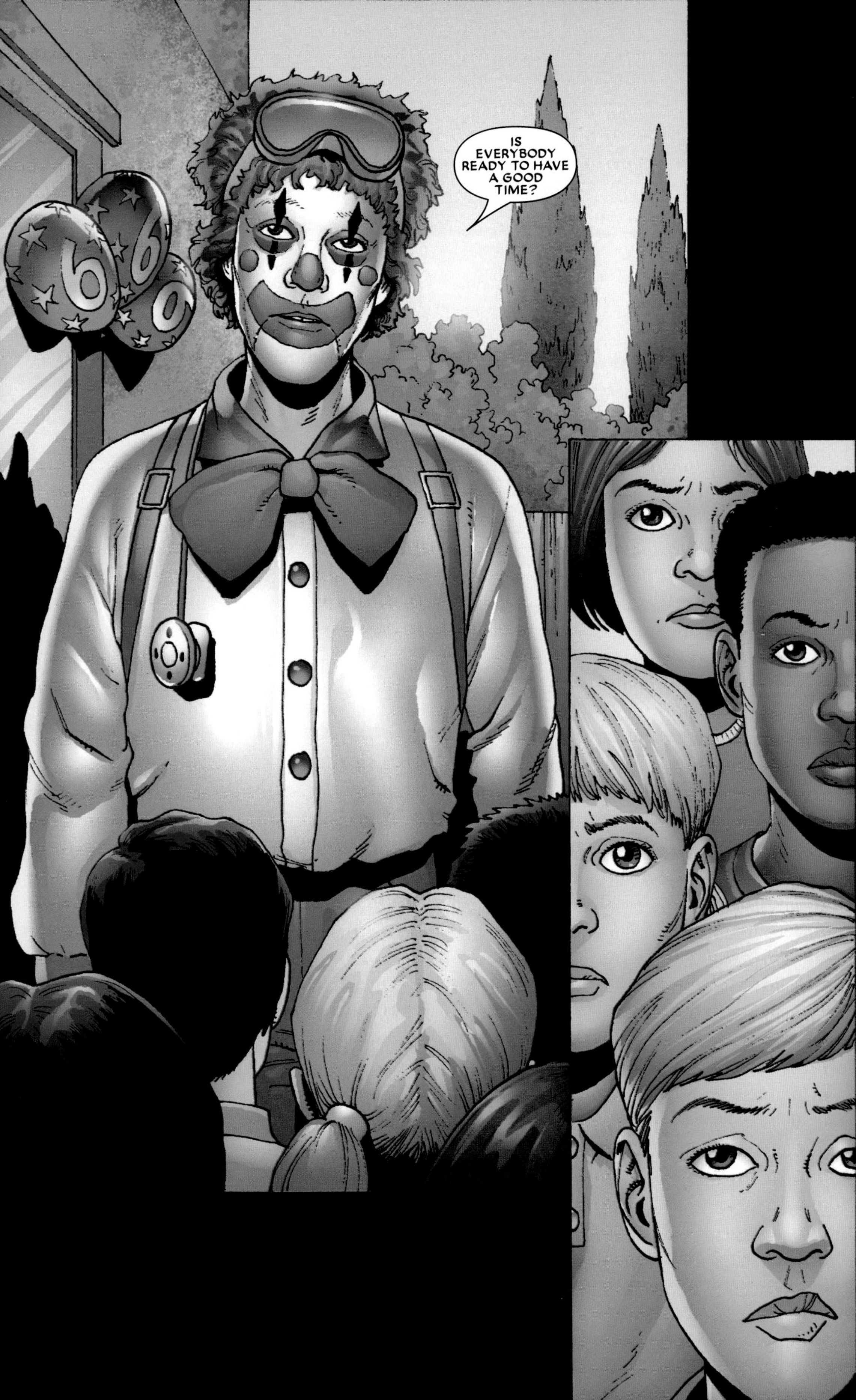
IS EVERYBODY READY TO HAVE A GOOD TIME?

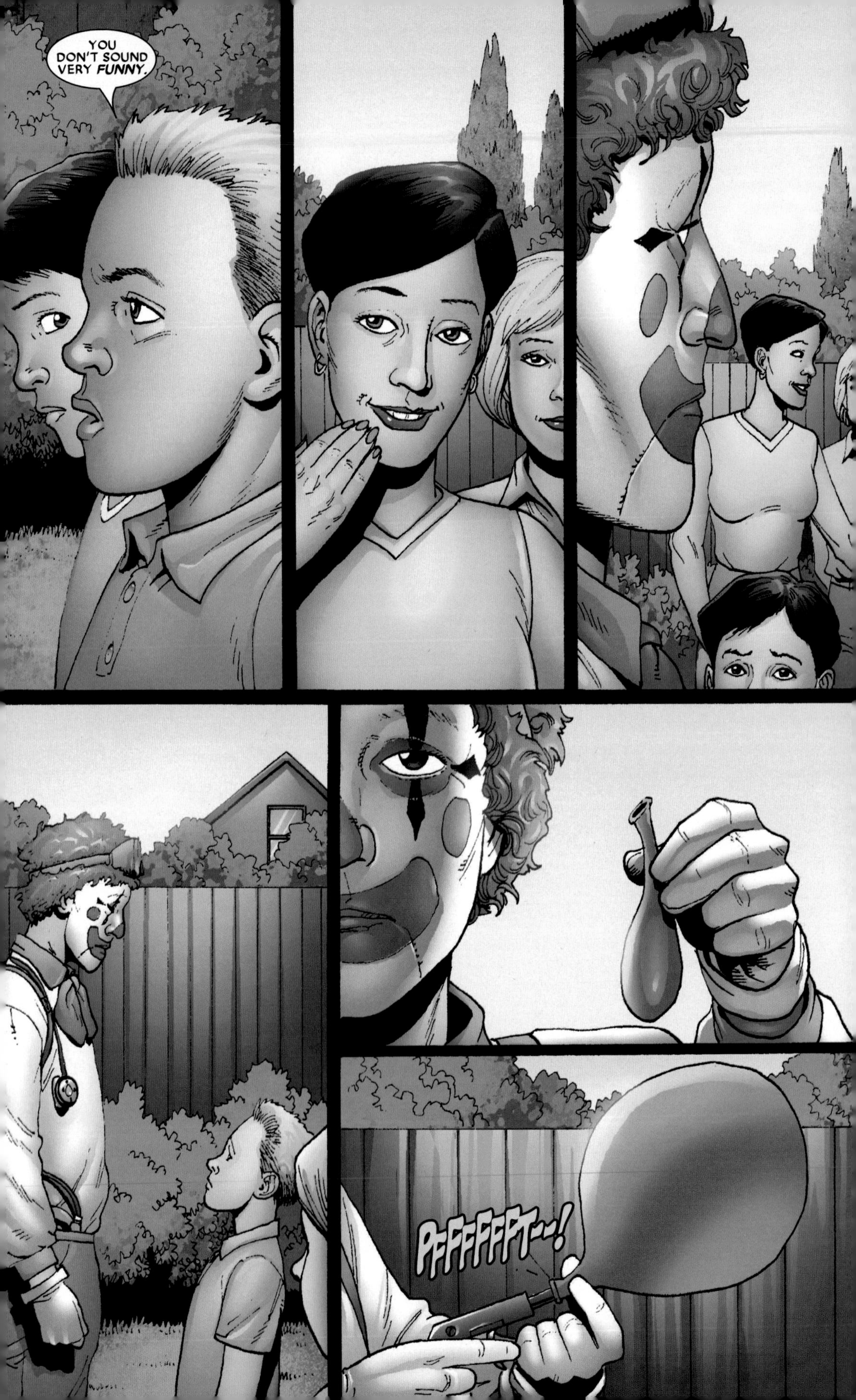
YOU DON'T SOUND VERY FUNNY.
PFFFFFPT--!

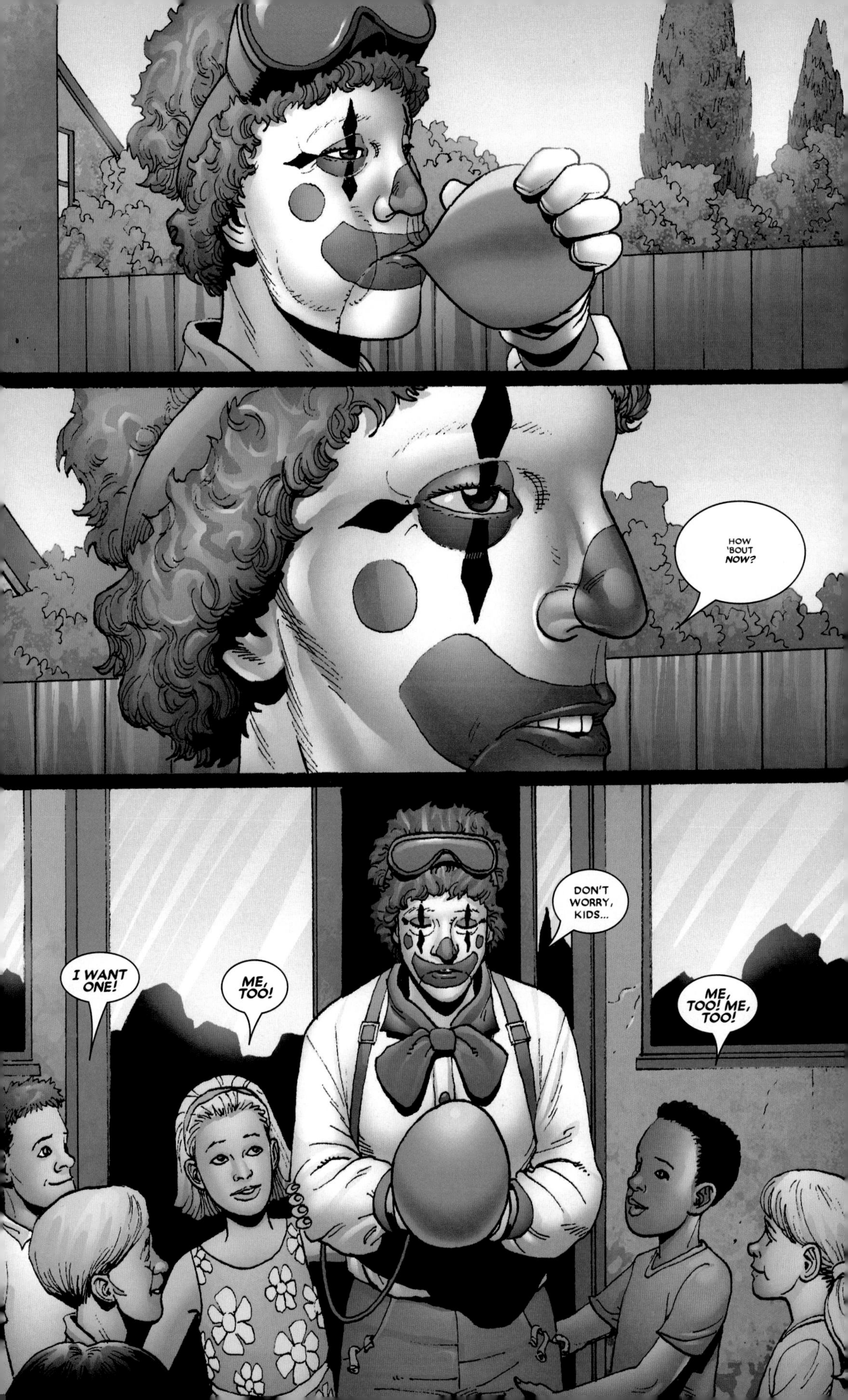
HOW 'BOUT NOW?
DON'T WORRY, KIDS...
I WANT ONE!
ME, TOO!
ME, TOO! ME, TOO!

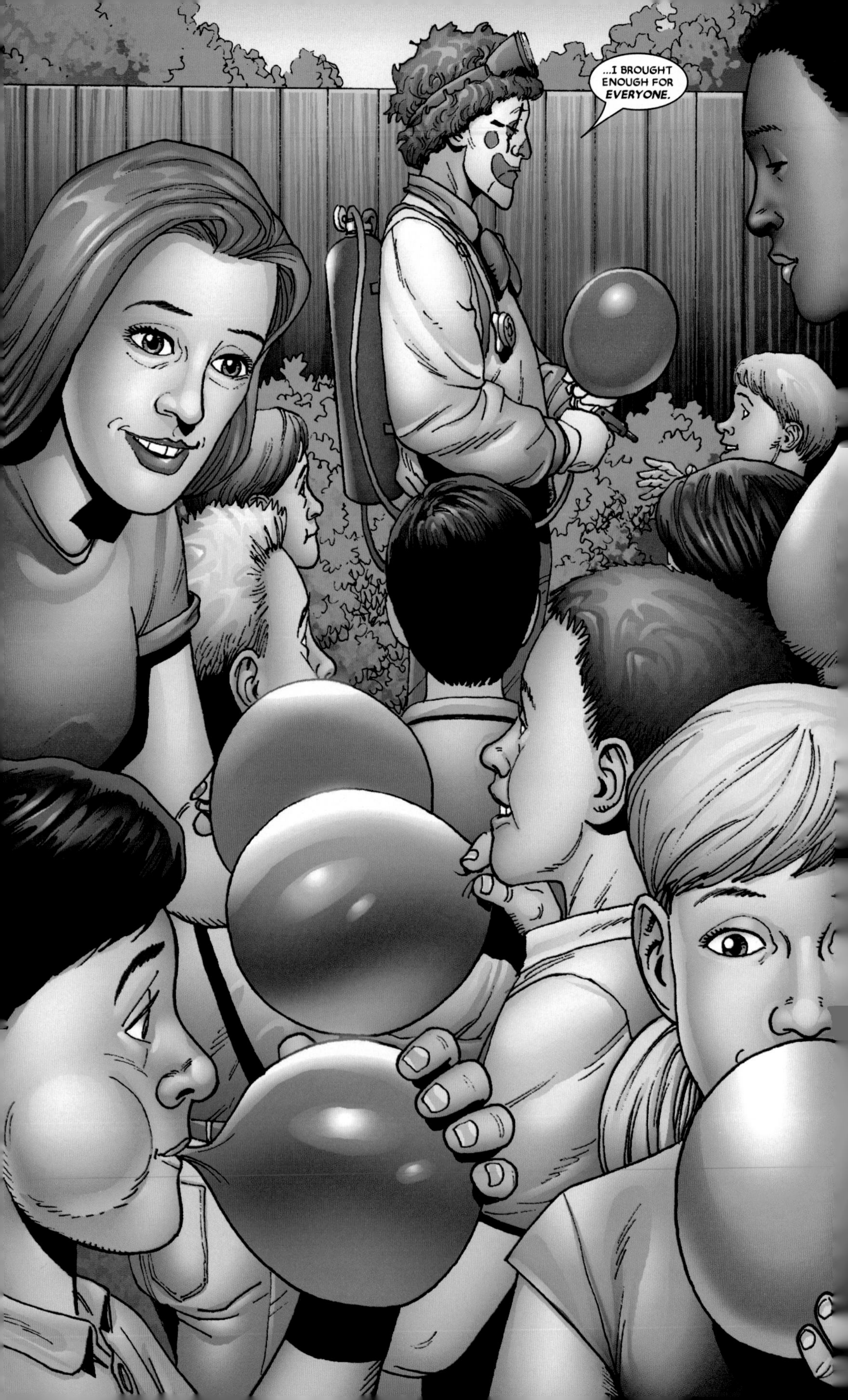
...I BROUGHT ENOUGH FOR EVERYONE.

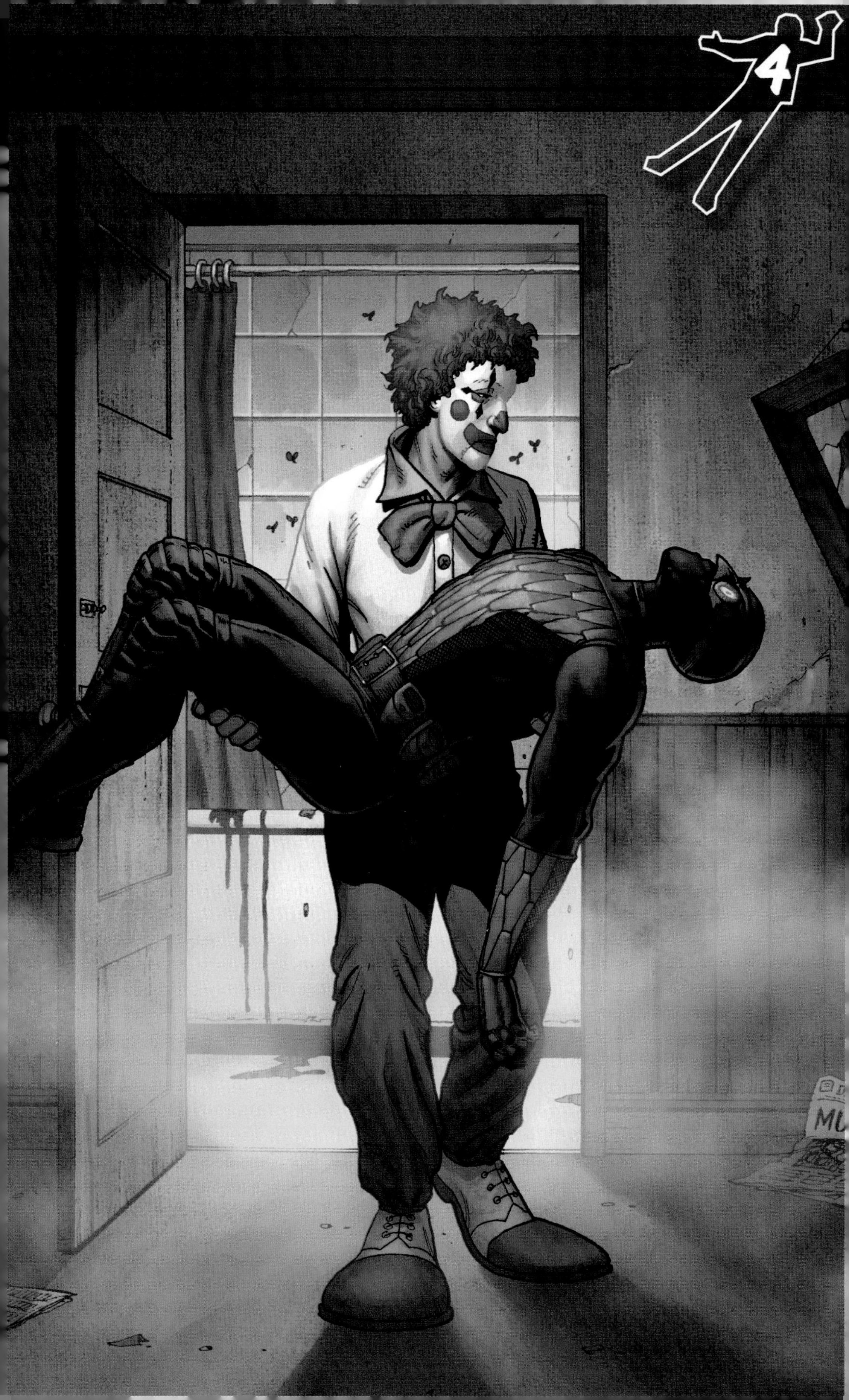
4

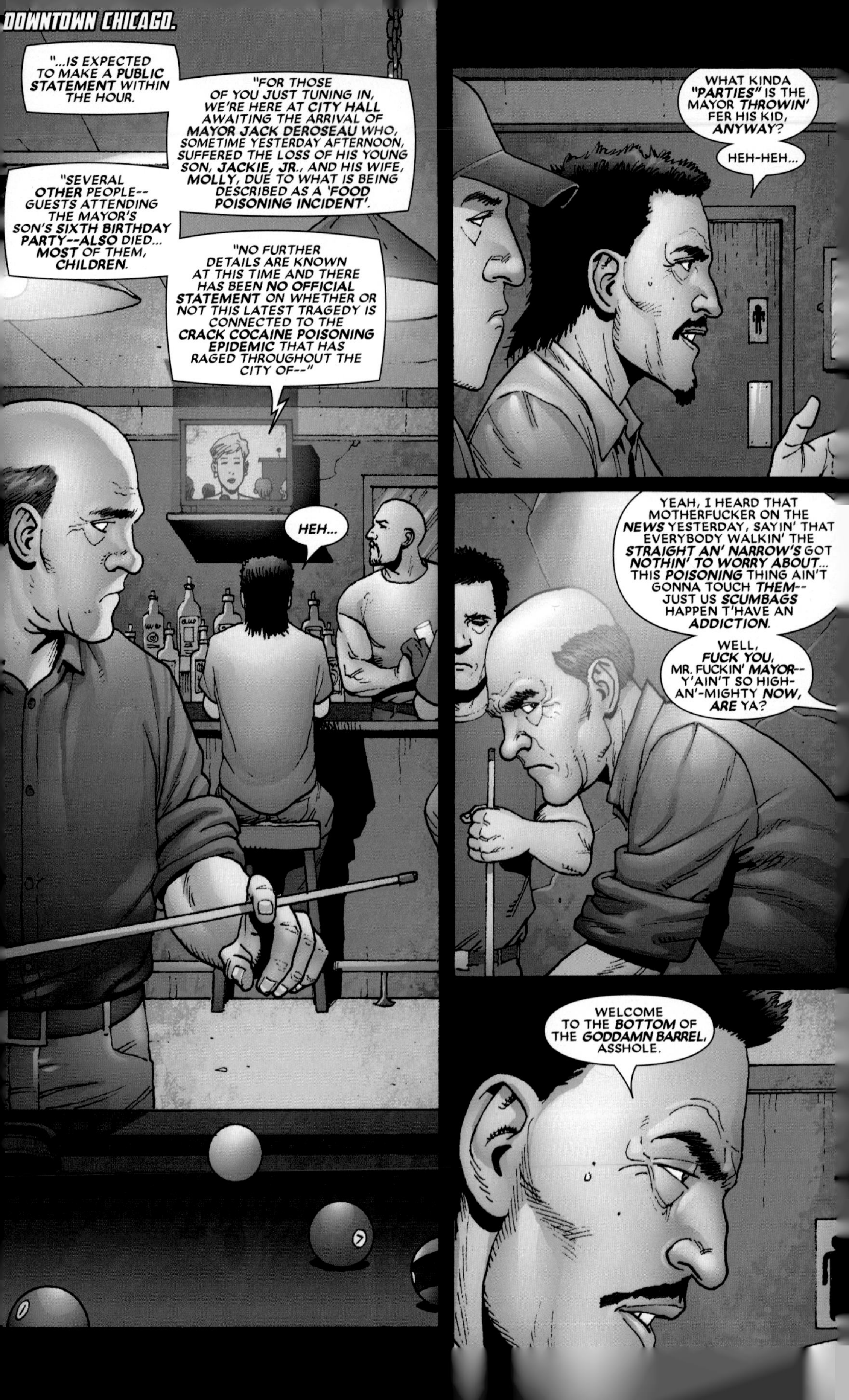
DOWNTOWN CHICAGO.
"...IS EXPECTED TO MAKE A PUBLIC STATEMENT WITHIN THE HOUR.
"FOR THOSE OF YOU JUST TUNING IN, WE'RE HERE AT CITY HALL AWAITING THE ARRIVAL OF MAYOR JACK DEROSEAU WHO, SOMETIME YESTERDAY AFTERNOON, SUFFERED THE LOSS OF HIS YOUNG SON, JACKIE, JR., AND HIS WIFE, MOLLY, DUE TO WHAT IS BEING DESCRIBED AS A 'FOOD POISONING INCIDENT'.
"SEVERAL OTHER PEOPLE-- GUESTS ATTENDING THE MAYOR'S SON'S SIXTH BIRTHDAY PARTY--ALSO DIED... MOST OF THEM, CHILDREN.
"NO FURTHER DETAILS ARE KNOWN AT THIS TIME AND THERE HAS BEEN NO OFFICIAL STATEMENT ON WHETHER OR NOT THIS LATEST TRAGEDY IS CONNECTED TO THE CRACK COCAINE POISONING EPIDEMIC THAT HAS RAGED THROUGHOUT THE CITY OF--"
HEH...
WHAT KINDA "PARTIES" IS THE MAYOR THROWIN' FER HIS KID, ANYWAY?
HEH-HEH...
YEAH, I HEARD THAT MOTHERFUCKER ON THE NEWS YESTERDAY, SAYIN' THAT EVERYBODY WALKIN' THE STRAIGHT AN' NARROW'S GOT NOTHIN' TO WORRY ABOUT... THIS POISONING THING AIN'T GONNA TOUCH THEM-- JUST US SCUMBAGS HAPPEN T'HAVE AN ADDICTION.
WELL, FUCK YOU, MR. FUCKIN' MAYOR-- Y'AIN'T SO HIGH-AN'-MIGHTY NOW, ARE YA?
WELCOME TO THE BOTTOM OF THE GODDAMN BARREL, ASSHOLE.

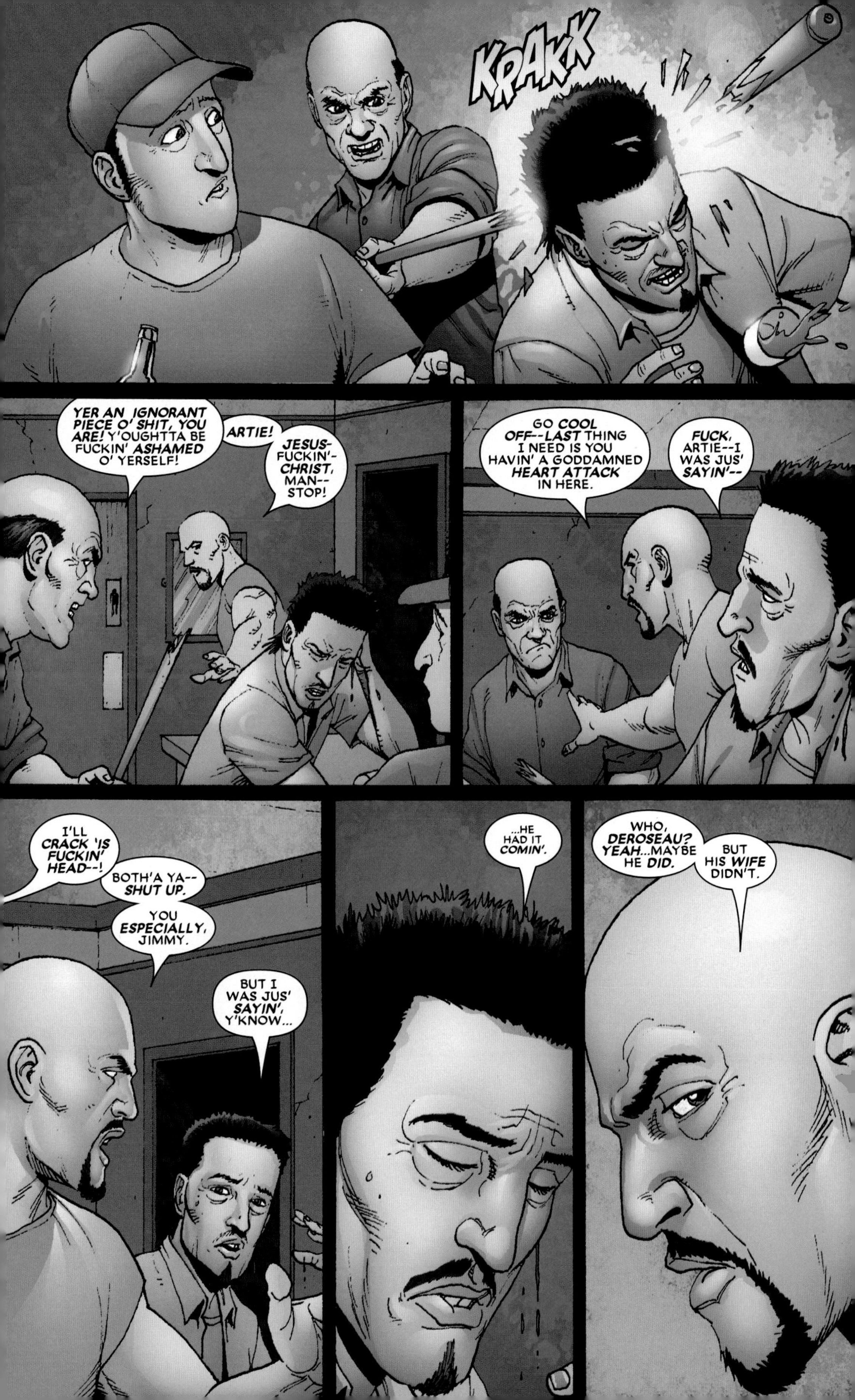
KRAKK
YER AN IGNORANT PIECE O' SHIT, YOU ARE! Y'OUGHTTA BE FUCKIN' ASHAMED O' YERSELF!
ARTIE!
JESUS-FUCKIN'-CHRIST, MAN--STOP!
GO COOL OFF--LAST THING I NEED IS YOU HAVIN' A GODDAMNED HEART ATTACK IN HERE.
FUCK, ARTIE--I WAS JUS' SAYIN'--
I'LL CRACK 'IS FUCKIN' HEAD--!
BOTH'A YA--SHUT UP.
YOU ESPECIALLY, JIMMY.
BUT I WAS JUS' SAYIN', Y'KNOW...
...HE HAD IT COMIN'.
WHO, DEROSEAU? YEAH...MAYBE HE DID.
BUT HIS WIFE DIDN'T.

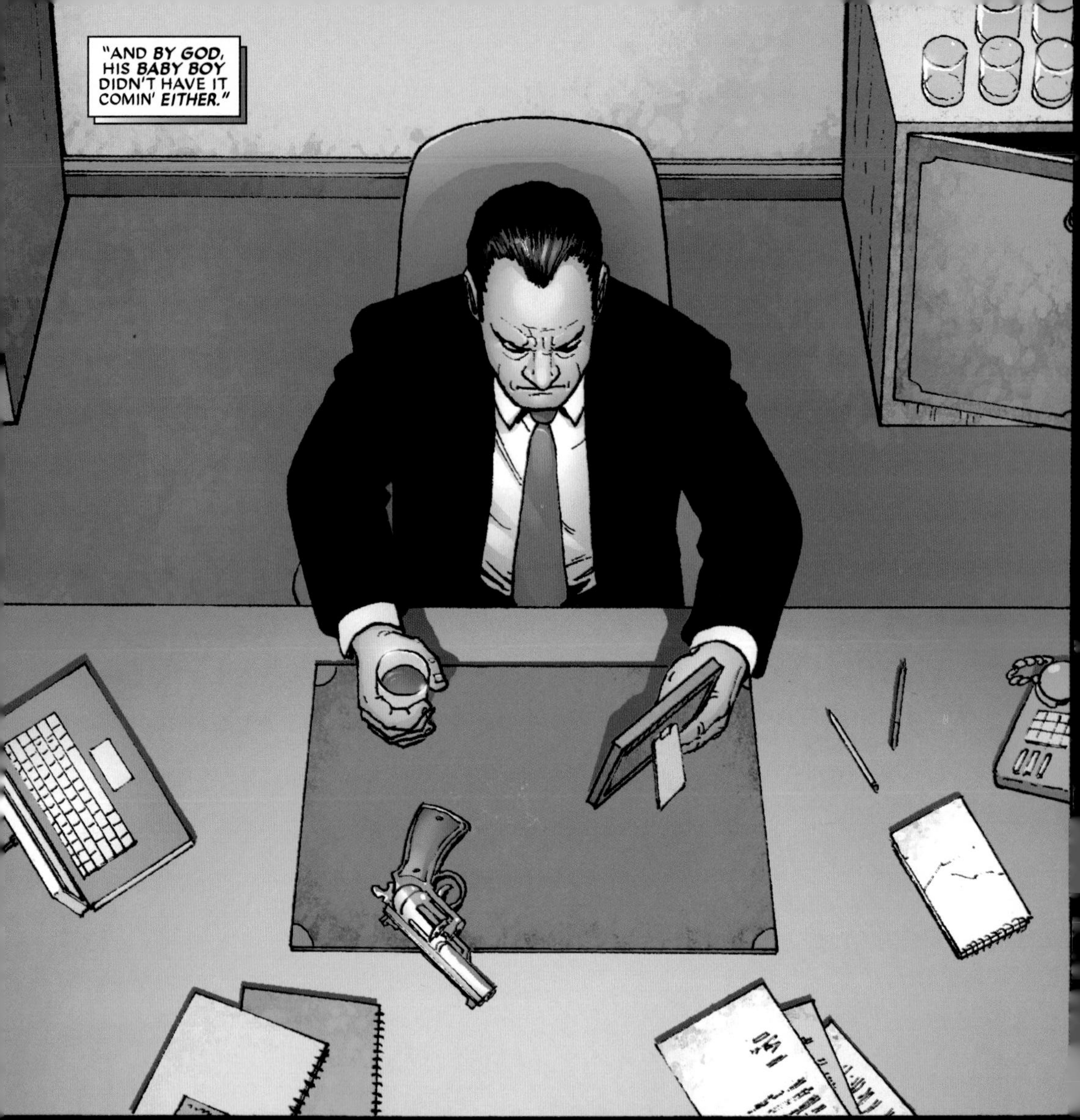
"AND BY GOD, HIS BABY BOY DIDN'T HAVE IT COMIN' EITHER."

The Joke's Over

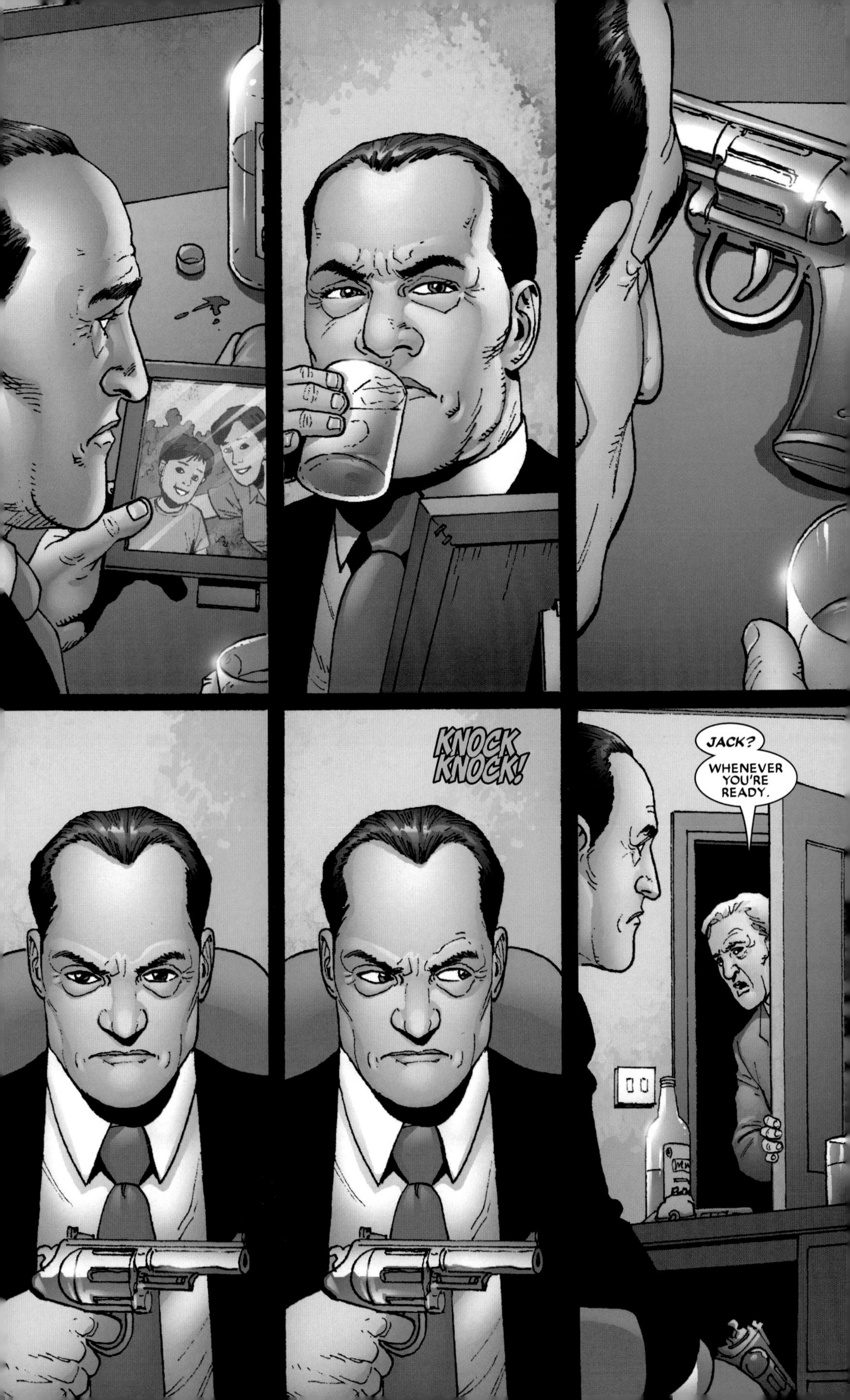
KNOCK KNOCK!
JACK?
WHENEVER YOU'RE READY.

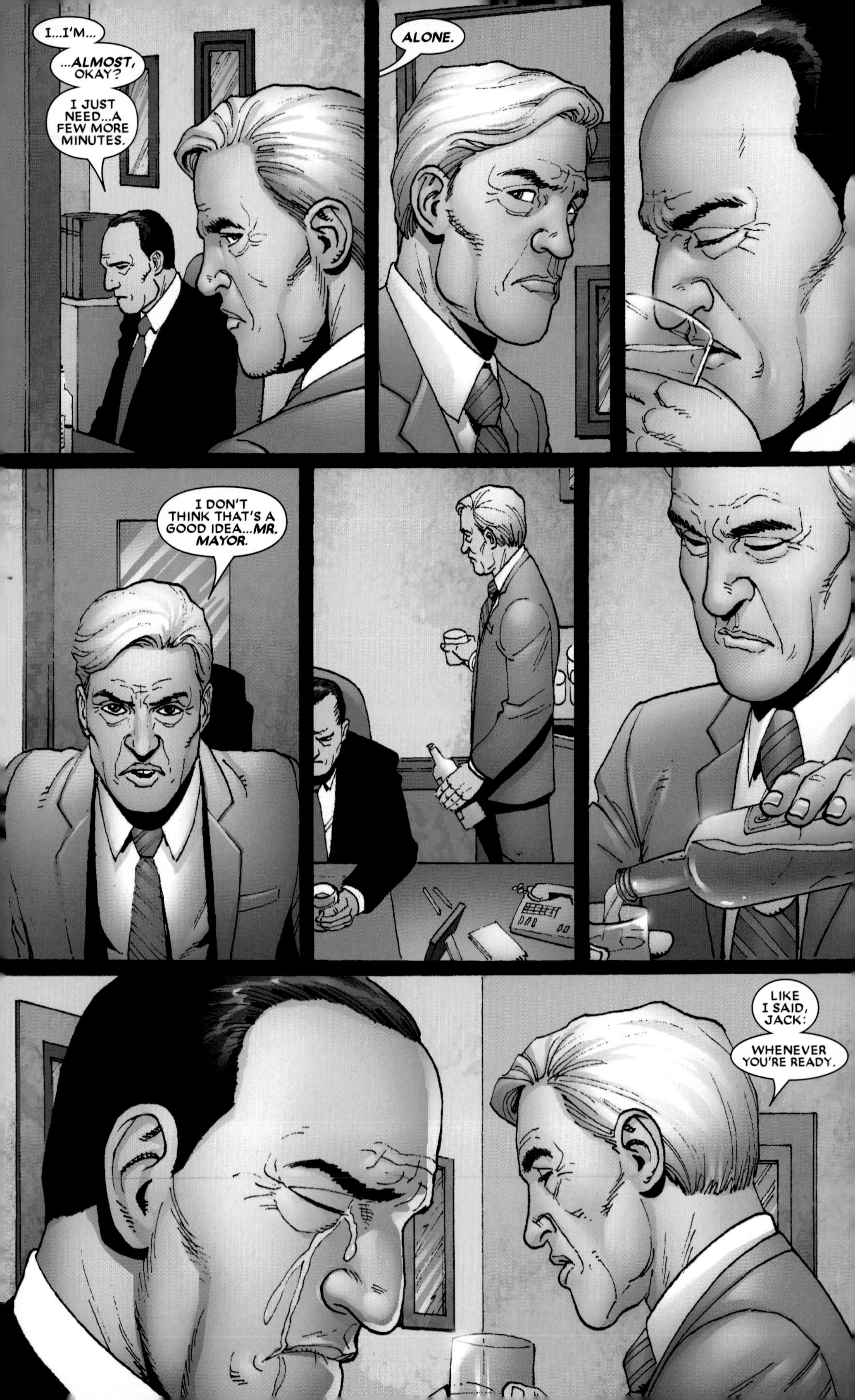

I...I'M...
...ALMOST, OKAY?
I JUST NEED...A FEW MORE MINUTES.
ALONE.
I DON'T THINK THAT'S A GOOD IDEA...MR. MAYOR.
LIKE I SAID, JACK:
WHENEVER YOU'RE READY.

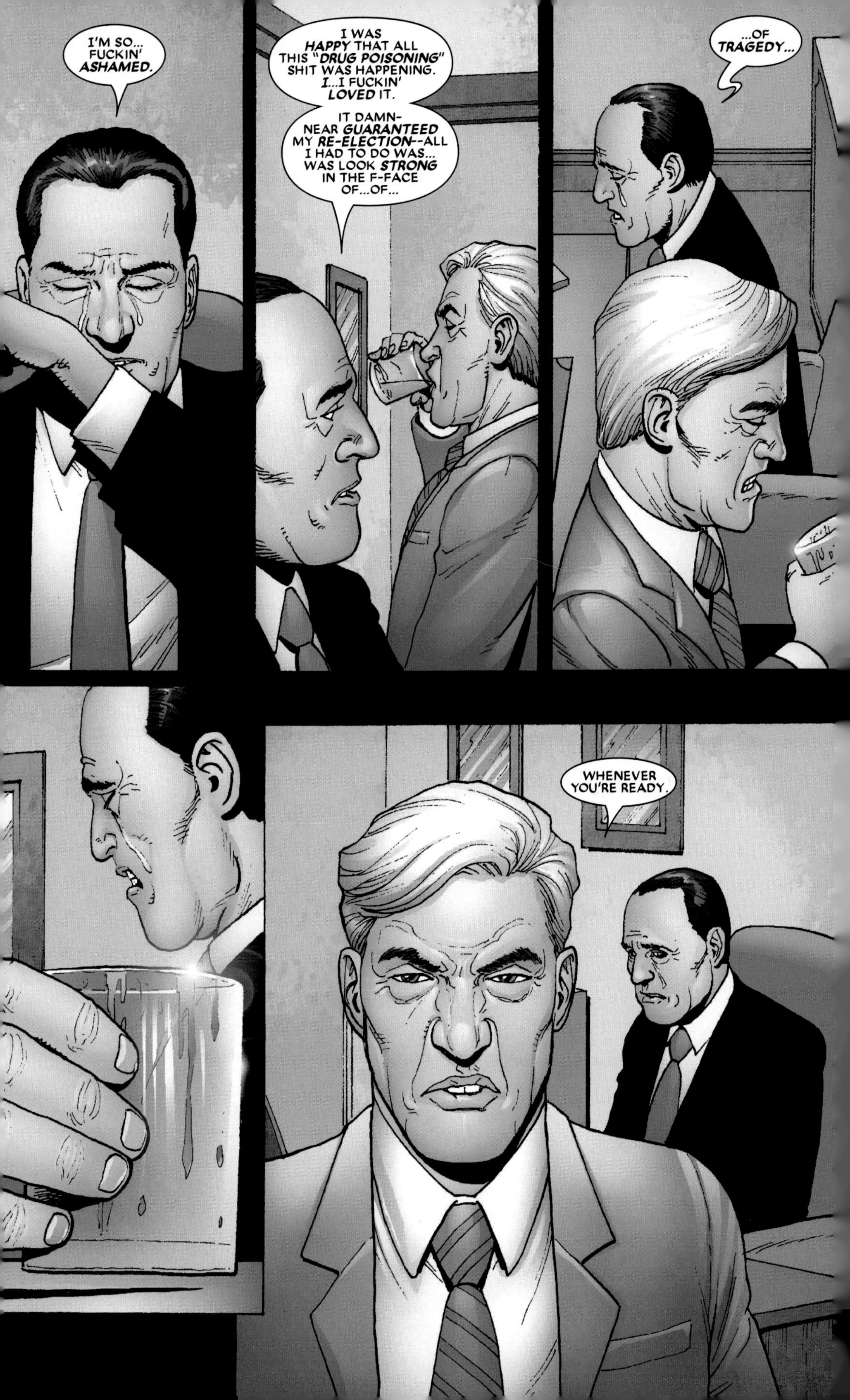
I'M SO... FUCKIN' ASHAMED.
I WAS HAPPY THAT ALL THIS "DRUG POISONING" SHIT WAS HAPPENING. I...I FUCKIN' LOVED IT.
IT DAMN-NEAR GUARANTEED MY RE-ELECTION--ALL I HAD TO DO WAS... WAS LOOK STRONG IN THE F-FACE OF...OF...
...OF TRAGEDY...
WHENEVER YOU'RE READY.

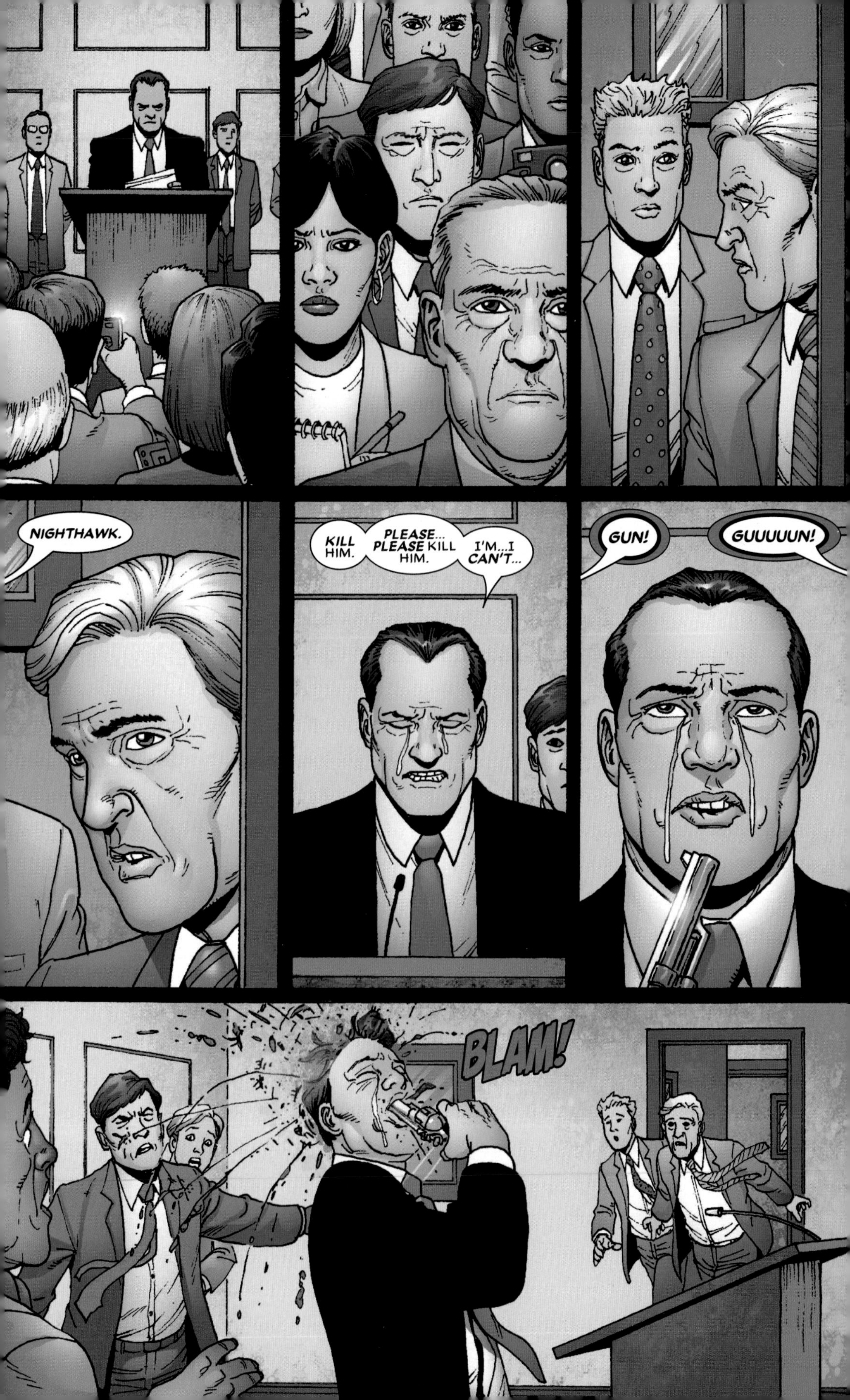
NIGHTHAWK.
KILL HIM.
PLEASE... PLEASE KILL HIM.
I'M...I CAN'T...
GUN!
GUUUUUN!
BLAM!

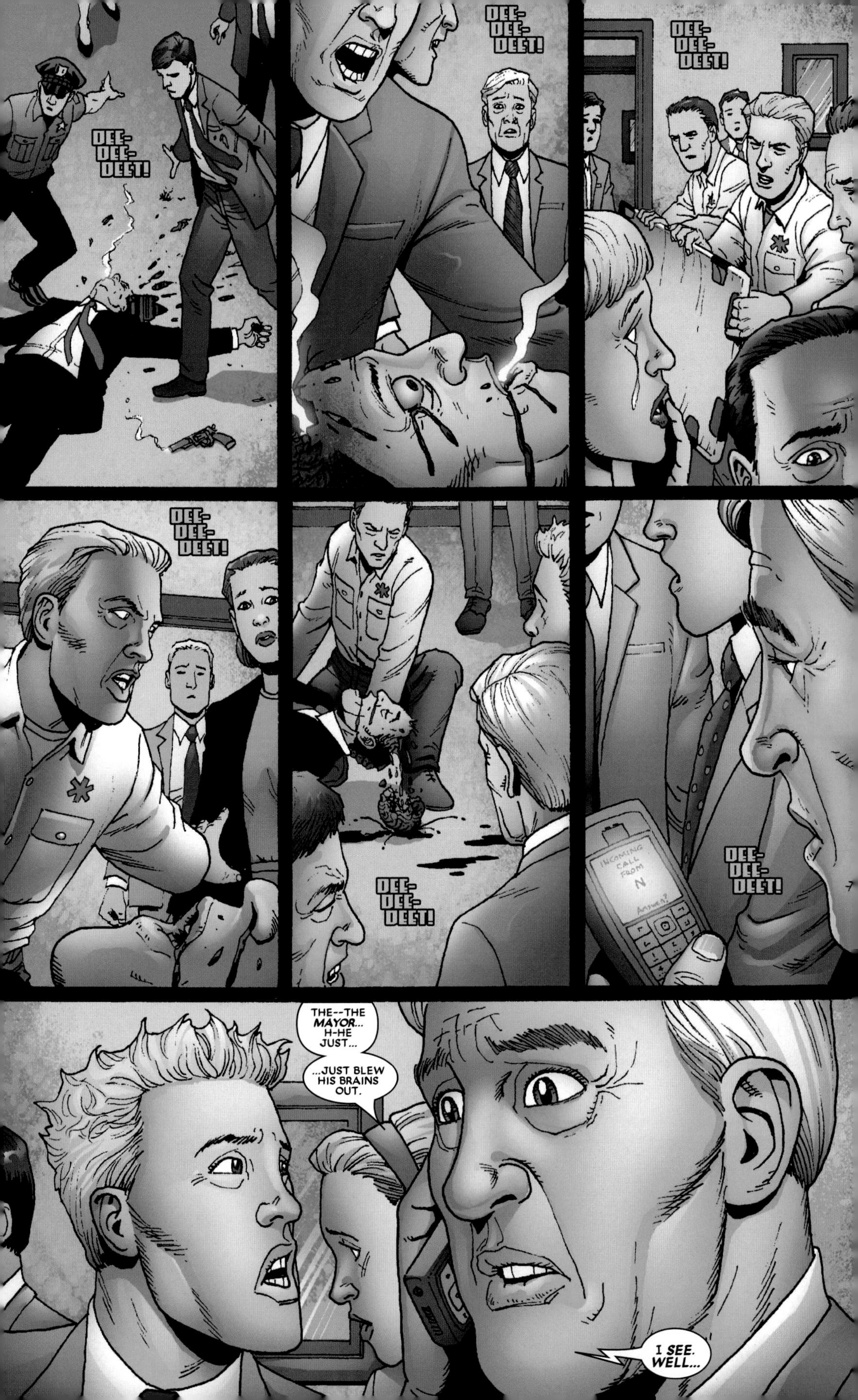
DEE-DEE-DEET!
DEE-DEE-DEET!
DEE-DEE-DEET!
DEE-DEE-DEET!
DEE-DEE-DEET!
INCOMING CALL FROM N
Answer?
DEE-DEE-DEET!
THE--THE MAYOR... H-HE JUST...
...JUST BLEW HIS BRAINS OUT.
I SEE. WELL...

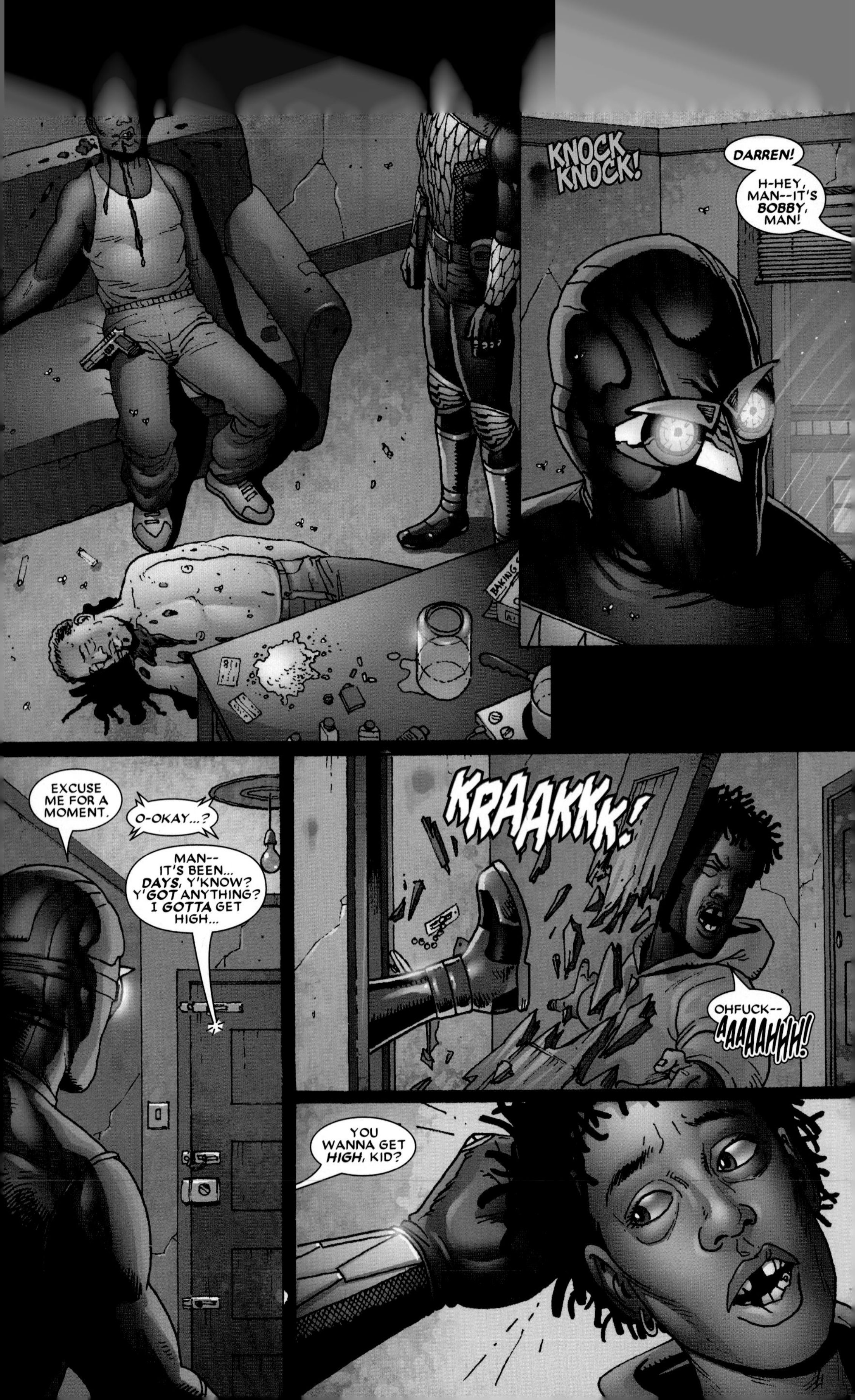
KNOCK KNOCK!
DARREN!
H-HEY, MAN--IT'S BOBBY, MAN!
EXCUSE ME FOR A MOMENT.
O-OKAY...?
MAN-- IT'S BEEN... DAYS, Y'KNOW? Y'GOT ANYTHING? I GOTTA GET HIGH...
KRAAKKK!
OHFUCK-- AAAAAHHH!
YOU WANNA GET HIGH, KID?

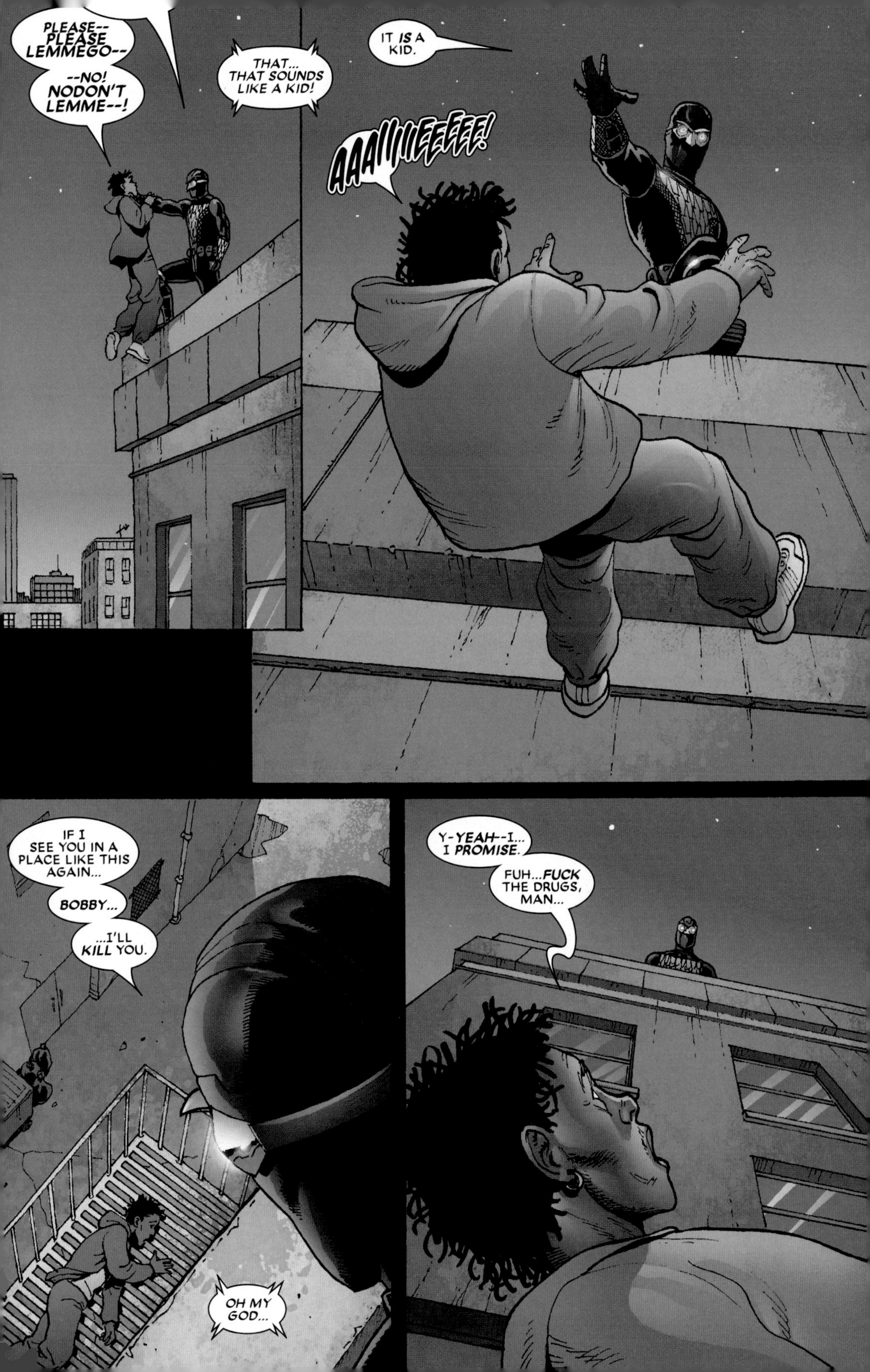
PLEASE--
PLEASE LEMMEGO--
--NO! NODON'T LEMME--!
THAT... THAT SOUNDS LIKE A KID!
IT IS A KID.
AAAIIIIIEEEEEE!
IF I SEE YOU IN A PLACE LIKE THIS AGAIN...
BOBBY...
...I'LL KILL YOU.
OH MY GOD...
Y-YEAH--I... I PROMISE.
FUH...FUCK THE DRUGS, MAN...

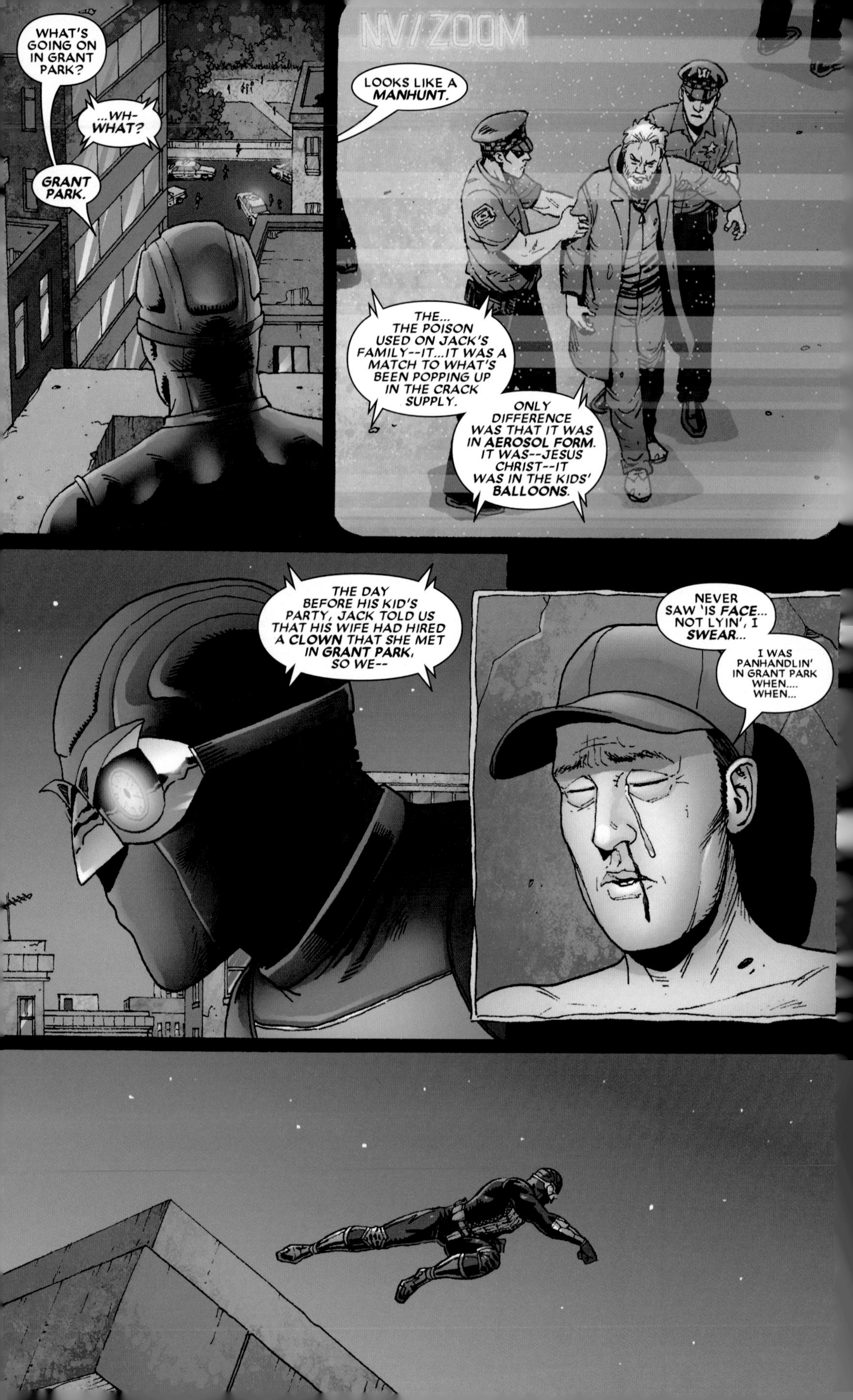
WHAT'S GOING ON IN GRANT PARK?
...WH-WHAT?
GRANT PARK.
NV/ZOOM
LOOKS LIKE A MANHUNT.
THE... THE POISON USED ON JACK'S FAMILY--IT...IT WAS A MATCH TO WHAT'S BEEN POPPING UP IN THE CRACK SUPPLY.
ONLY DIFFERENCE WAS THAT IT WAS IN AEROSOL FORM. IT WAS--JESUS CHRIST--IT WAS IN THE KIDS' BALLOONS.
THE DAY BEFORE HIS KID'S PARTY, JACK TOLD US THAT HIS WIFE HAD HIRED A CLOWN THAT SHE MET IN GRANT PARK, SO WE--
NEVER SAW 'IS FACE... NOT LYIN', I SWEAR...
I WAS PANHANDLIN' IN GRANT PARK WHEN.... WHEN...

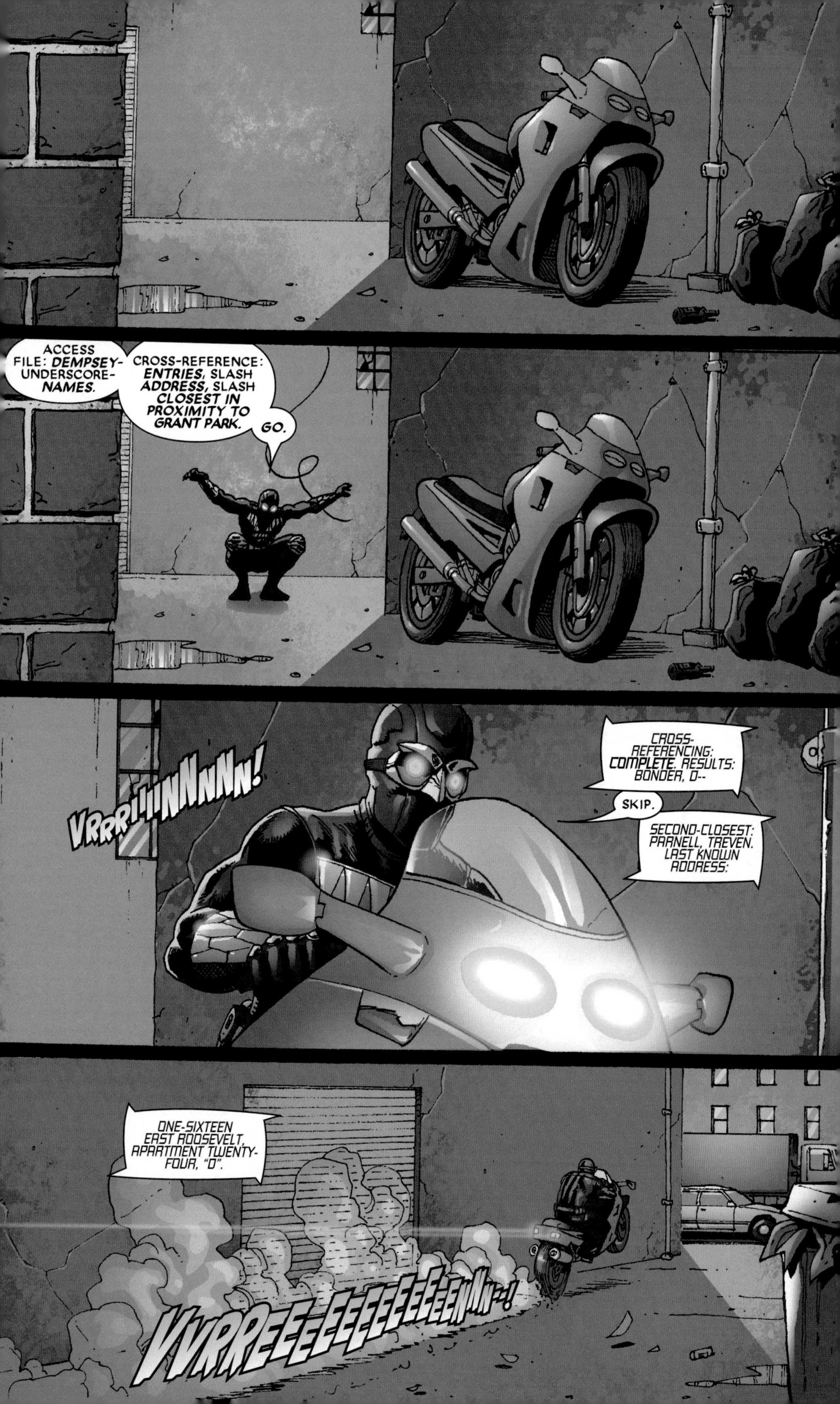
ACCESS FILE: DEMPSEY-UNDERSCORE-NAMES.
CROSS-REFERENCE: ENTRIES, SLASH ADDRESS, SLASH CLOSEST IN PROXIMITY TO GRANT PARK.
GO.
VRRRIIIIINNNNN!
CROSS-REFERENCING: COMPLETE. RESULTS: BONDER, D--
SKIP.
SECOND-CLOSEST: PARNELL, TREVEN. LAST KNOWN ADDRESS:
ONE-SIXTEEN EAST ROOSEVELT, APARTMENT TWENTY-FOUR, "D".
VVRREEEEEEEEEEEEENNN--!

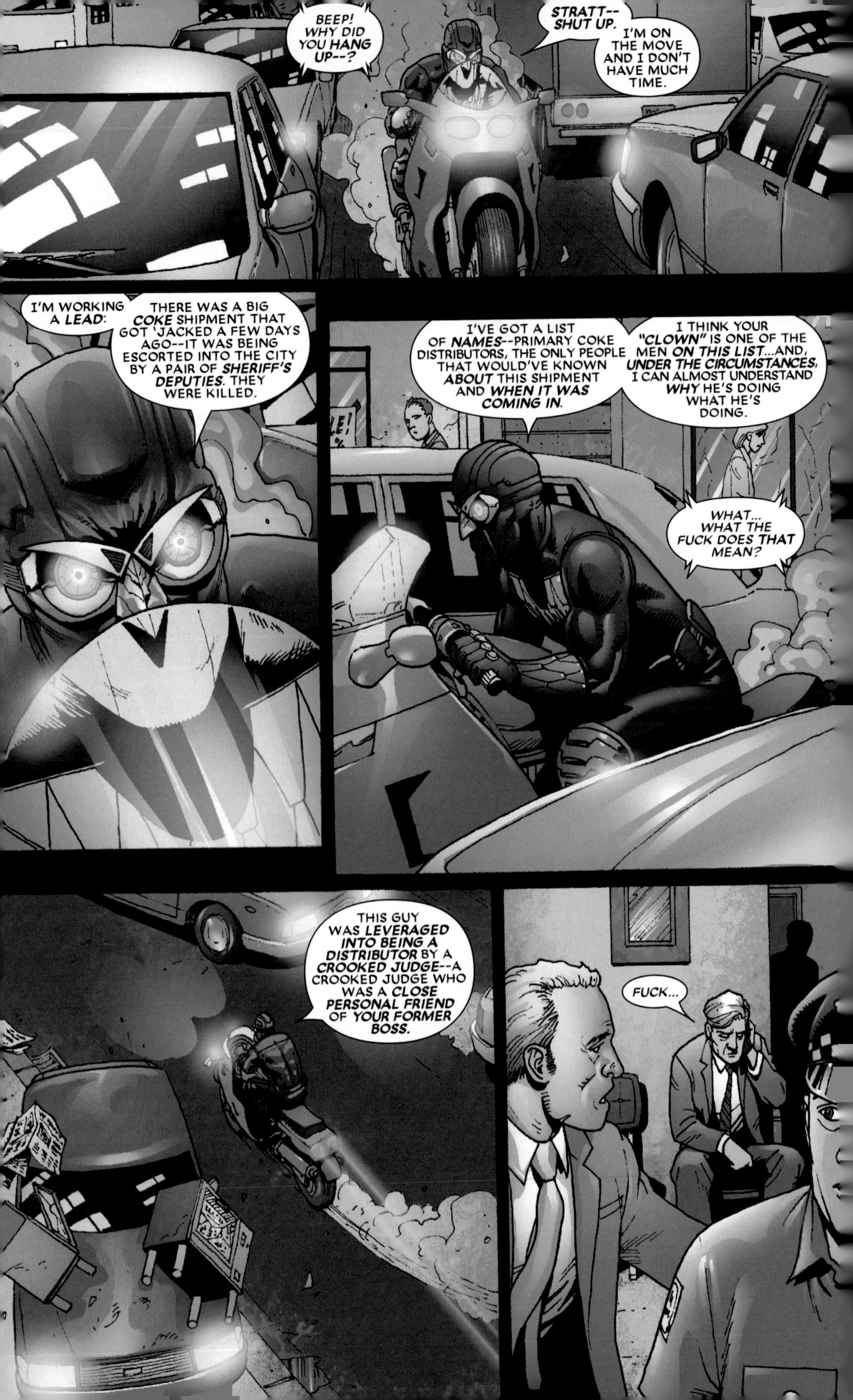
BEEP! WHY DID YOU HANG UP--?
STRATT-- SHUT UP.
I'M ON THE MOVE AND I DON'T HAVE MUCH TIME.
I'M WORKING A LEAD:
THERE WAS A BIG COKE SHIPMENT THAT GOT 'JACKED A FEW DAYS AGO--IT WAS BEING ESCORTED INTO THE CITY BY A PAIR OF SHERIFF'S DEPUTIES. THEY WERE KILLED.
I'VE GOT A LIST OF NAMES--PRIMARY COKE DISTRIBUTORS, THE ONLY PEOPLE THAT WOULD'VE KNOWN ABOUT THIS SHIPMENT AND WHEN IT WAS COMING IN.
I THINK YOUR "CLOWN" IS ONE OF THE MEN ON THIS LIST...AND, UNDER THE CIRCUMSTANCES, I CAN ALMOST UNDERSTAND WHY HE'S DOING WHAT HE'S DOING.
WHAT... WHAT THE FUCK DOES THAT MEAN?
THIS GUY WAS LEVERAGED INTO BEING A DISTRIBUTOR BY A CROOKED JUDGE--A CROOKED JUDGE WHO WAS A CLOSE PERSONAL FRIEND OF YOUR FORMER BOSS.
FUCK...

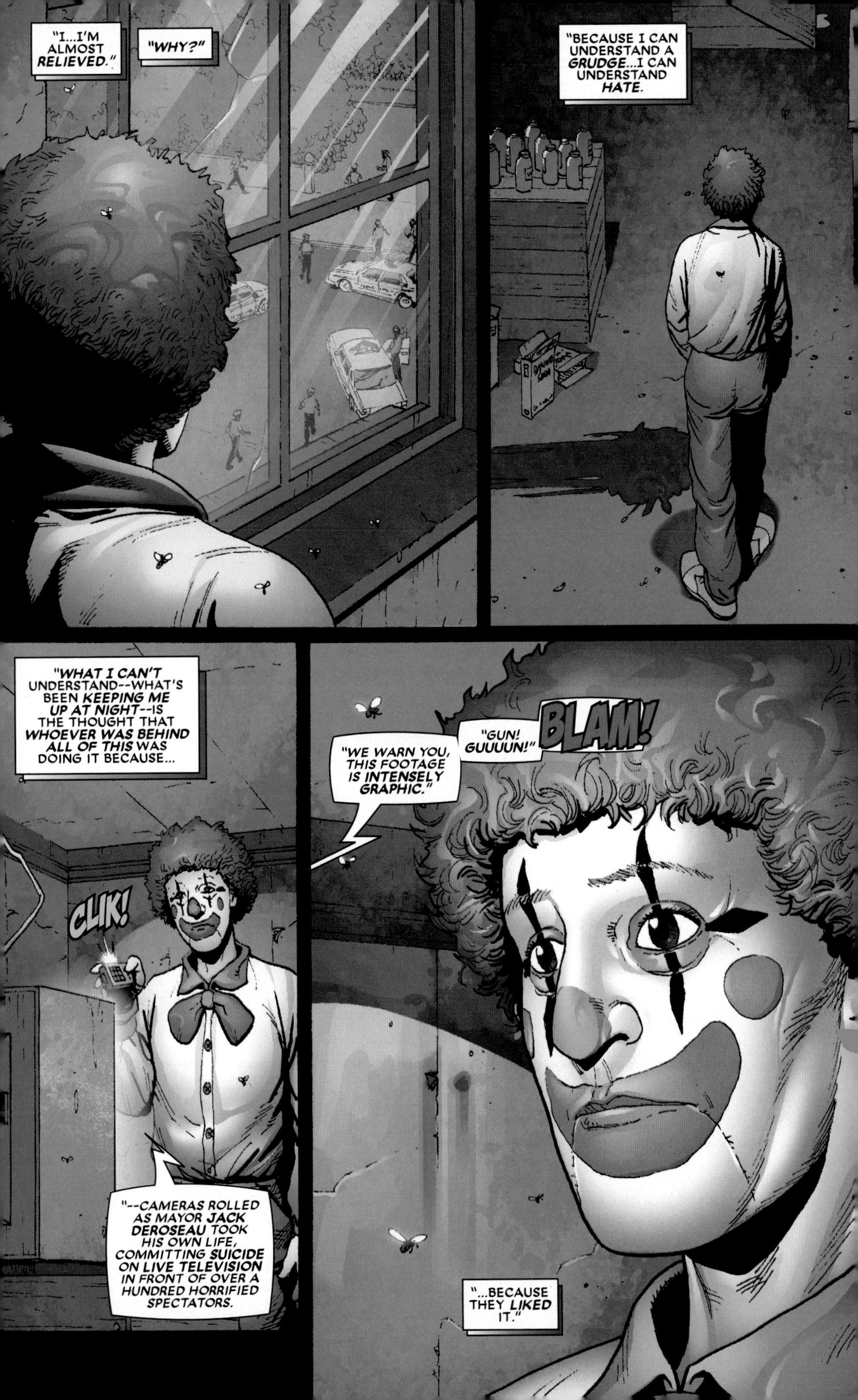
"I...I'M ALMOST RELIEVED."
"WHY?"
"BECAUSE I CAN UNDERSTAND A GRUDGE...I CAN UNDERSTAND HATE.
"WHAT I CAN'T UNDERSTAND--WHAT'S BEEN KEEPING ME UP AT NIGHT--IS THE THOUGHT THAT WHOEVER WAS BEHIND ALL OF THIS WAS DOING IT BECAUSE...
CLIK!
"--CAMERAS ROLLED AS MAYOR JACK DEROSEAU TOOK HIS OWN LIFE, COMMITTING SUICIDE ON LIVE TELEVISION IN FRONT OF OVER A HUNDRED HORRIFIED SPECTATORS.
"WE WARN YOU, THIS FOOTAGE IS INTENSELY GRAPHIC."
"GUN! GUUUUN!"
BLAM!
"...BECAUSE THEY LIKED IT."

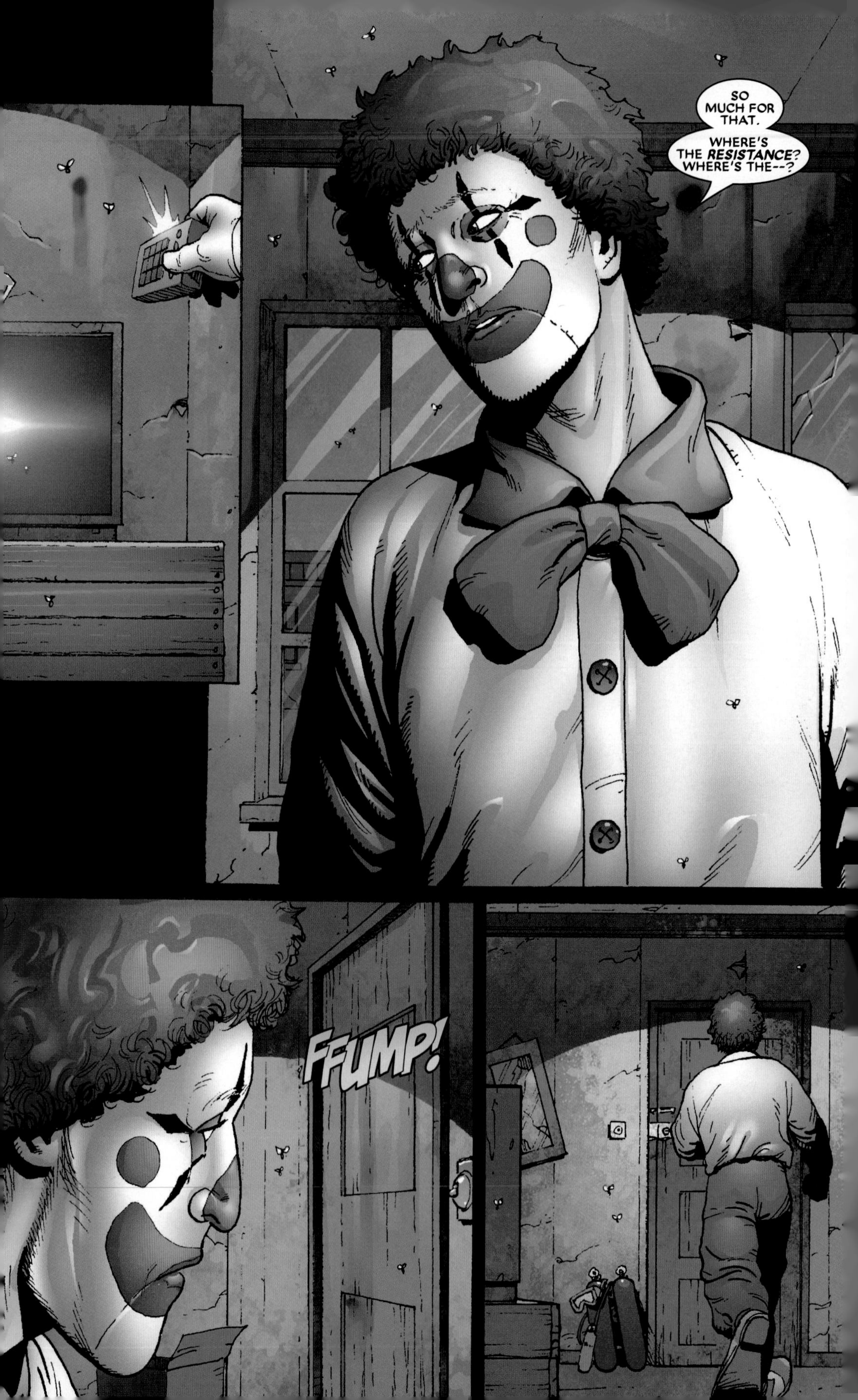
SO MUCH FOR THAT.
WHERE'S THE *RESISTANCE?* WHERE'S THE--?
FFUMP!

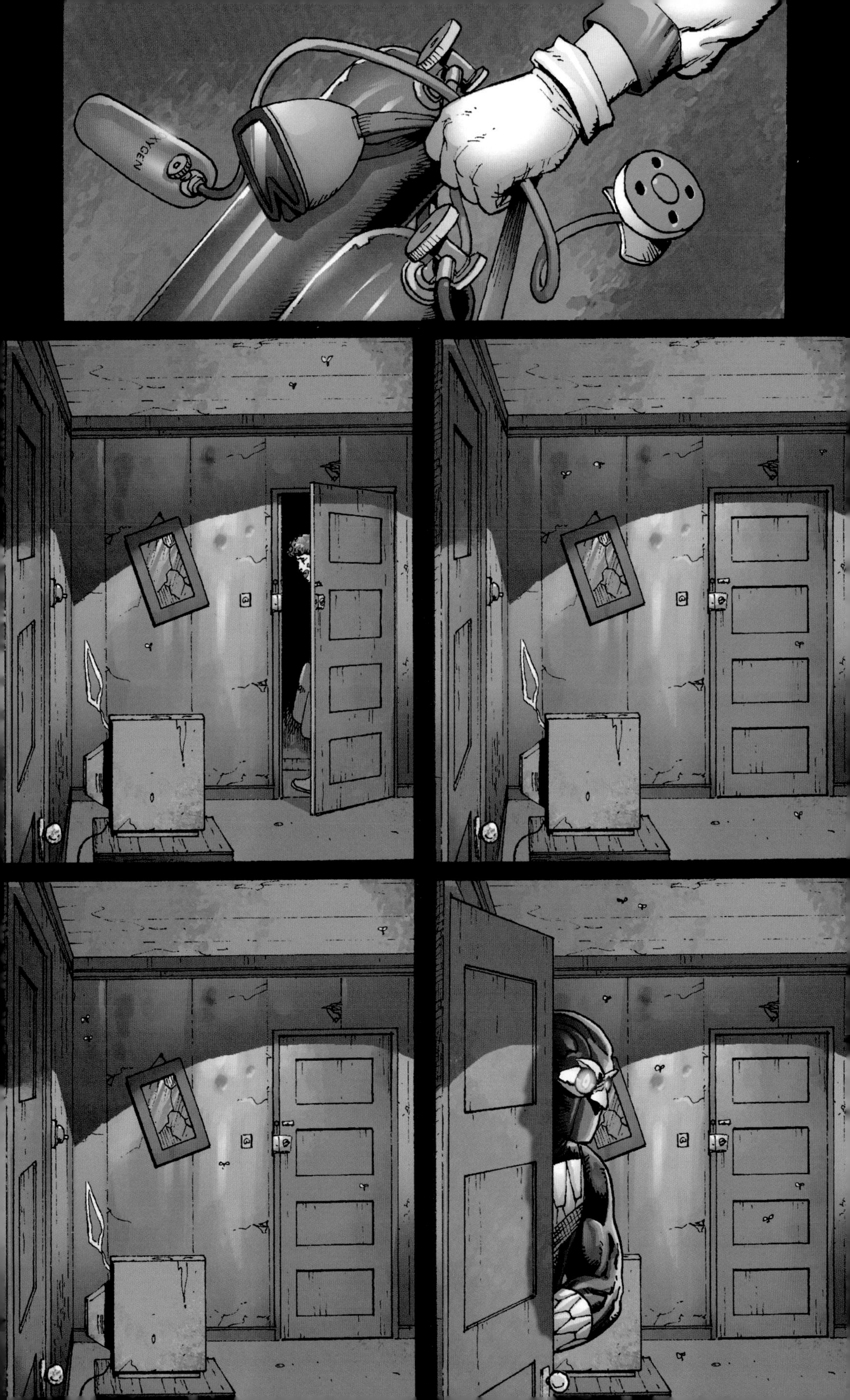
XYGEN

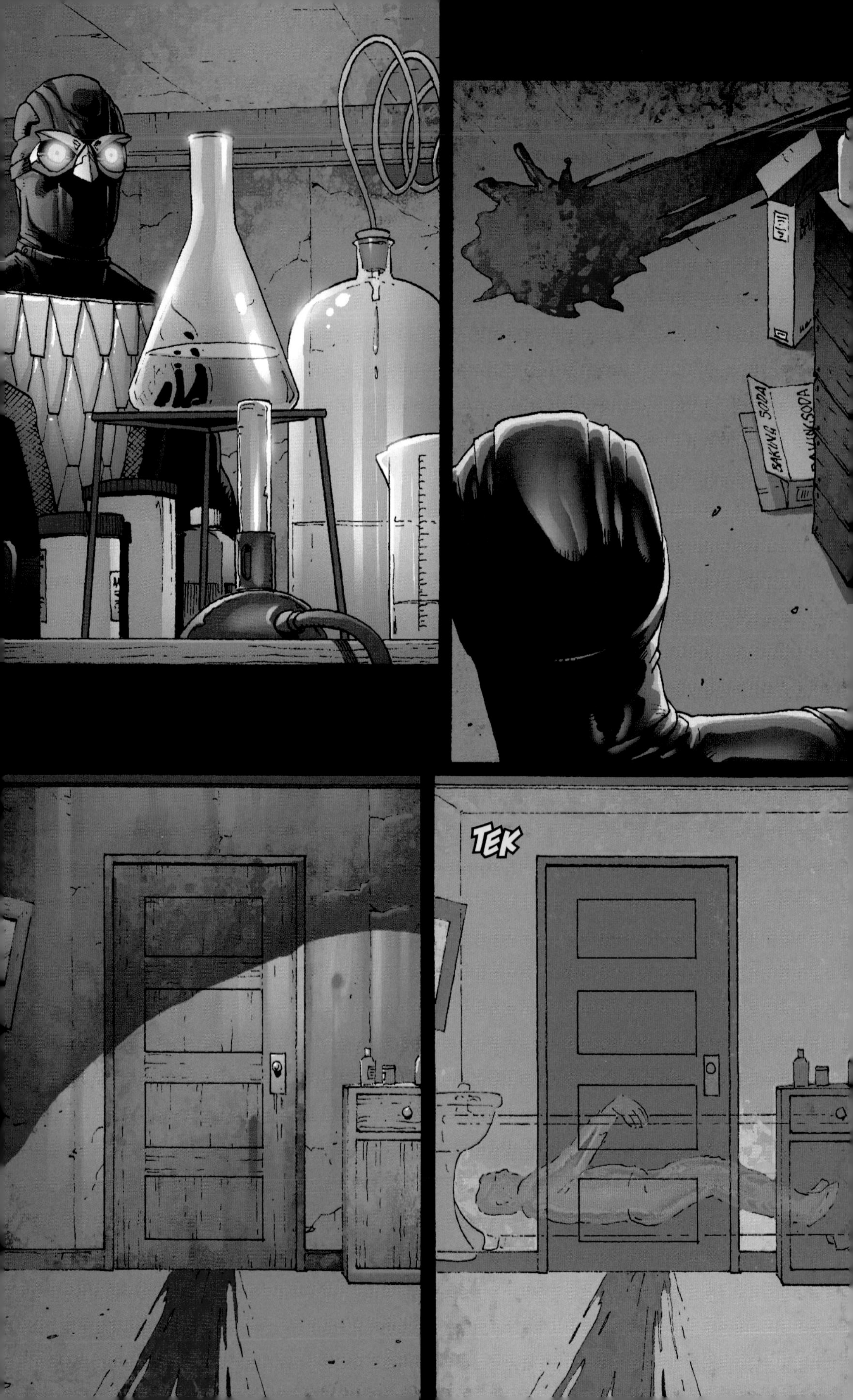
BAKING SODA
TEK

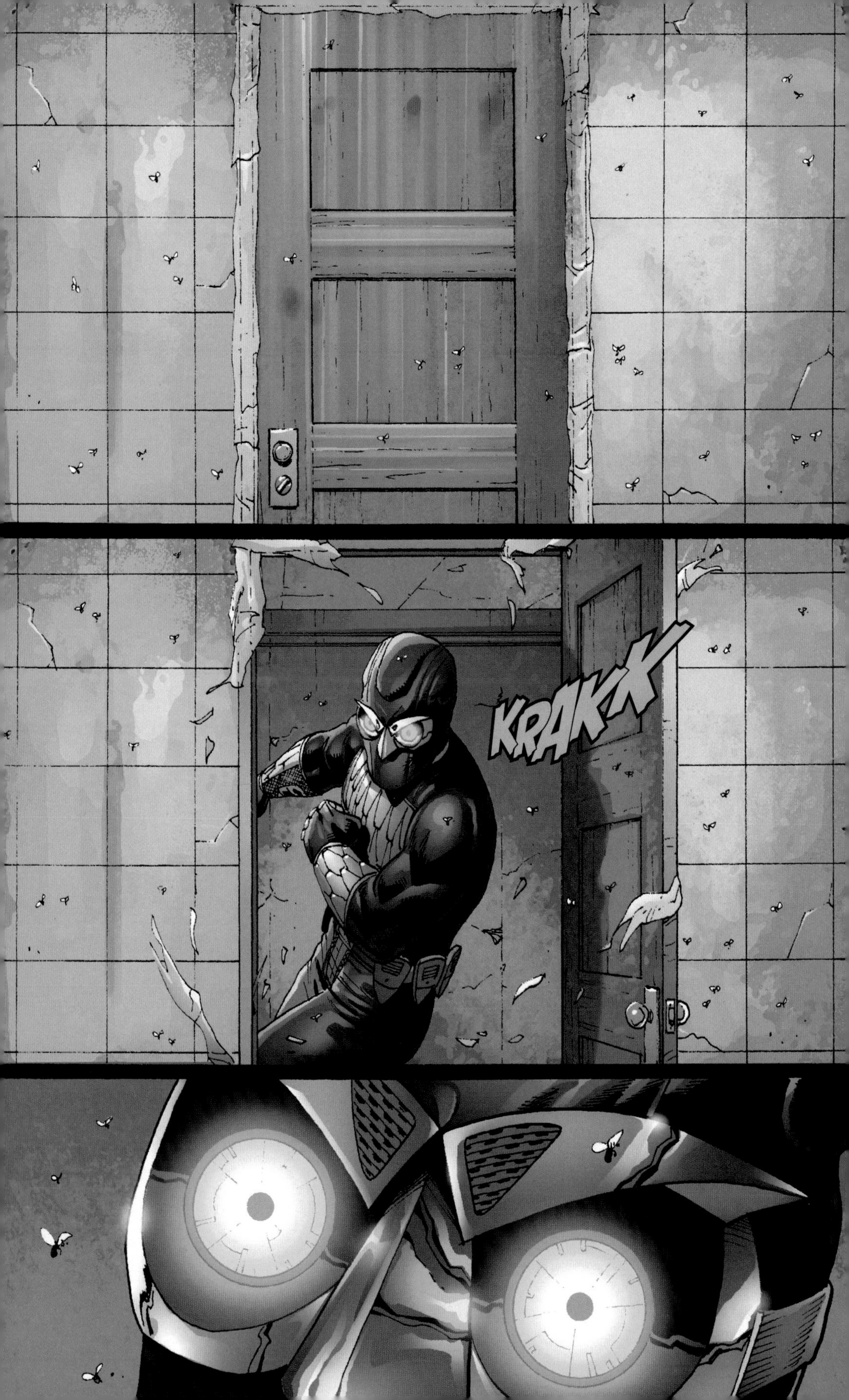
KRAK-K

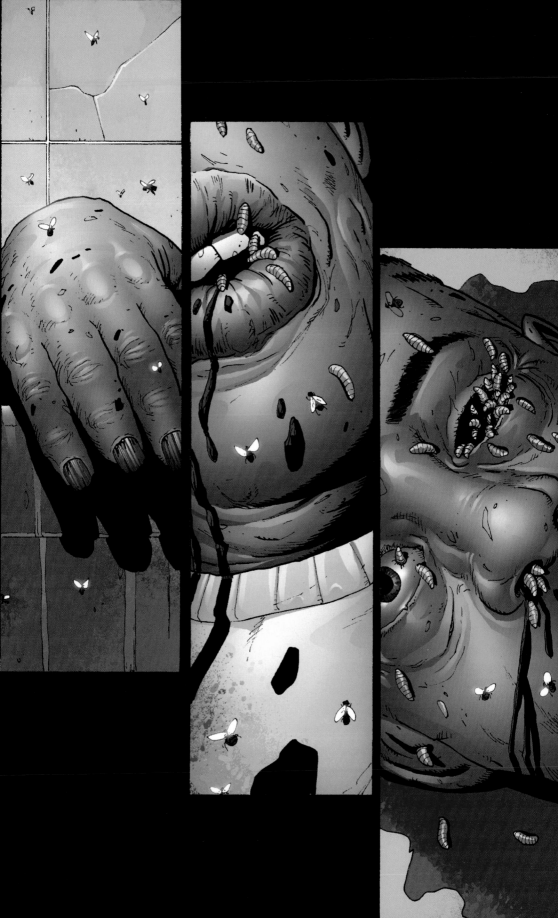

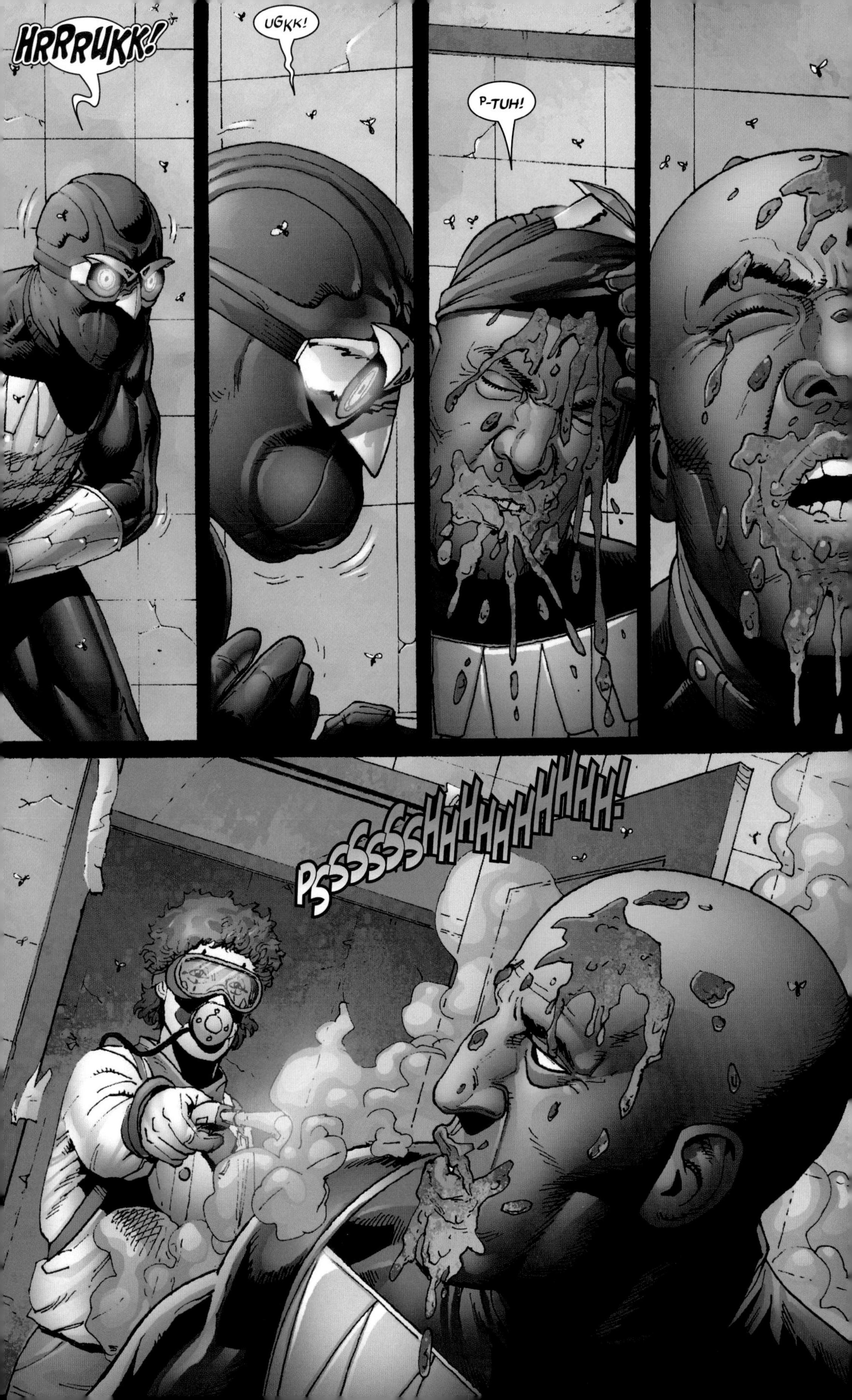
HRRRUKK!
UGKK!
P-TUH!
PSSSSSSHHHHHHHHHHH!

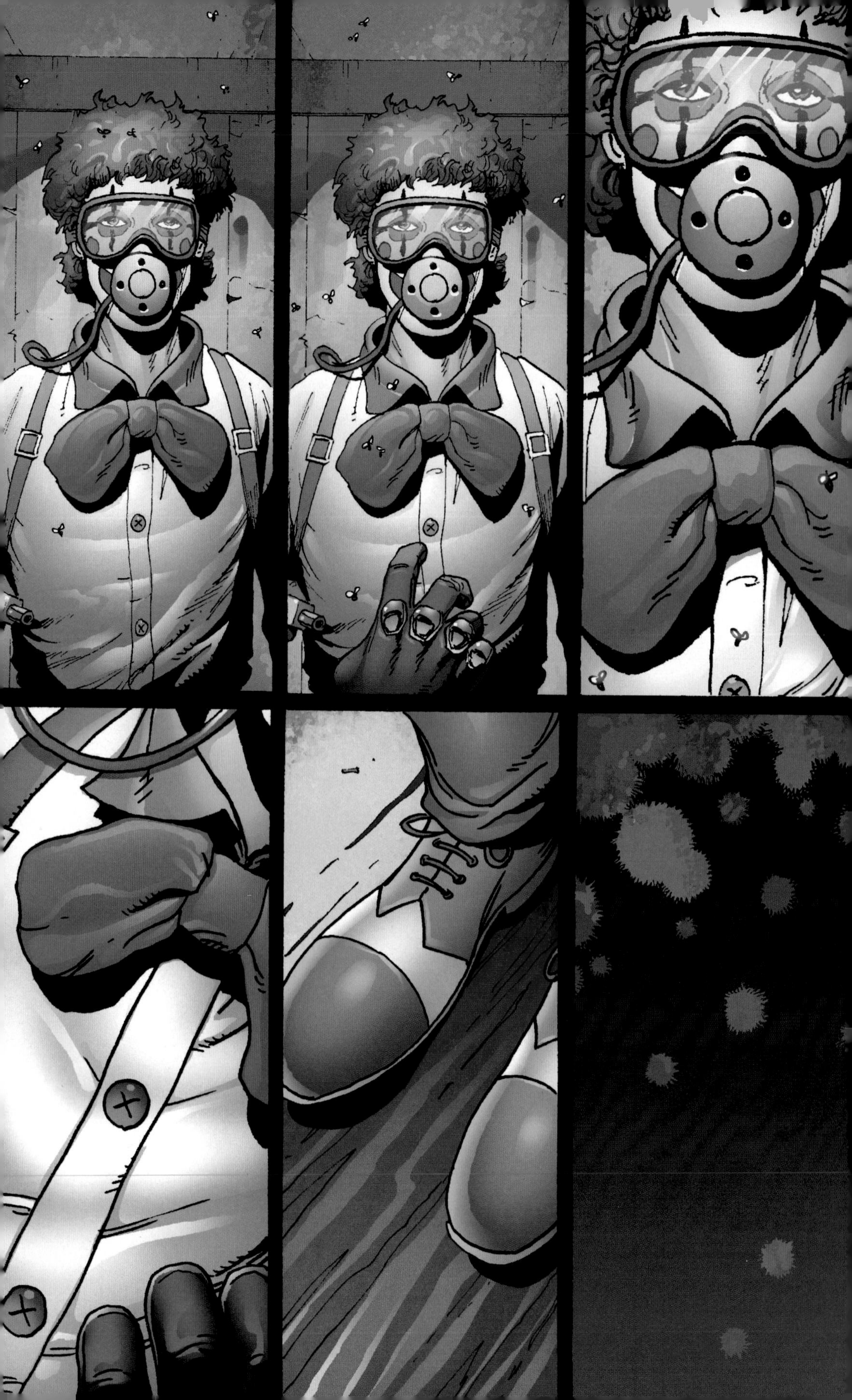

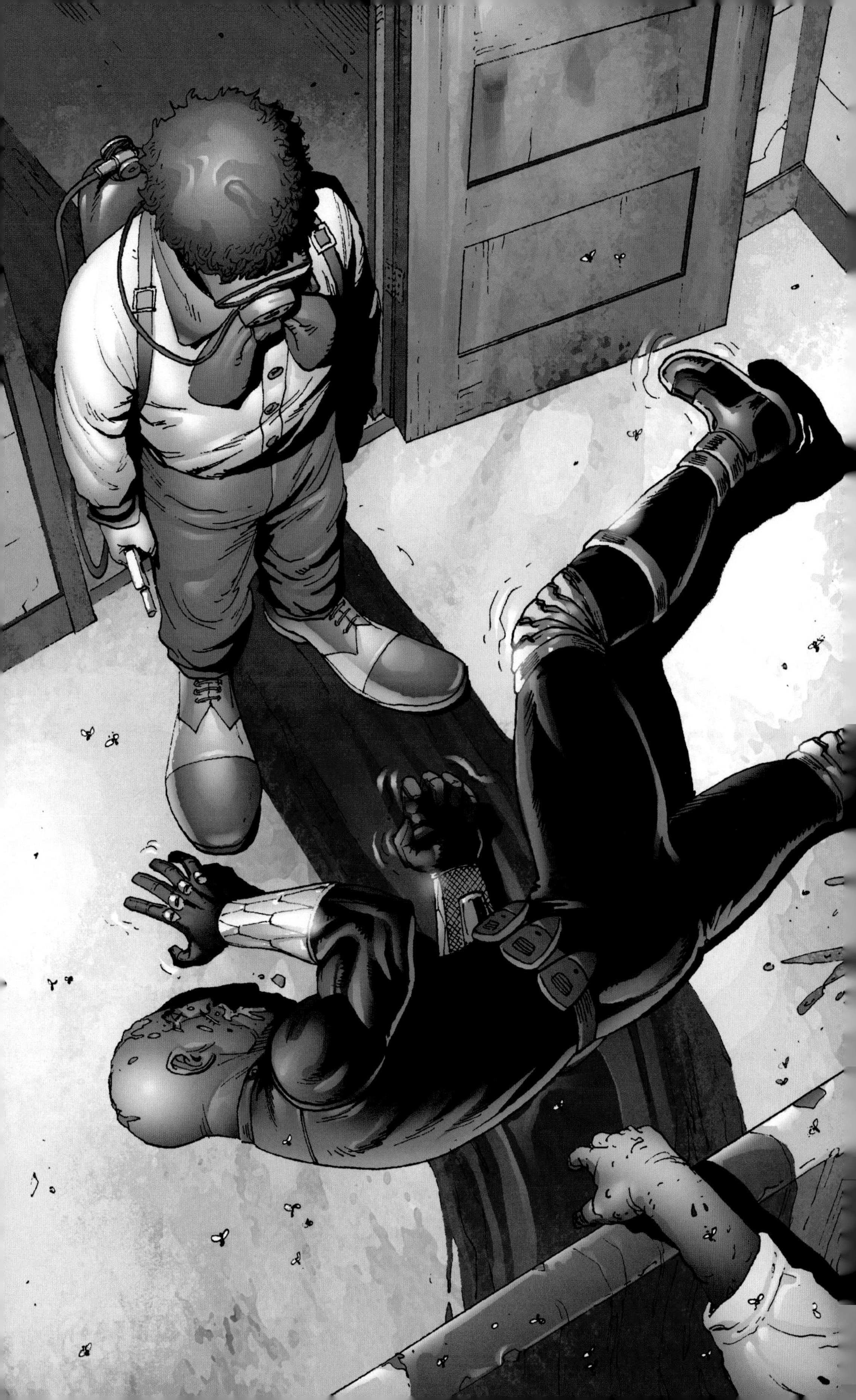

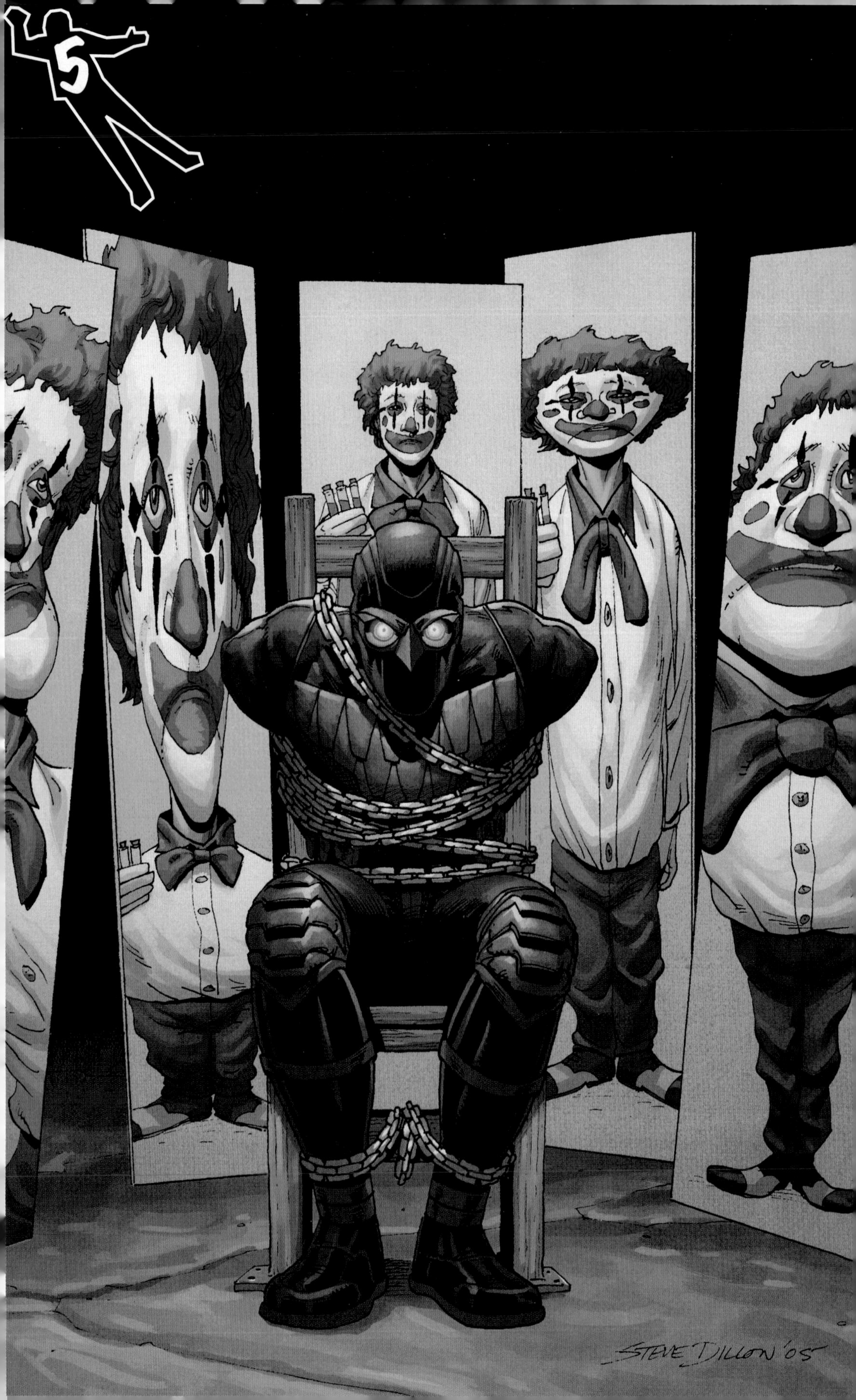
5
STEVE DILLON '05

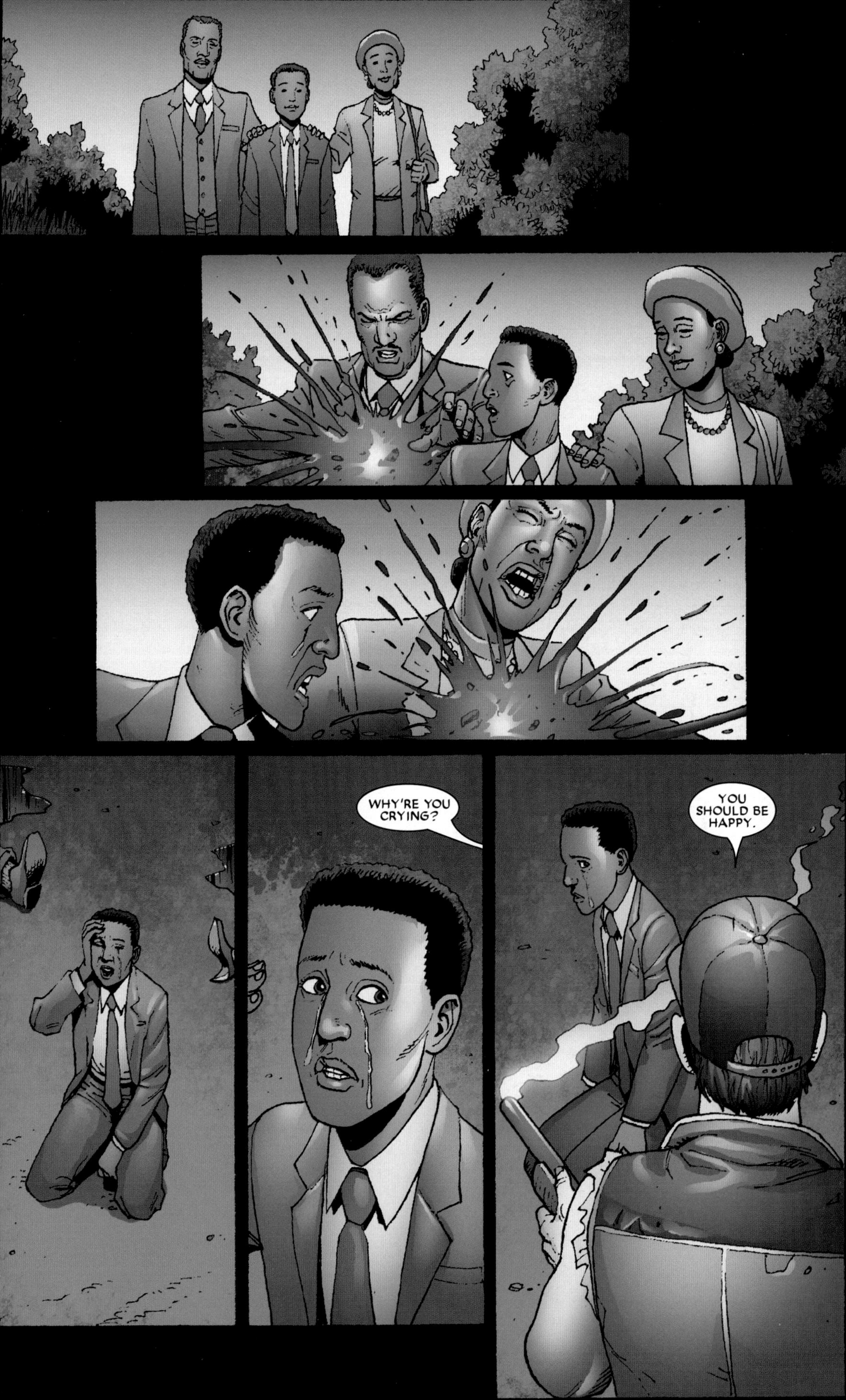
WHY'RE YOU CRYING?
YOU SHOULD BE HAPPY.

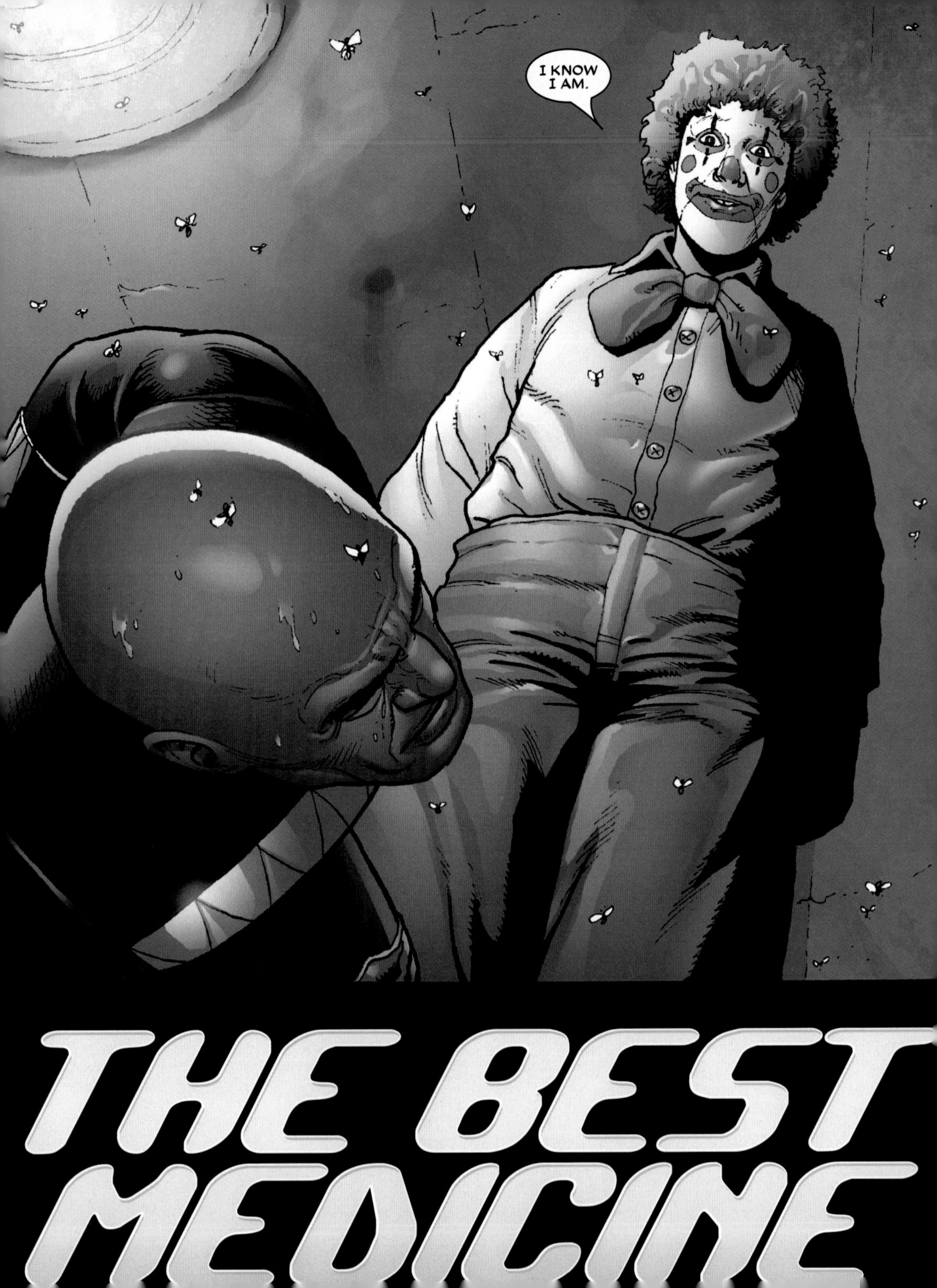
I KNOW I AM.
THE BEST MEDICINE

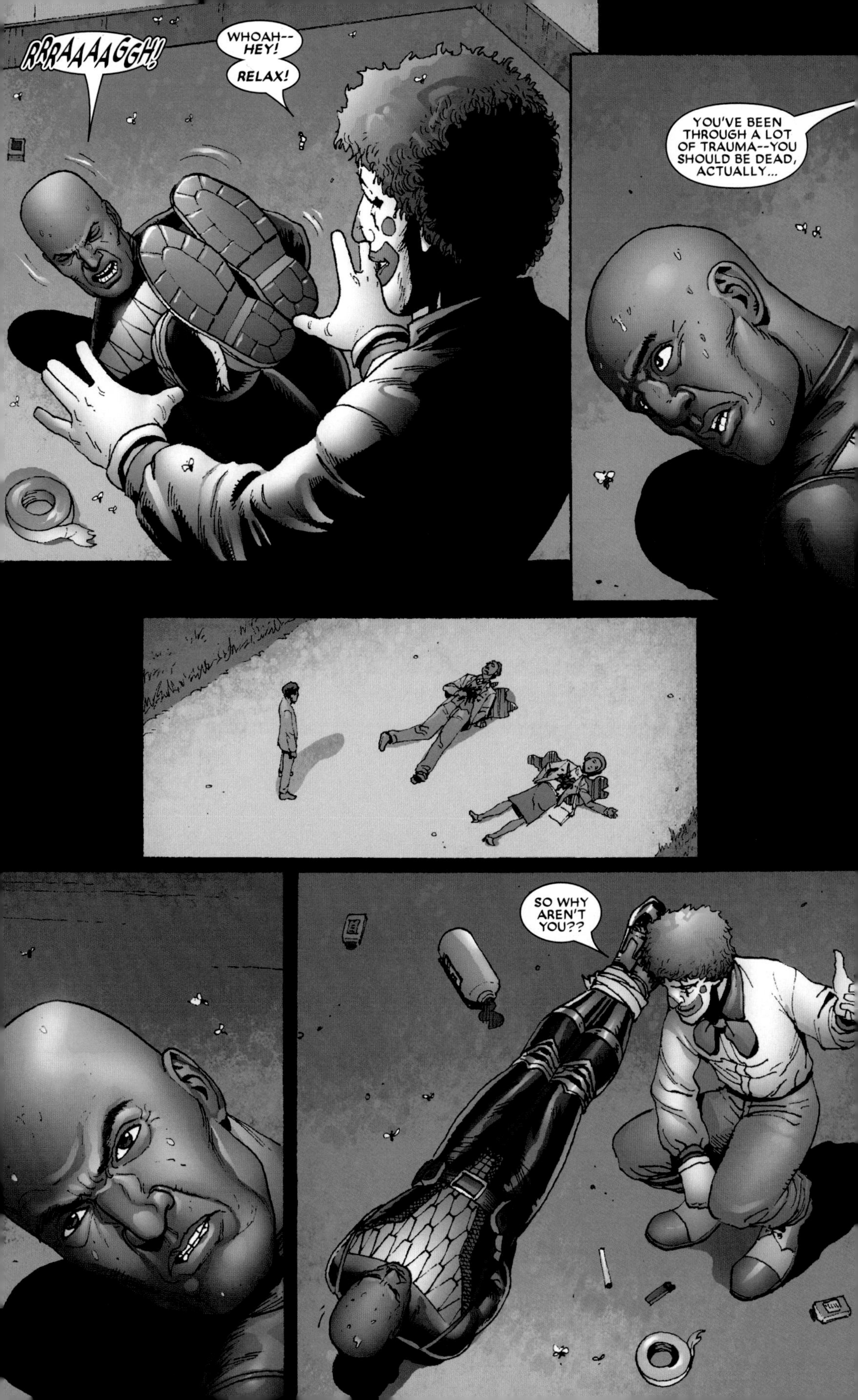
RRRAAAAGGH!
WHOAH--HEY!
RELAX!
YOU'VE BEEN THROUGH A LOT OF TRAUMA--YOU SHOULD BE DEAD, ACTUALLY...
SO WHY AREN'T YOU??

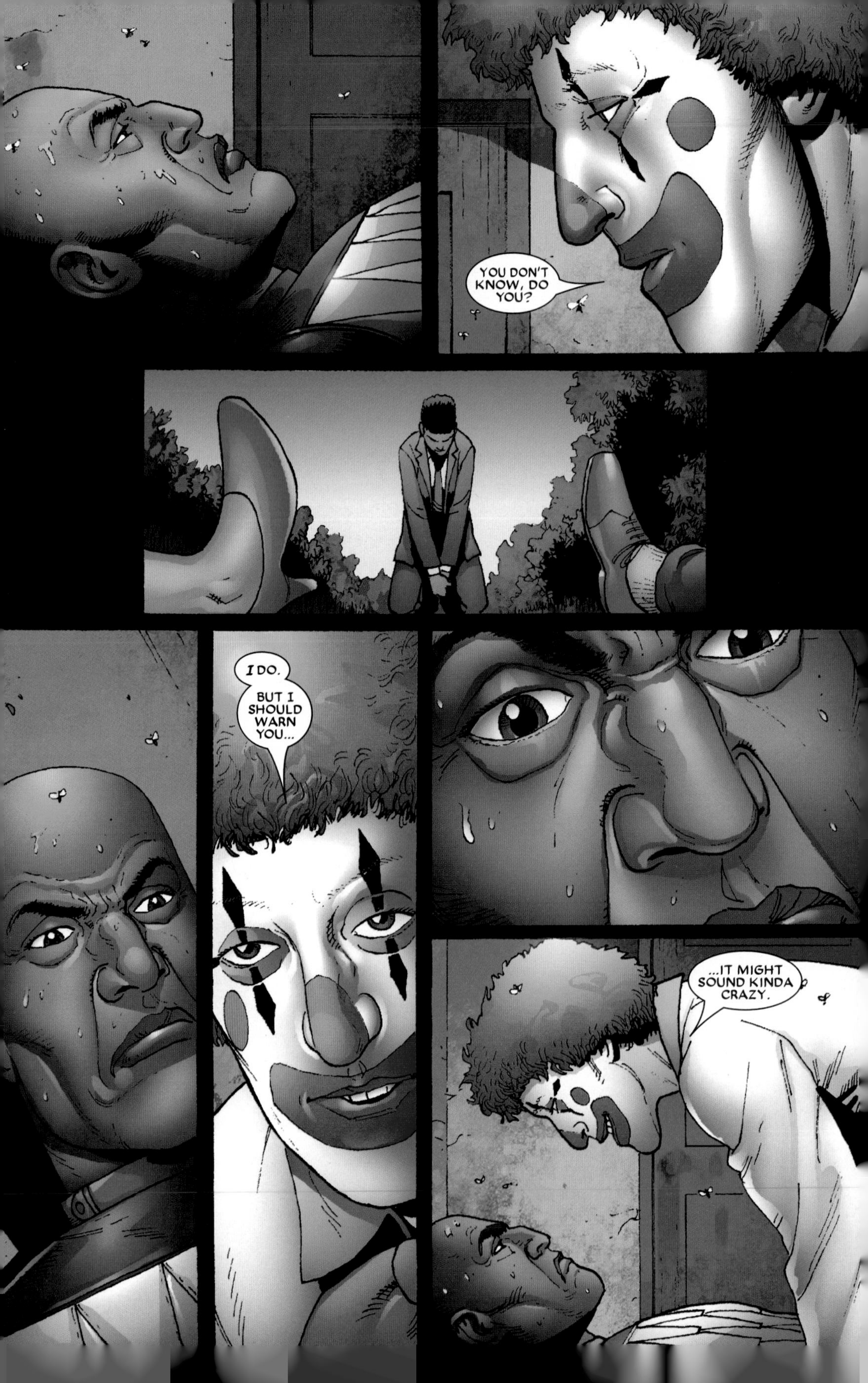
YOU DON'T KNOW, DO YOU?
I DO.
BUT I SHOULD WARN YOU...
...IT MIGHT SOUND KINDA CRAZY.

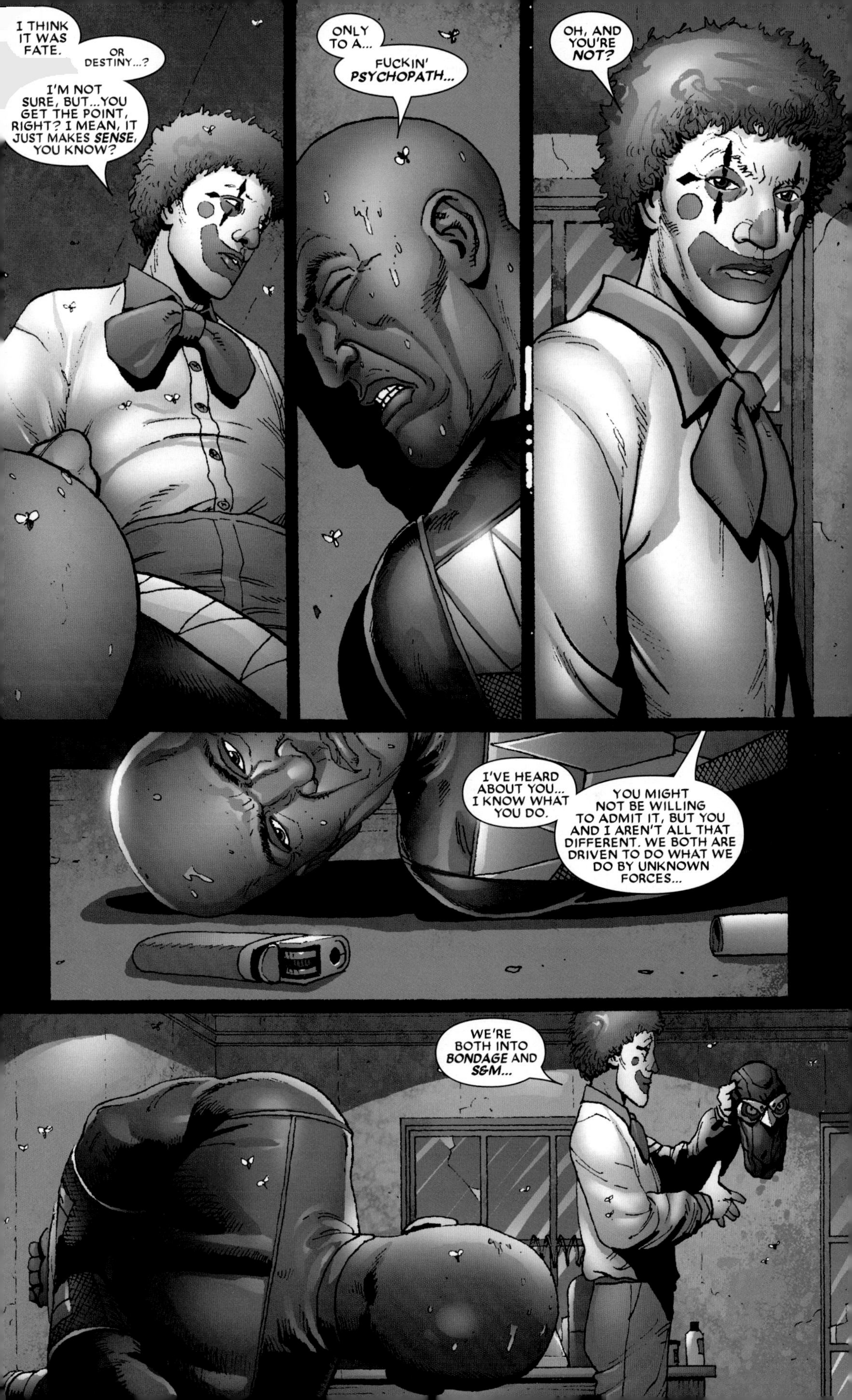
I THINK IT WAS FATE.
OR DESTINY...?
I'M NOT SURE, BUT...YOU GET THE POINT, RIGHT? I MEAN, IT JUST MAKES *SENSE*, YOU KNOW?
ONLY TO A...
FUCKIN' *PSYCHOPATH...*
OH, AND YOU'RE *NOT?*
I'VE HEARD ABOUT YOU... I KNOW WHAT YOU DO.
YOU MIGHT NOT BE WILLING TO ADMIT IT, BUT YOU AND I AREN'T ALL THAT DIFFERENT. WE BOTH ARE DRIVEN TO DO WHAT WE DO BY UNKNOWN FORCES...
WE'RE BOTH INTO *BONDAGE* AND *S&M...*

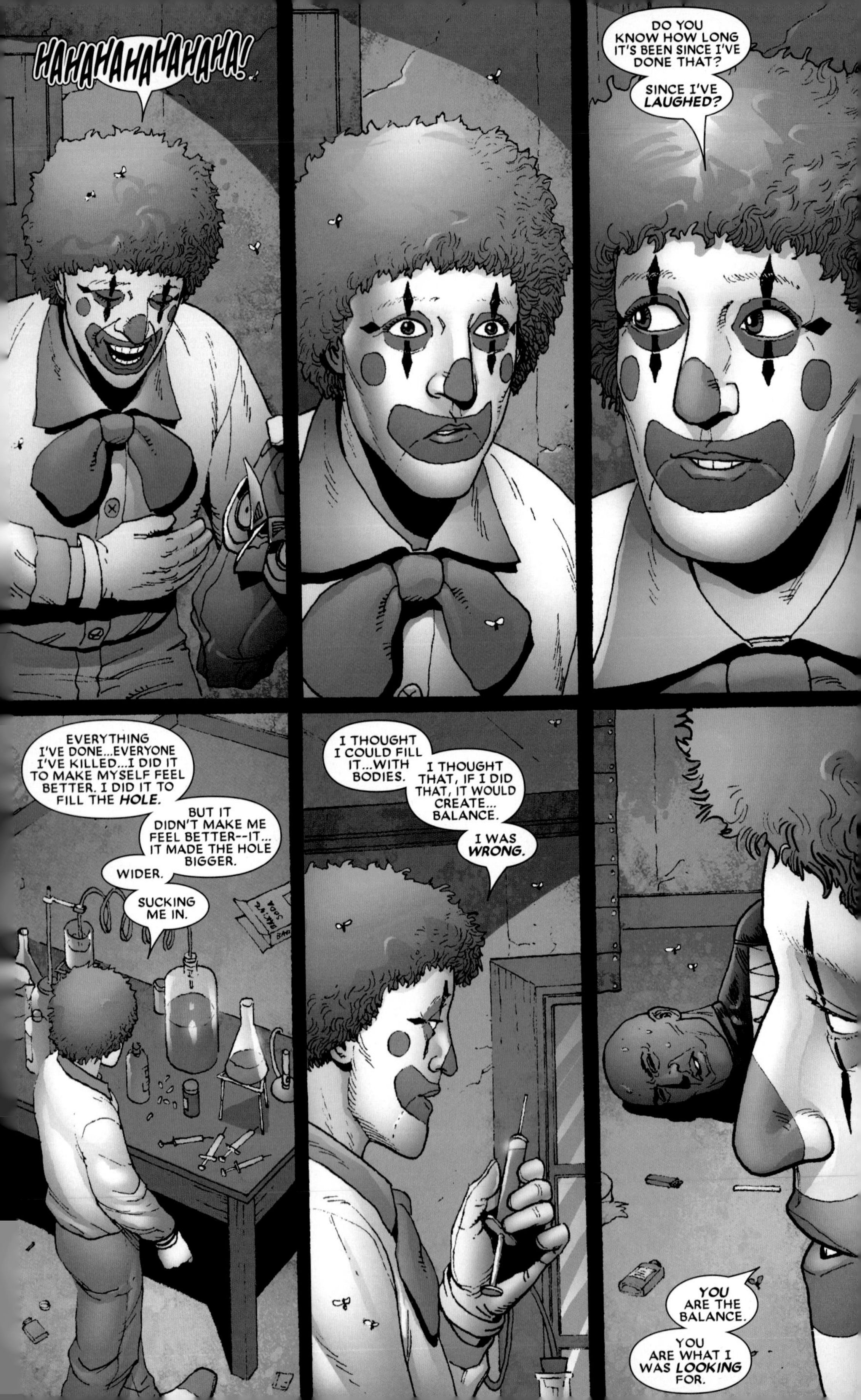
HAHAHAHAHAHAHA!
DO YOU KNOW HOW LONG IT'S BEEN SINCE I'VE DONE THAT?
SINCE I'VE LAUGHED?
EVERYTHING I'VE DONE...EVERYONE I'VE KILLED...I DID IT TO MAKE MYSELF FEEL BETTER. I DID IT TO FILL THE HOLE.
BUT IT DIDN'T MAKE ME FEEL BETTER--IT... IT MADE THE HOLE BIGGER.
WIDER.
SUCKING ME IN.
I THOUGHT I COULD FILL IT...WITH BODIES.
I THOUGHT THAT, IF I DID THAT, IT WOULD CREATE... BALANCE.
I WAS WRONG.
YOU ARE THE BALANCE.
YOU ARE WHAT I WAS LOOKING FOR.

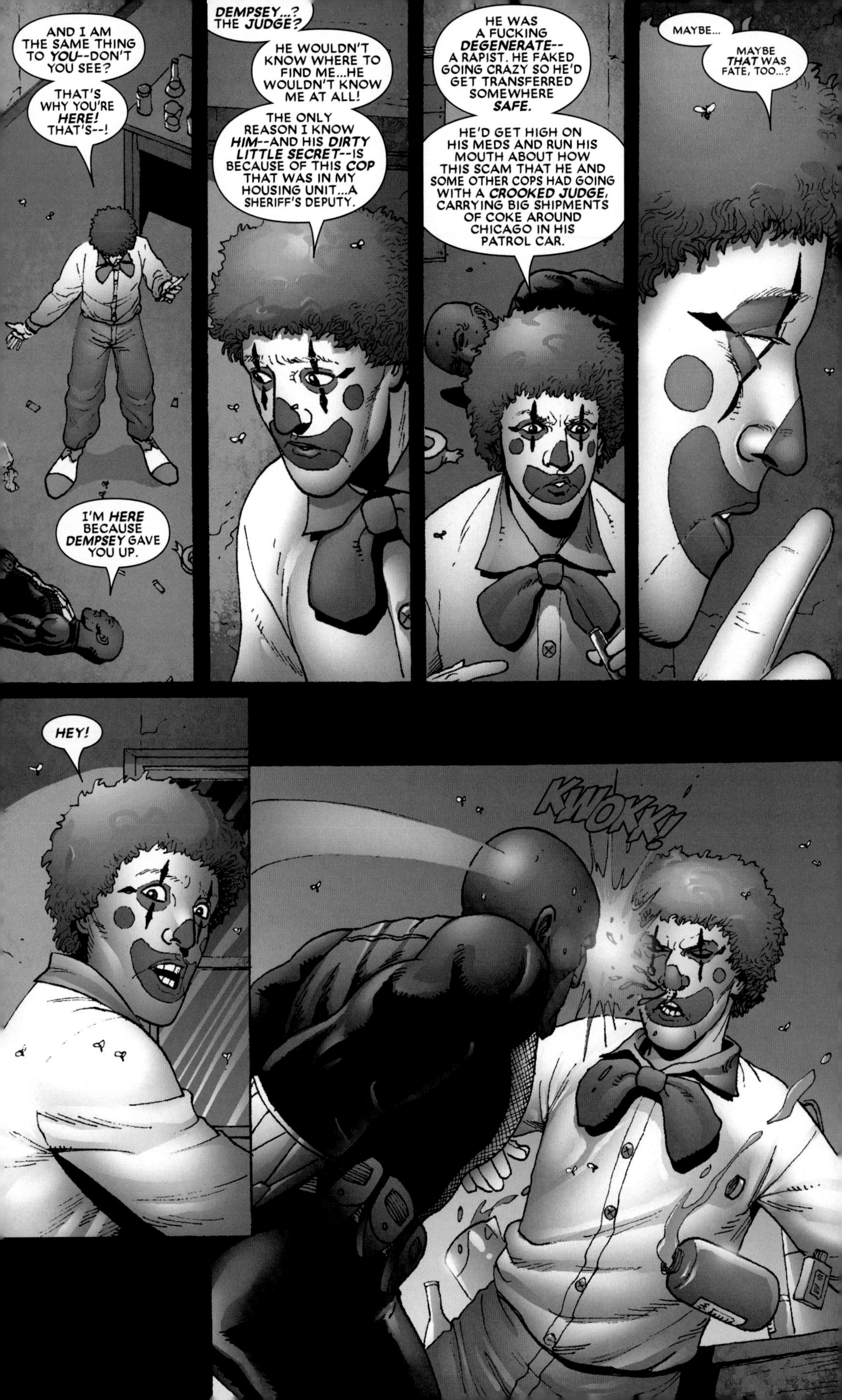

AND I AM THE SAME THING TO YOU--DON'T YOU SEE?
THAT'S WHY YOU'RE HERE! THAT'S--!
I'M HERE BECAUSE DEMPSEY GAVE YOU UP.
DEMPSEY...? THE JUDGE?
HE WOULDN'T KNOW WHERE TO FIND ME...HE WOULDN'T KNOW ME AT ALL!
THE ONLY REASON I KNOW HIM--AND HIS DIRTY LITTLE SECRET--IS BECAUSE OF THIS COP THAT WAS IN MY HOUSING UNIT...A SHERIFF'S DEPUTY.
HE WAS A FUCKING DEGENERATE--A RAPIST. HE FAKED GOING CRAZY SO HE'D GET TRANSFERRED SOMEWHERE SAFE.
HE'D GET HIGH ON HIS MEDS AND RUN HIS MOUTH ABOUT HOW THIS SCAM THAT HE AND SOME OTHER COPS HAD GOING WITH A CROOKED JUDGE, CARRYING BIG SHIPMENTS OF COKE AROUND CHICAGO IN HIS PATROL CAR.
MAYBE...
MAYBE THAT WAS FATE, TOO...?
HEY!
KWOKK!

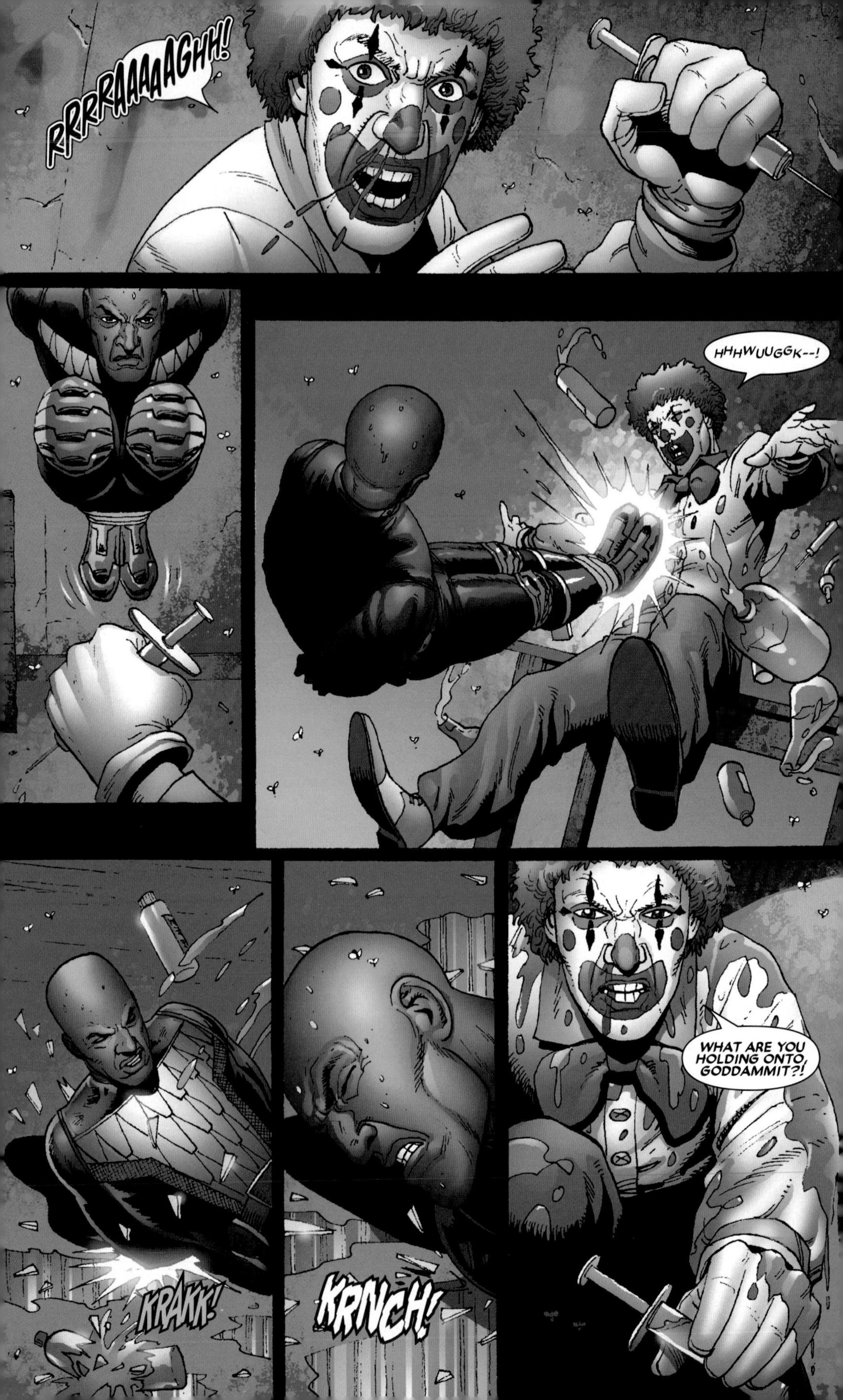
RRRRAAAAAGHH!
HHHWUUGGK--!
KRAKK!
KRNCH!
WHAT ARE YOU HOLDING ONTO, GODDAMMIT?!

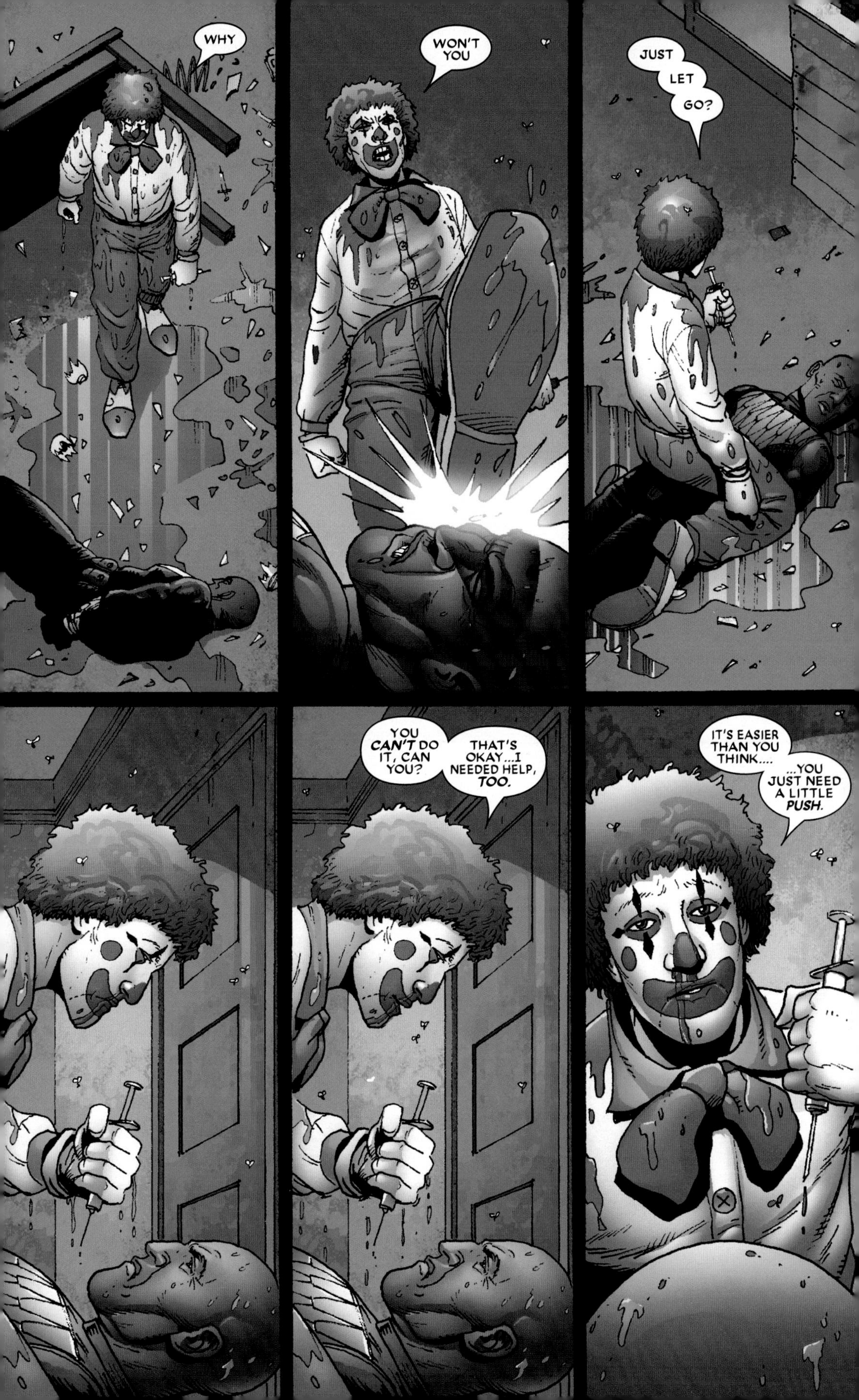
WHY
WON'T YOU
JUST LET GO?
YOU *CAN'T* DO IT, CAN YOU?
THAT'S OKAY...I NEEDED HELP, *TOO.*
IT'S EASIER THAN YOU THINK....
...YOU JUST NEED A LITTLE *PUSH*.

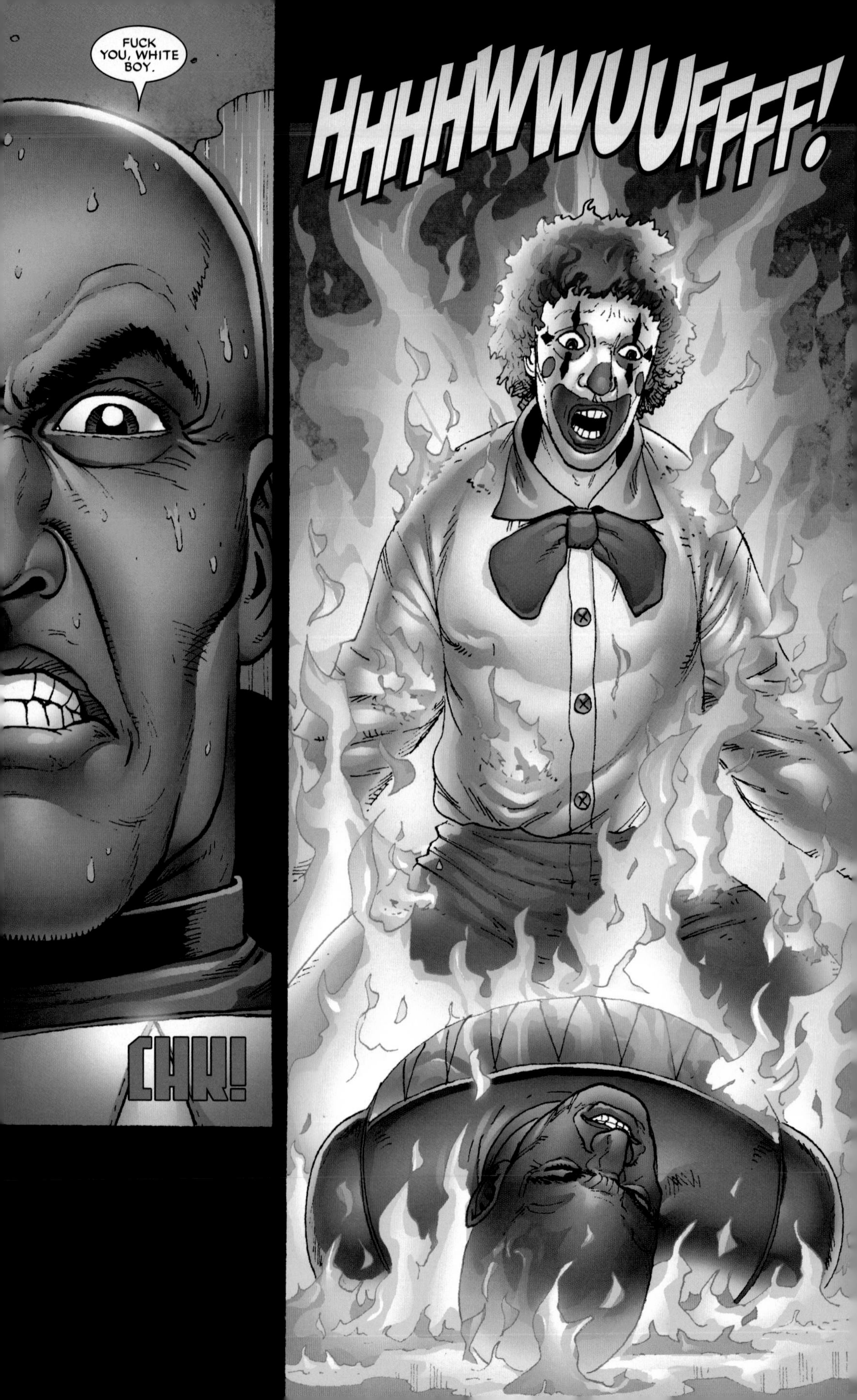
FUCK YOU, WHITE BOY.
CHK!
HHHHWWUUFFFF!

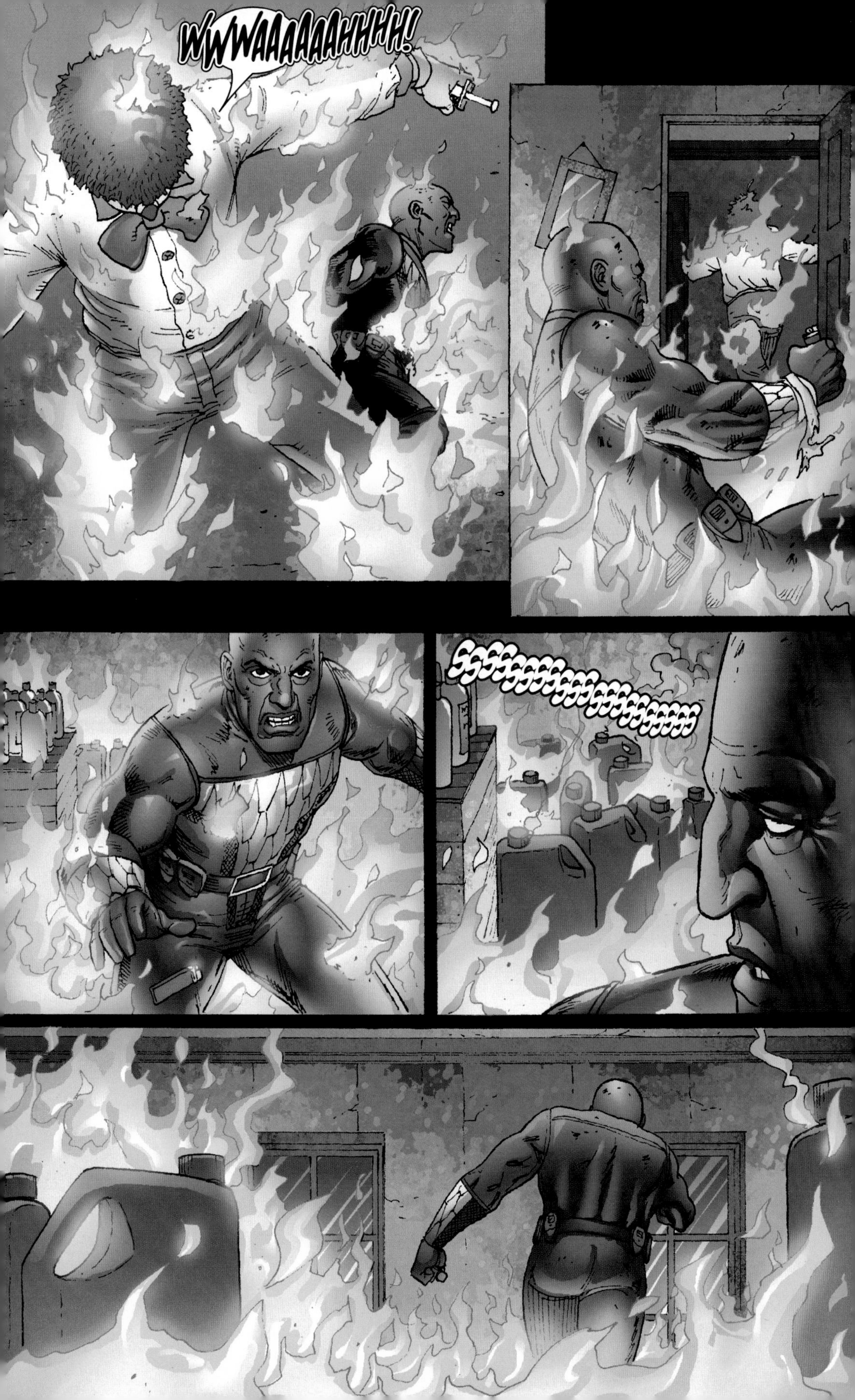
WWWAAAAAAAHHHH!
SSSSSSSSSSSSSSSSSSSSS

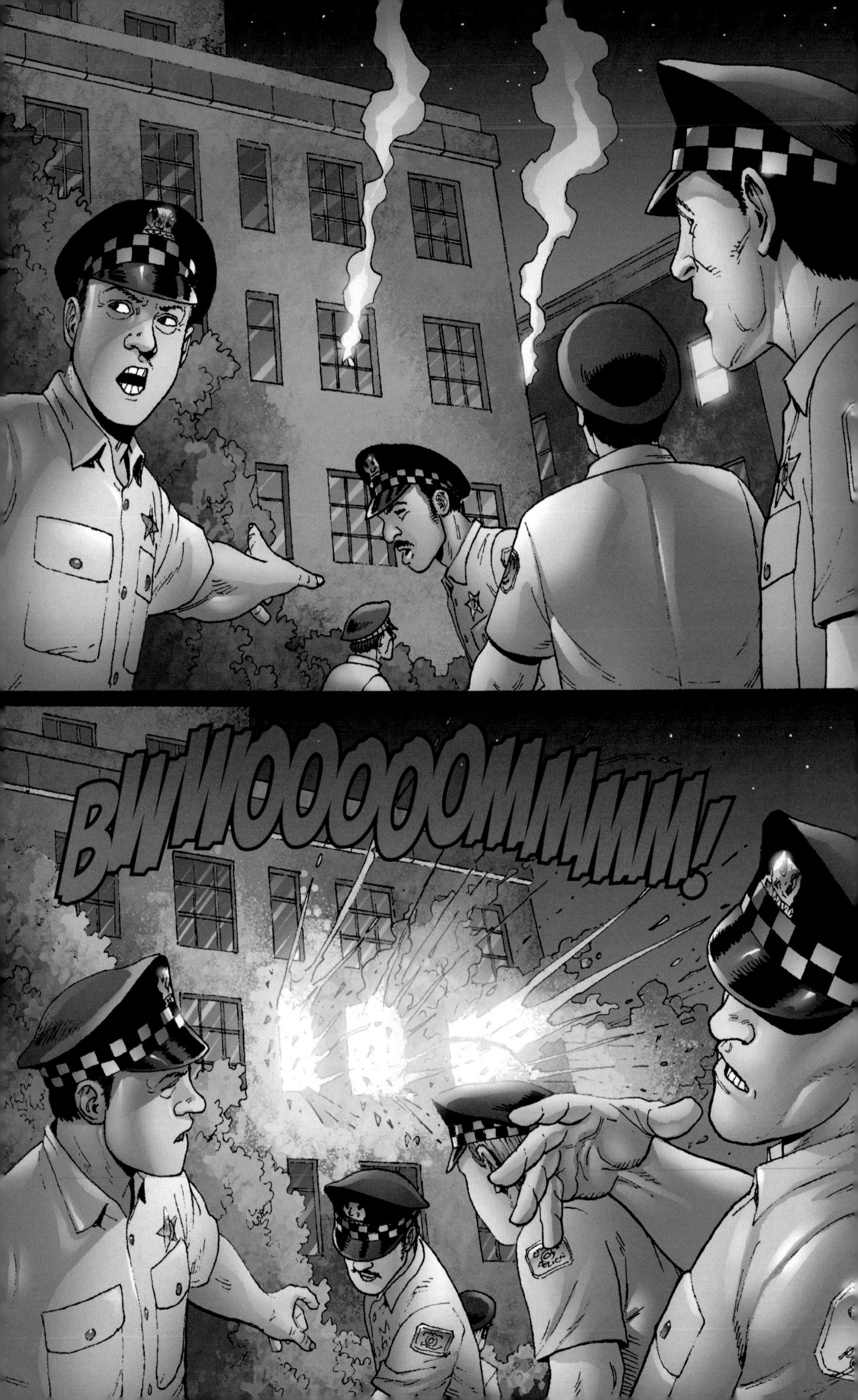
BWOOOOOMMMMM!

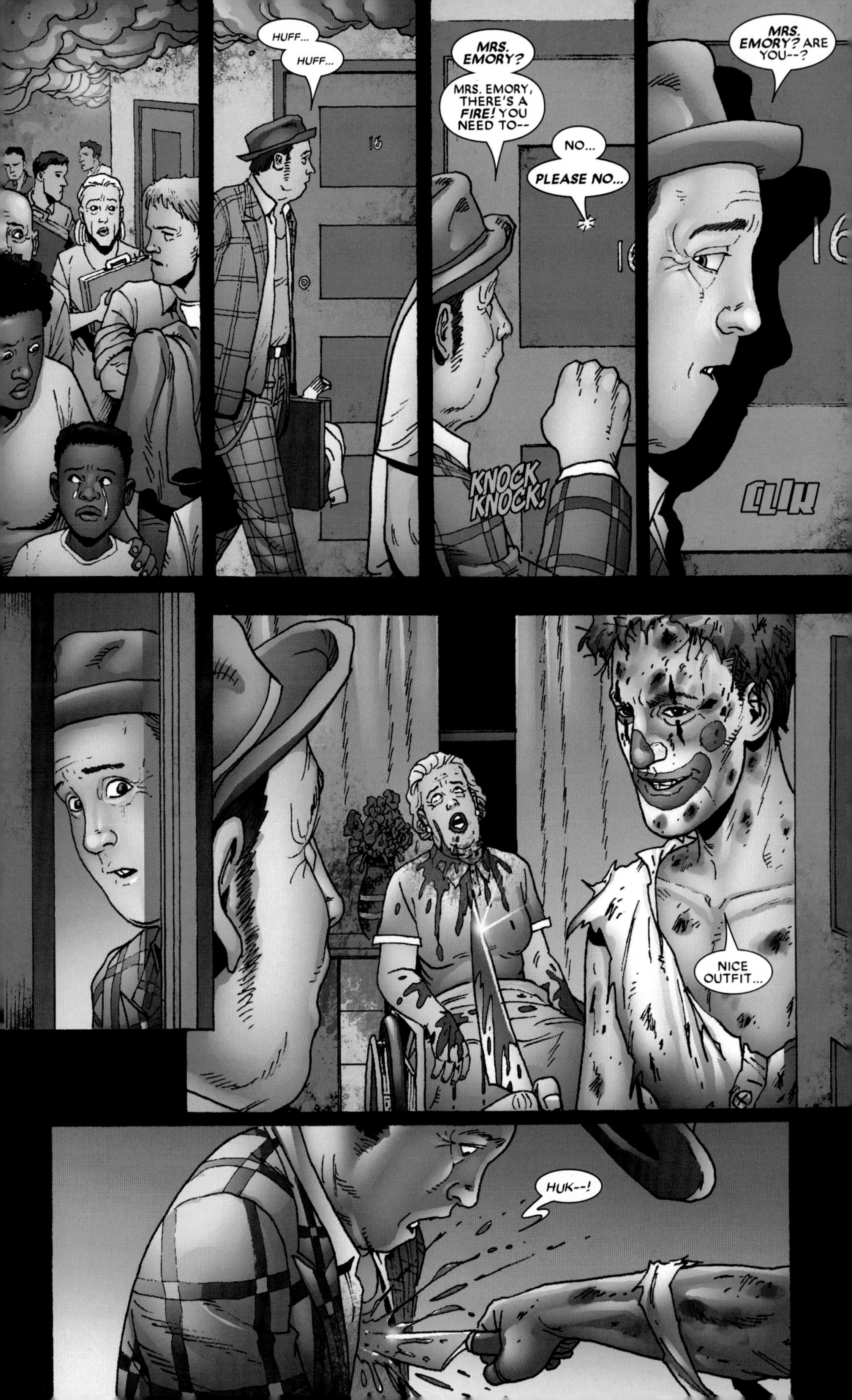
HUFF...
HUFF...
MRS. EMORY?
MRS. EMORY, THERE'S A FIRE! YOU NEED TO--
NO...
PLEASE NO...
KNOCK KNOCK!
MRS. EMORY? ARE YOU--?
CLIK
NICE OUTFIT...
HUK--!

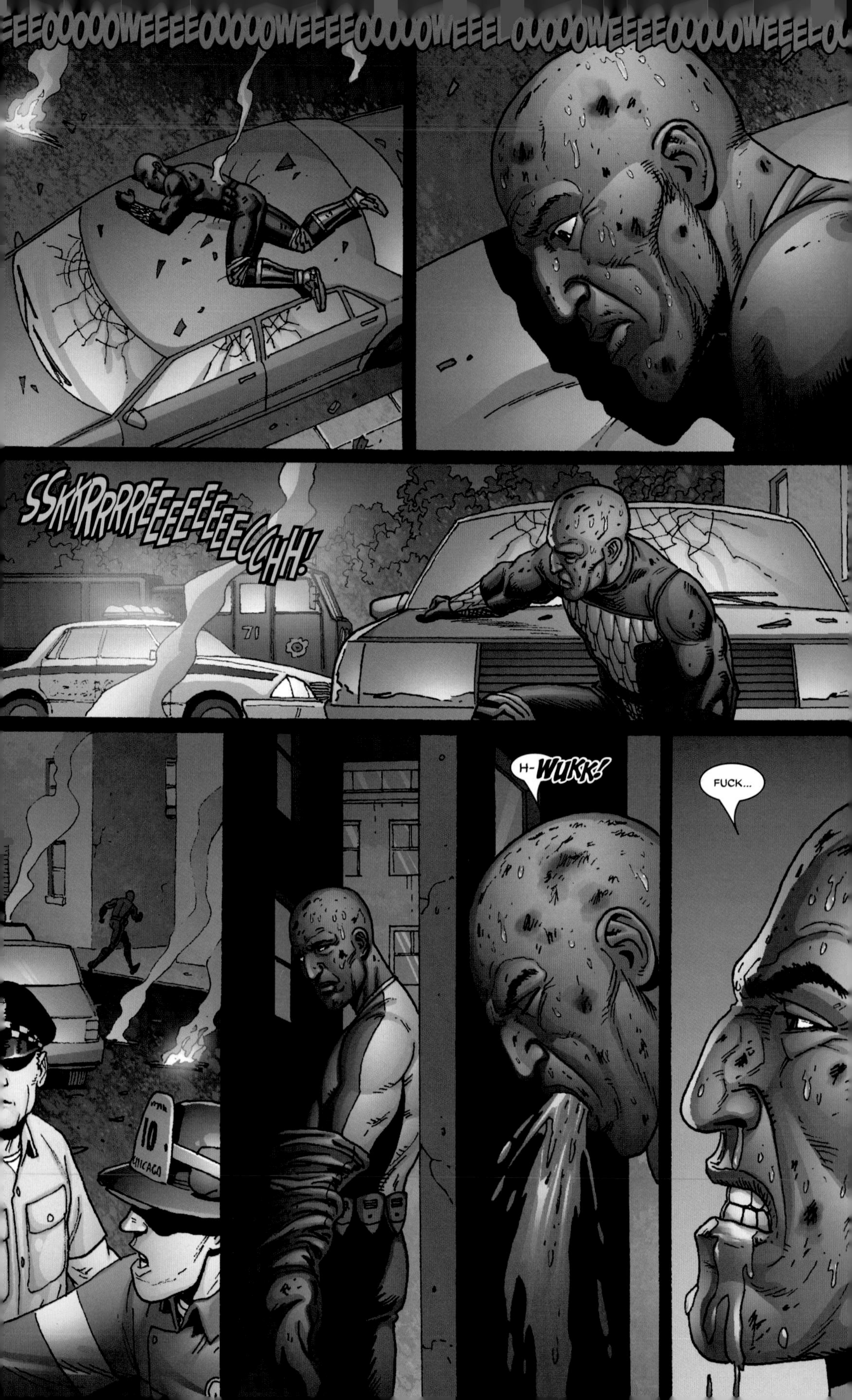
EEEOOOOOWEEEEOOOOOWEEEEOOOOOWEEEL OOOOOWEEEEOOOOOWEEEL-OO
SSKKRRRRREEEEEEEEEECCHH!
71
10
CHICAGO
H-WUKK!
FUCK...

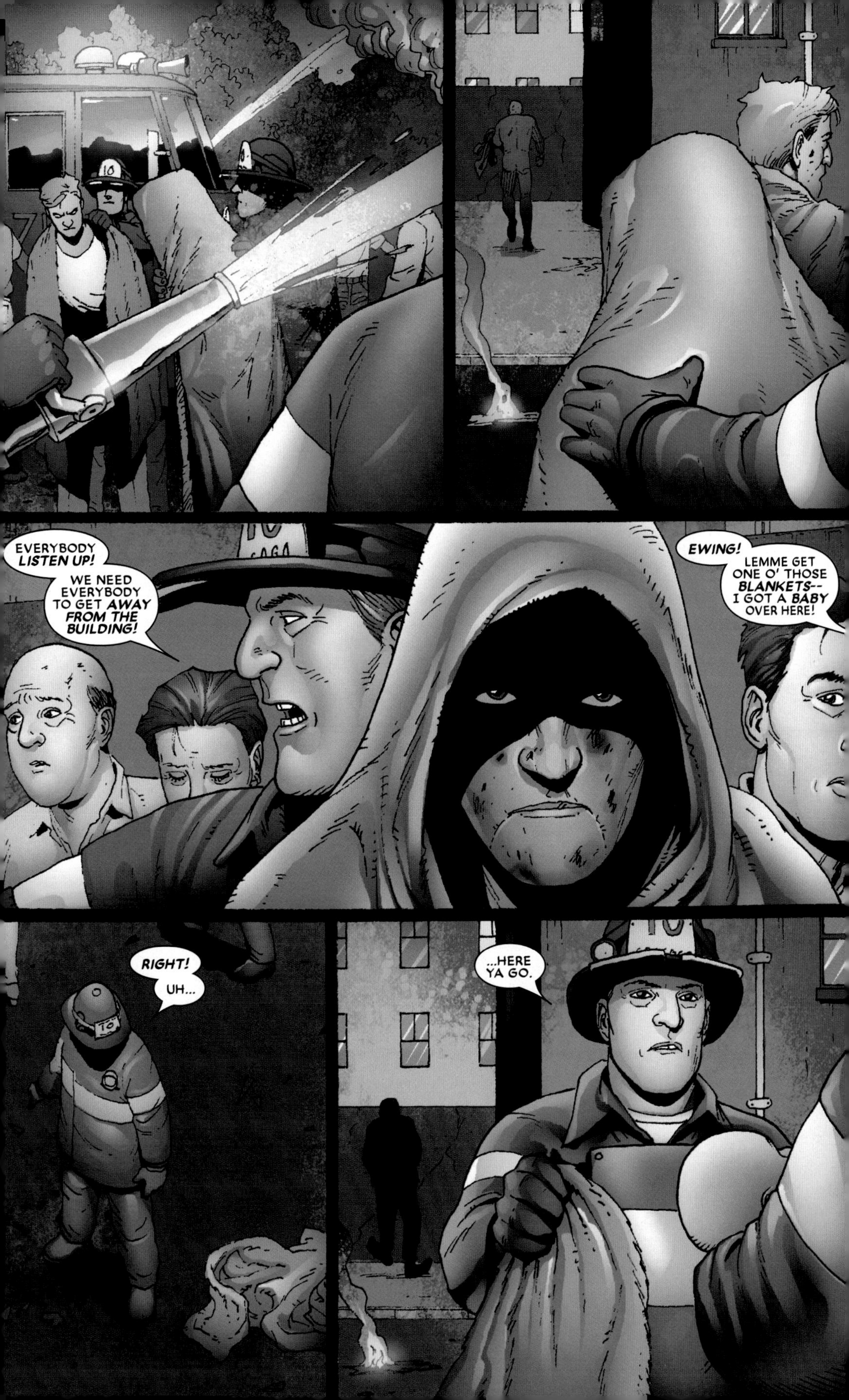
EVERYBODY LISTEN UP!
WE NEED EVERYBODY TO GET AWAY FROM THE BUILDING!
EWING!
LEMME GET ONE O' THOSE BLANKETS-- I GOT A BABY OVER HERE!
RIGHT!
UH...
...HERE YA GO.

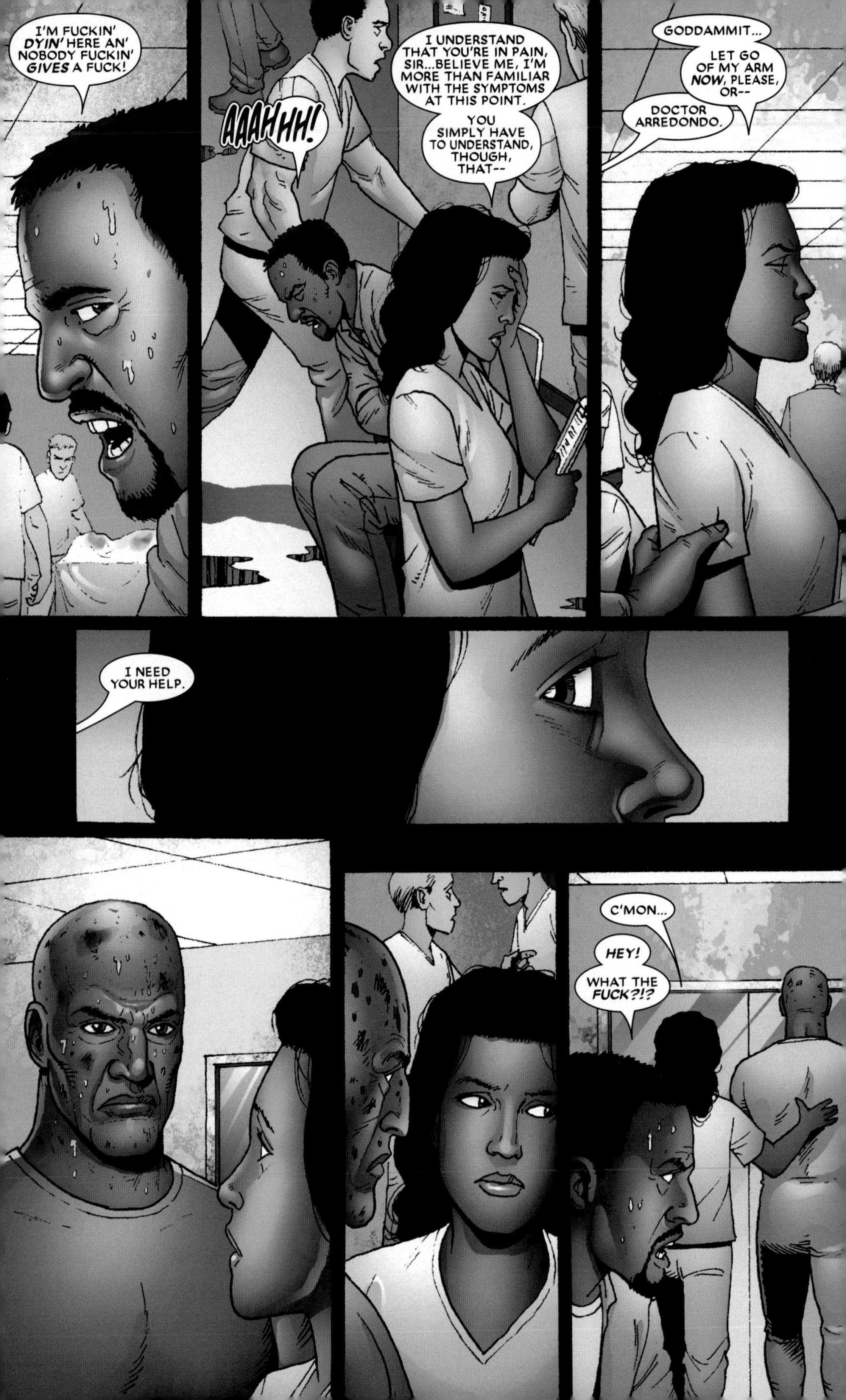

I'M FUCKIN' *DYIN'* HERE AN' NOBODY FUCKIN' *GIVES* A FUCK!
AAAHHH!
I UNDERSTAND THAT YOU'RE IN PAIN, SIR...BELIEVE ME, I'M MORE THAN FAMILIAR WITH THE SYMPTOMS AT THIS POINT.
YOU SIMPLY HAVE TO UNDERSTAND, THOUGH, THAT--
GODDAMMIT...
LET GO OF MY ARM *NOW*, PLEASE, OR--
DOCTOR ARREDONDO.
I NEED YOUR HELP.
C'MON...
HEY!
WHAT THE *FUCK?!?*

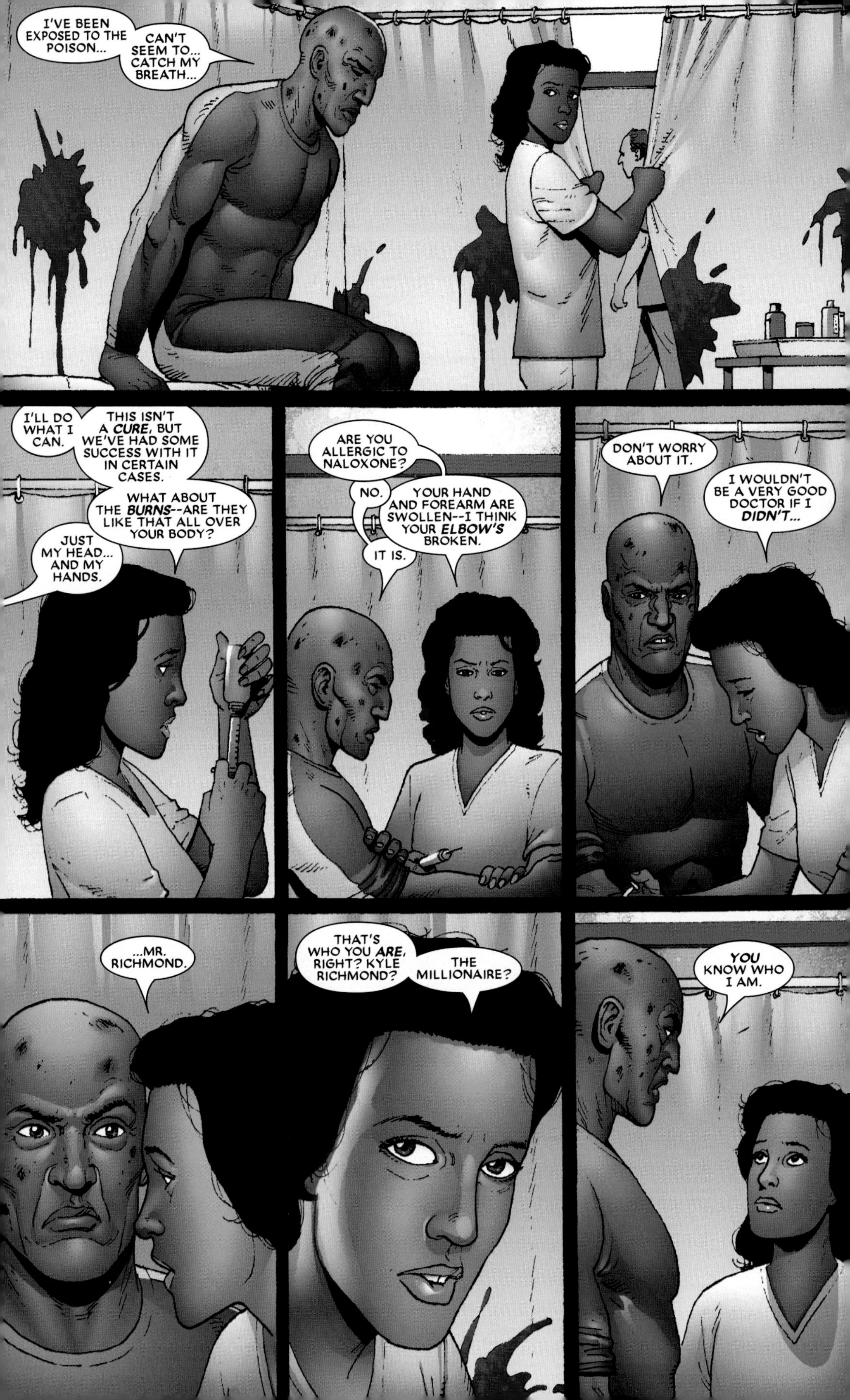
I'VE BEEN EXPOSED TO THE POISON...
CAN'T SEEM TO... CATCH MY BREATH...
I'LL DO WHAT I CAN.
THIS ISN'T A *CURE*, BUT WE'VE HAD SOME SUCCESS WITH IT IN CERTAIN CASES.
WHAT ABOUT THE *BURNS*--ARE THEY LIKE THAT ALL OVER YOUR BODY?
JUST MY HEAD... AND MY HANDS.
ARE YOU ALLERGIC TO NALOXONE?
NO.
YOUR HAND AND FOREARM ARE SWOLLEN--I THINK YOUR *ELBOW'S* BROKEN.
IT IS.
DON'T WORRY ABOUT IT.
I WOULDN'T BE A VERY GOOD DOCTOR IF I *DIDN'T...*
...MR. RICHMOND.
THAT'S WHO YOU *ARE*, RIGHT? KYLE RICHMOND?
THE MILLIONAIRE?
YOU KNOW WHO I AM.

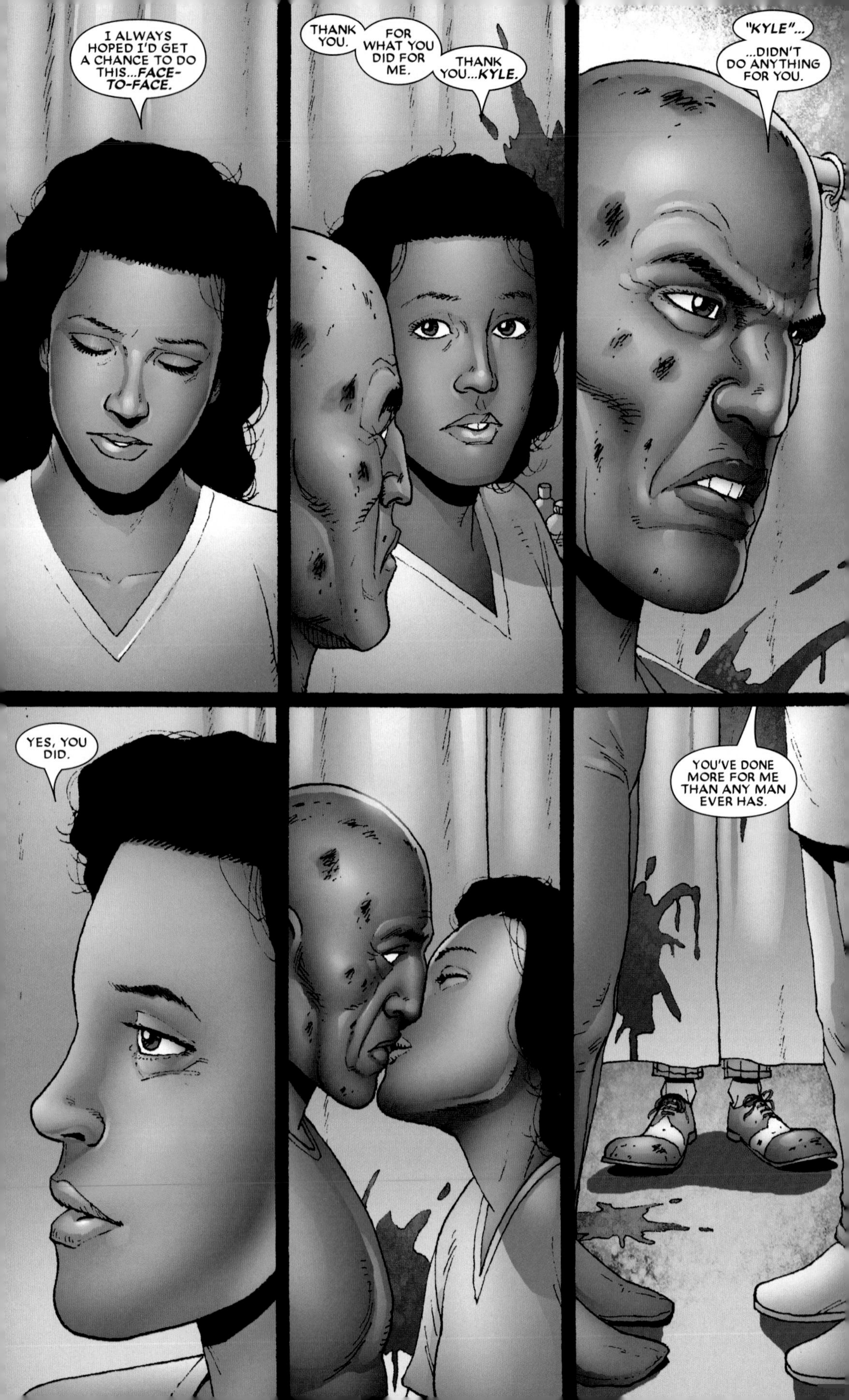
I ALWAYS HOPED I'D GET A CHANCE TO DO THIS...*FACE-TO-FACE.*
THANK YOU.
FOR WHAT YOU DID FOR ME.
THANK YOU...*KYLE.*
"KYLE"...
...DIDN'T DO ANYTHING FOR YOU.
YES, YOU DID.
YOU'VE DONE MORE FOR ME THAN ANY MAN EVER HAS.

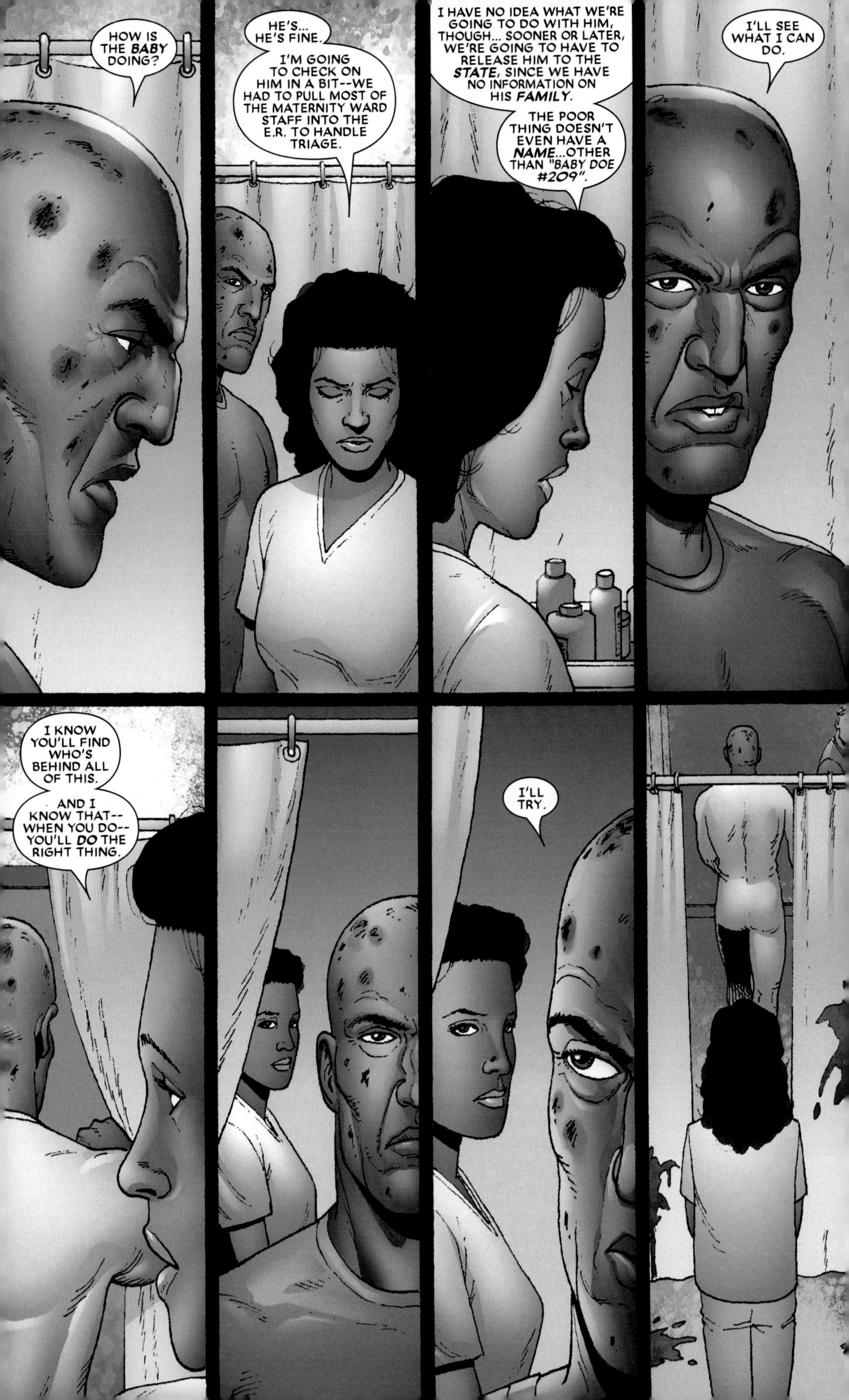
HOW IS THE BABY DOING?
HE'S... HE'S FINE.
I'M GOING TO CHECK ON HIM IN A BIT--WE HAD TO PULL MOST OF THE MATERNITY WARD STAFF INTO THE E.R. TO HANDLE TRIAGE.
I HAVE NO IDEA WHAT WE'RE GOING TO DO WITH HIM, THOUGH... SOONER OR LATER, WE'RE GOING TO HAVE TO RELEASE HIM TO THE STATE, SINCE WE HAVE NO INFORMATION ON HIS FAMILY.
THE POOR THING DOESN'T EVEN HAVE A NAME...OTHER THAN "BABY DOE #209".
I'LL SEE WHAT I CAN DO.
I KNOW YOU'LL FIND WHO'S BEHIND ALL OF THIS.
AND I KNOW THAT--WHEN YOU DO--YOU'LL DO THE RIGHT THING.
I'LL TRY.

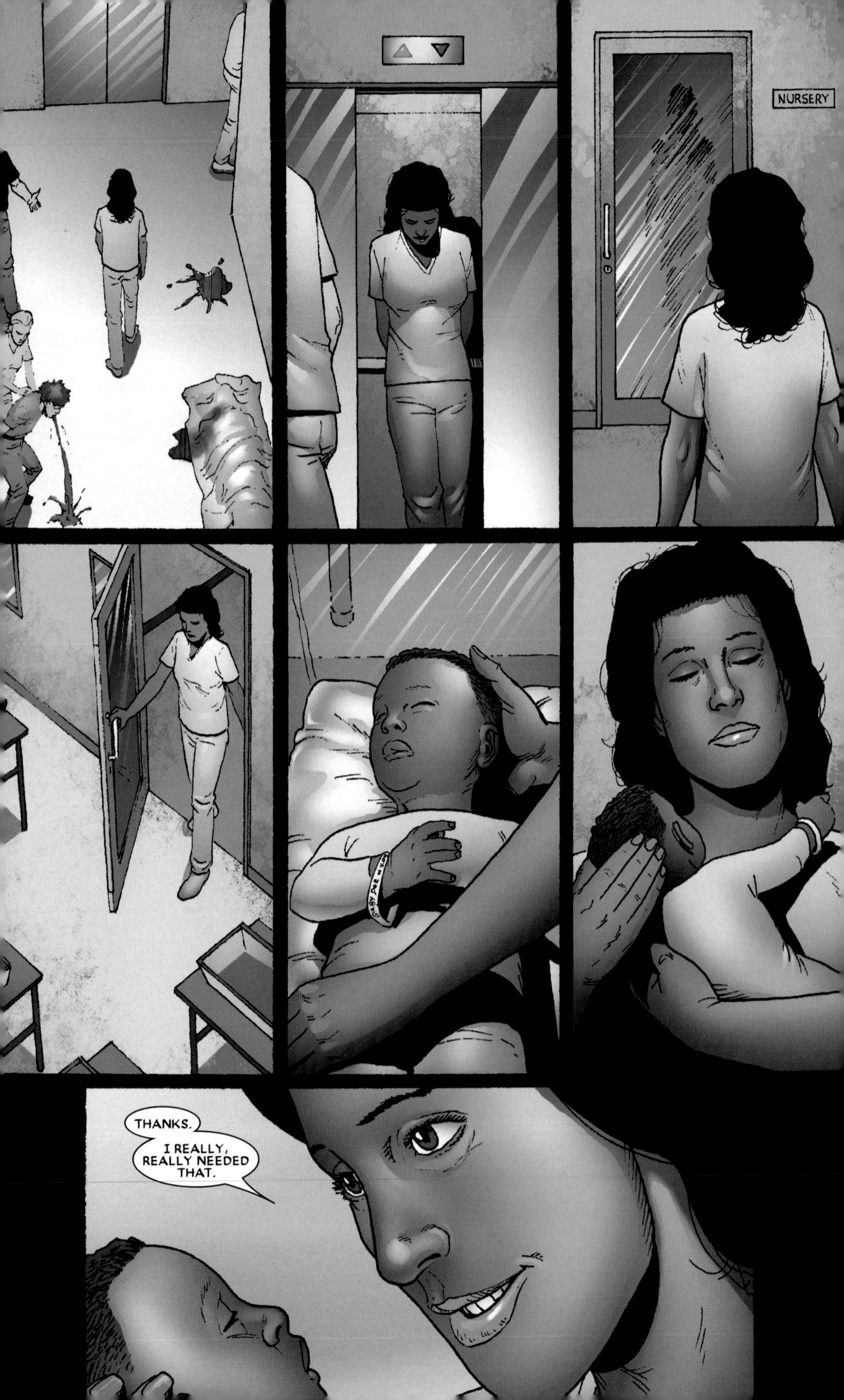
NURSERY
THANKS.
I REALLY, REALLY NEEDED THAT.

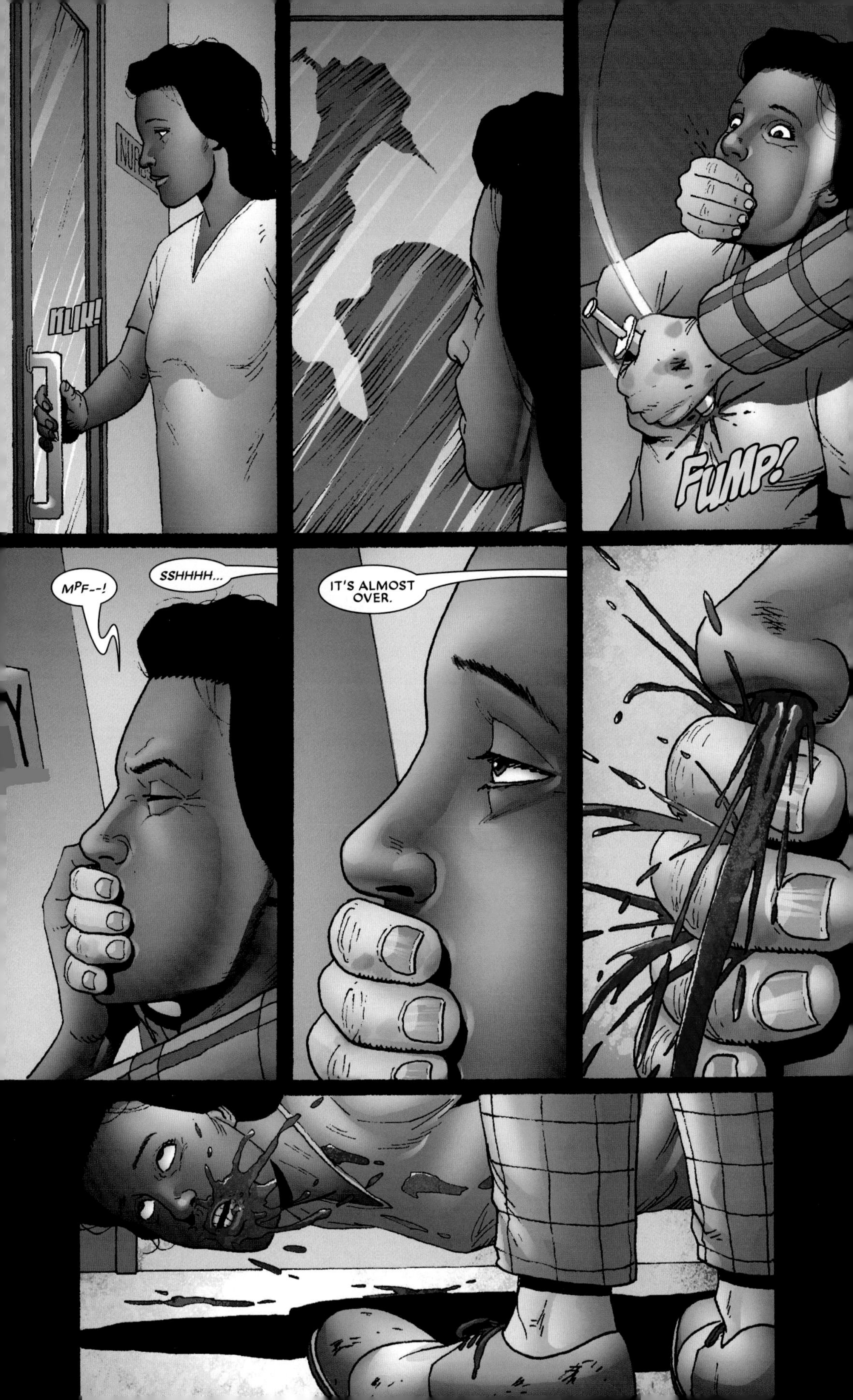
KLIK!
FUMP!
MPF--!
SSHHHH...
IT'S ALMOST OVER.

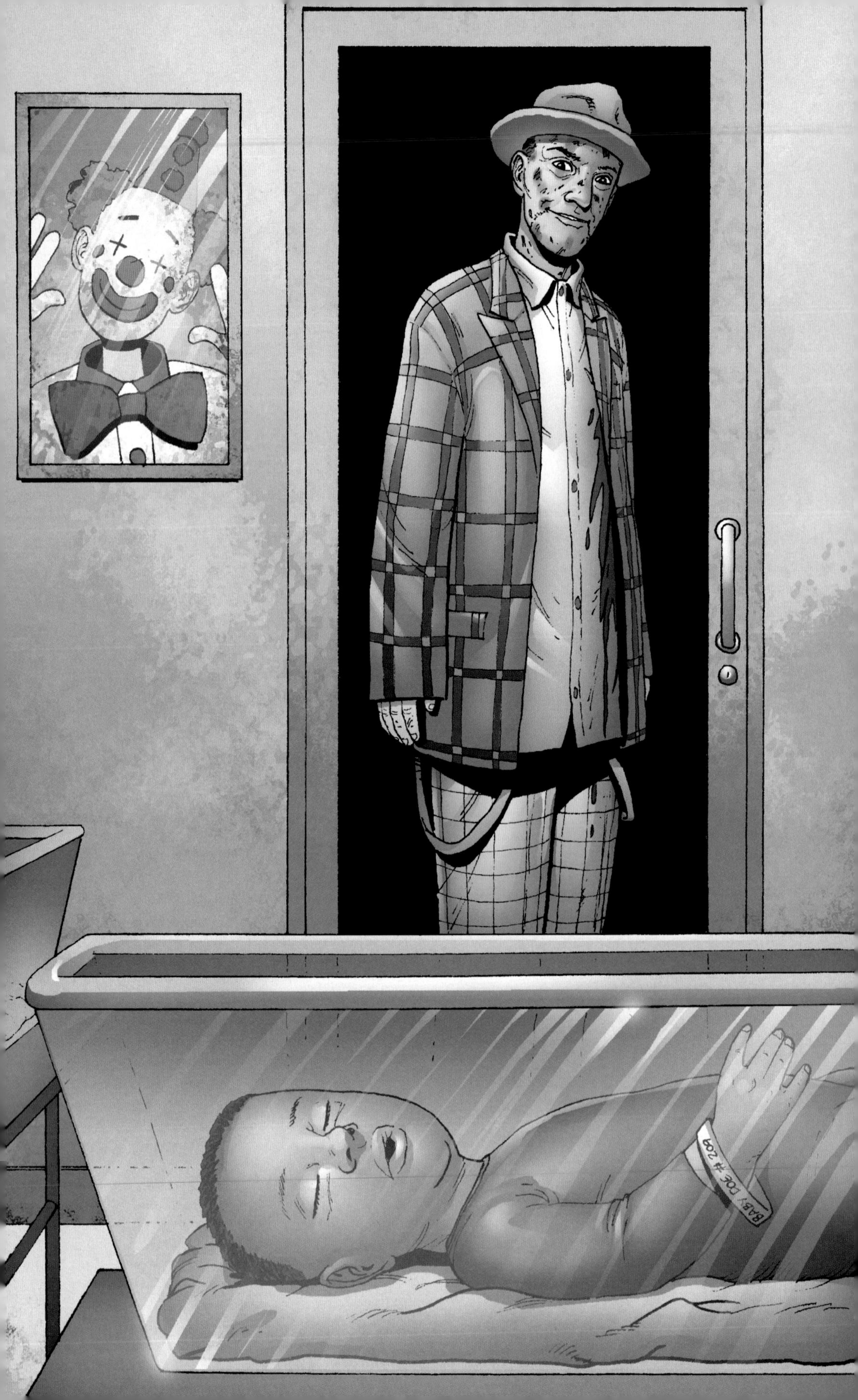
BABY DOE # 209

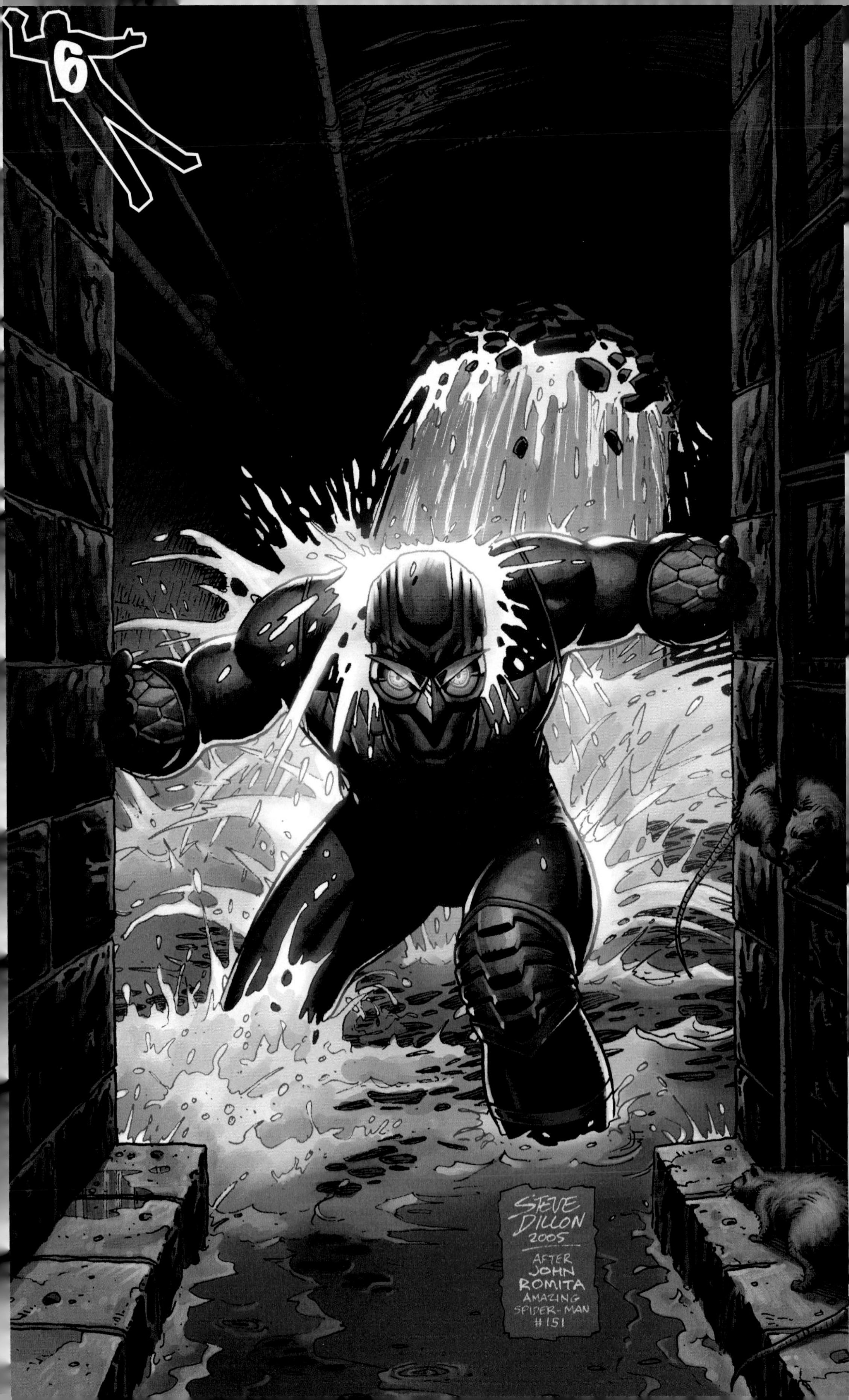
6
STEVE DILLON 2005
AFTER JOHN ROMITA AMAZING SPIDER-MAN #151

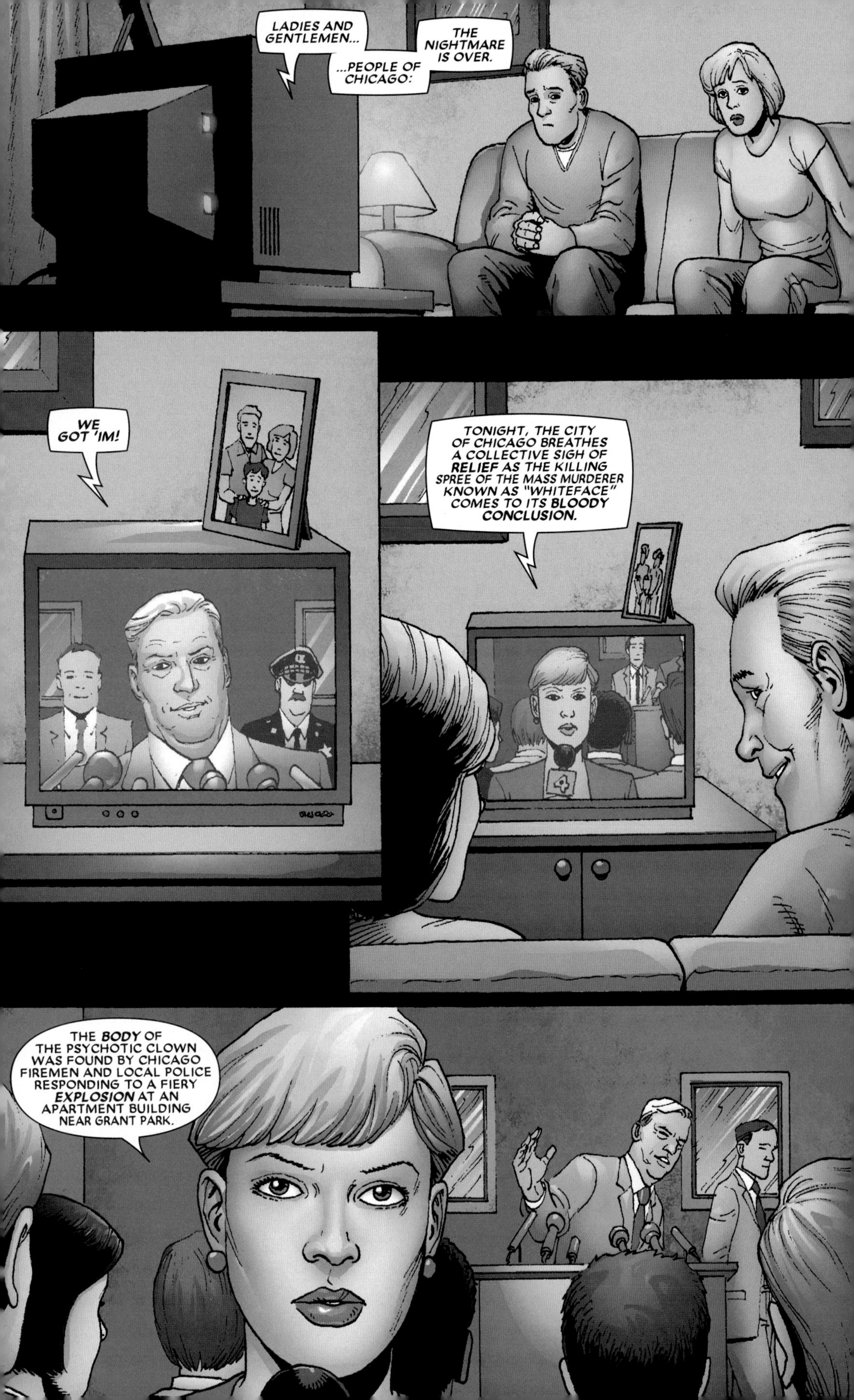
LADIES AND GENTLEMEN...
...PEOPLE OF CHICAGO:
THE NIGHTMARE IS OVER.
WE GOT 'IM!
TONIGHT, THE CITY OF CHICAGO BREATHES A COLLECTIVE SIGH OF RELIEF AS THE KILLING SPREE OF THE MASS MURDERER KNOWN AS "WHITEFACE" COMES TO ITS BLOODY CONCLUSION.
THE BODY OF THE PSYCHOTIC CLOWN WAS FOUND BY CHICAGO FIREMEN AND LOCAL POLICE RESPONDING TO A FIERY EXPLOSION AT AN APARTMENT BUILDING NEAR GRANT PARK.

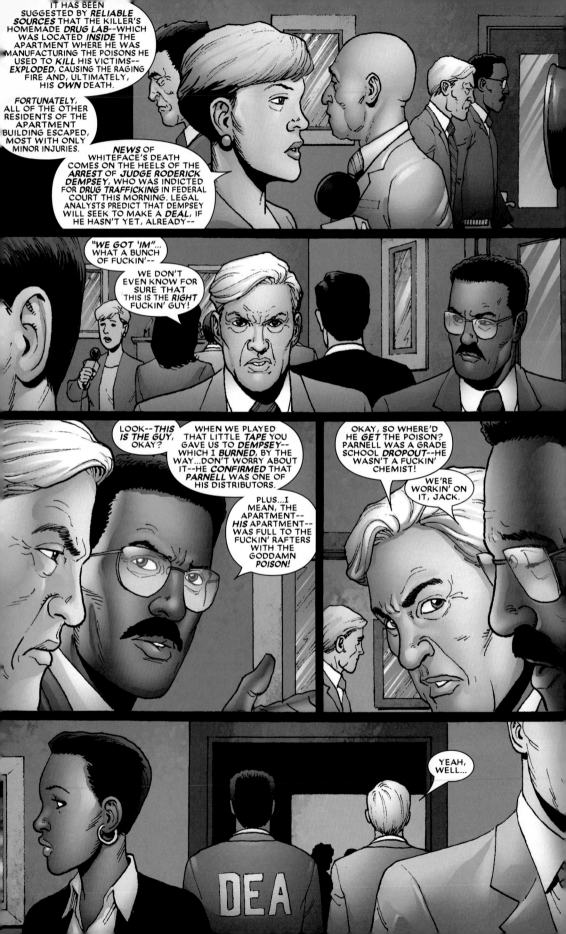

IT HAS BEEN SUGGESTED BY *RELIABLE SOURCES* THAT THE KILLER'S HOMEMADE *DRUG LAB*--WHICH WAS LOCATED *INSIDE* THE APARTMENT WHERE HE WAS MANUFACTURING THE POISONS HE USED TO *KILL* HIS VICTIMS-- *EXPLODED*, CAUSING THE RAGING FIRE AND, ULTIMATELY, HIS *OWN* DEATH.

FORTUNATELY, ALL OF THE OTHER RESIDENTS OF THE APARTMENT BUILDING ESCAPED, MOST WITH ONLY MINOR INJURIES.

NEWS OF *WHITEFACE'S* DEATH COMES ON THE HEELS OF THE *ARREST* OF *JUDGE RODERICK DEMPSEY,* WHO WAS INDICTED FOR *DRUG TRAFFICKING* IN FEDERAL COURT THIS MORNING. LEGAL ANALYSTS PREDICT THAT DEMPSEY WILL SEEK TO MAKE A *DEAL,* IF HE HASN'T YET, ALREADY--

"WE GOT 'IM"... WHAT A BUNCH OF FUCKIN'--

WE DON'T EVEN KNOW FOR SURE THAT THIS IS THE *RIGHT* FUCKIN' GUY!

LOOK--*THIS IS THE GUY,* OKAY?

WHEN WE PLAYED THAT LITTLE *TAPE* YOU GAVE US TO *DEMPSEY*--WHICH I *BURNED,* BY THE WAY...DON'T WORRY ABOUT IT--HE *CONFIRMED* THAT *PARNELL* WAS ONE OF HIS DISTRIBUTORS.

PLUS...I MEAN, THE APARTMENT-- *HIS* APARTMENT-- WAS FULL TO THE FUCKIN' RAFTERS WITH THE GODDAMN *POISON!*

OKAY, SO WHERE'D HE *GET* THE POISON? PARNELL WAS A GRADE SCHOOL *DROPOUT*--HE WASN'T A FUCKIN' CHEMIST!

WE'RE *WORKIN'* ON IT, JACK.

YEAH, WELL...

DEA

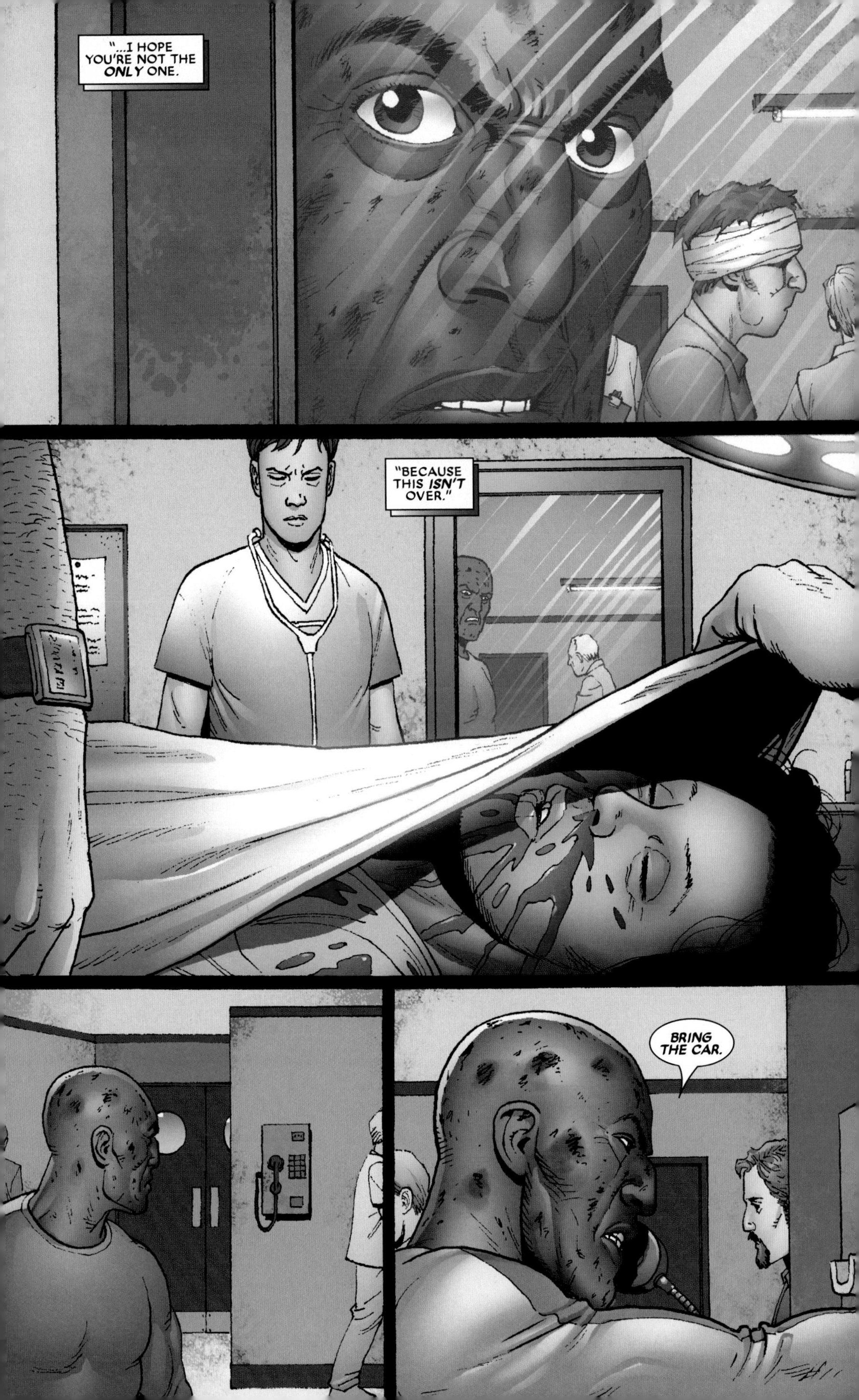
"...I HOPE YOU'RE NOT THE *ONLY* ONE.
"BECAUSE THIS *ISN'T* OVER."
BRING THE CAR.

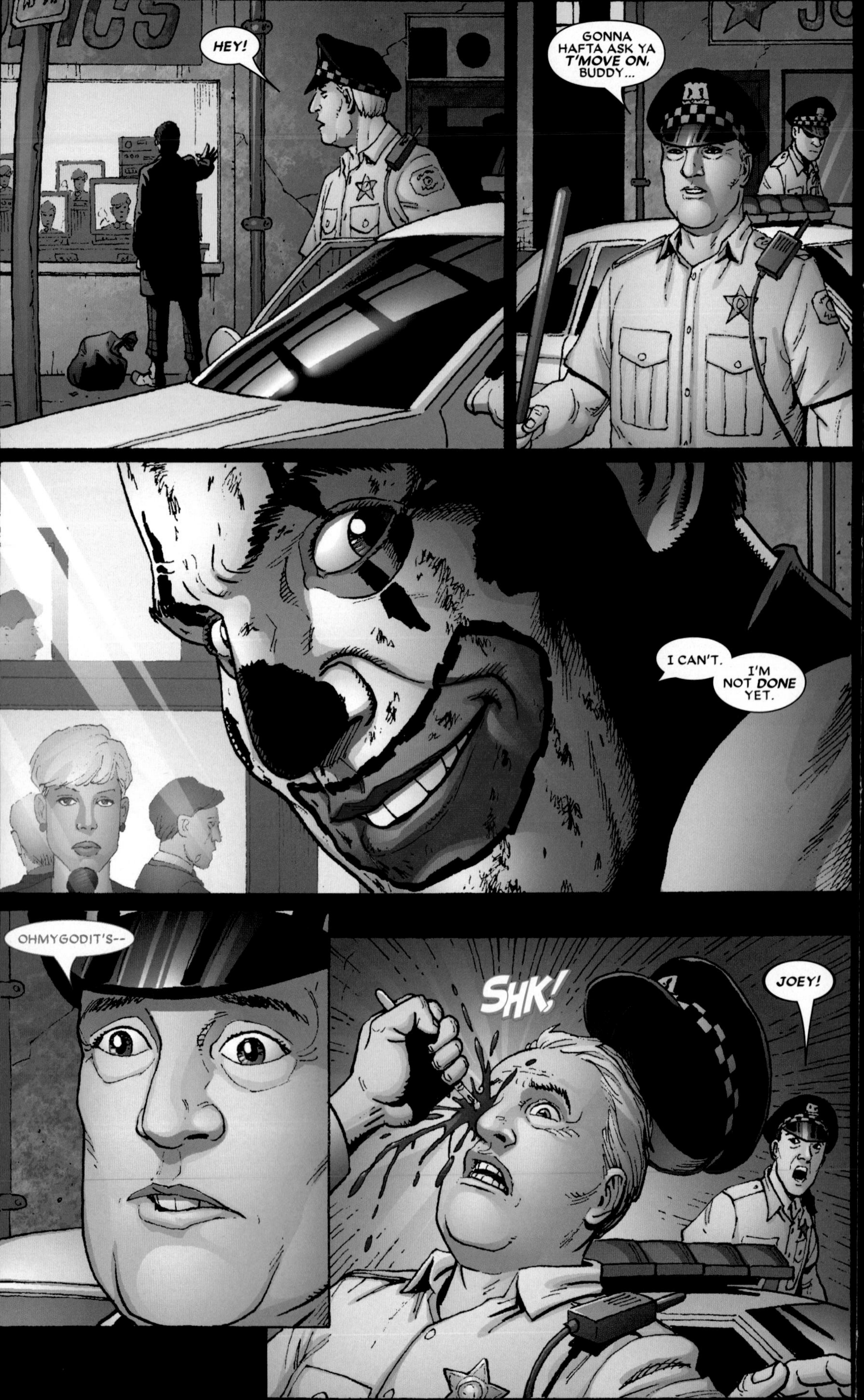
HEY!
GONNA HAFTA ASK YA T'MOVE ON, BUDDY...
I CAN'T.
I'M NOT DONE YET.
OHMYGODIT'S--
SHK!
JOEY!

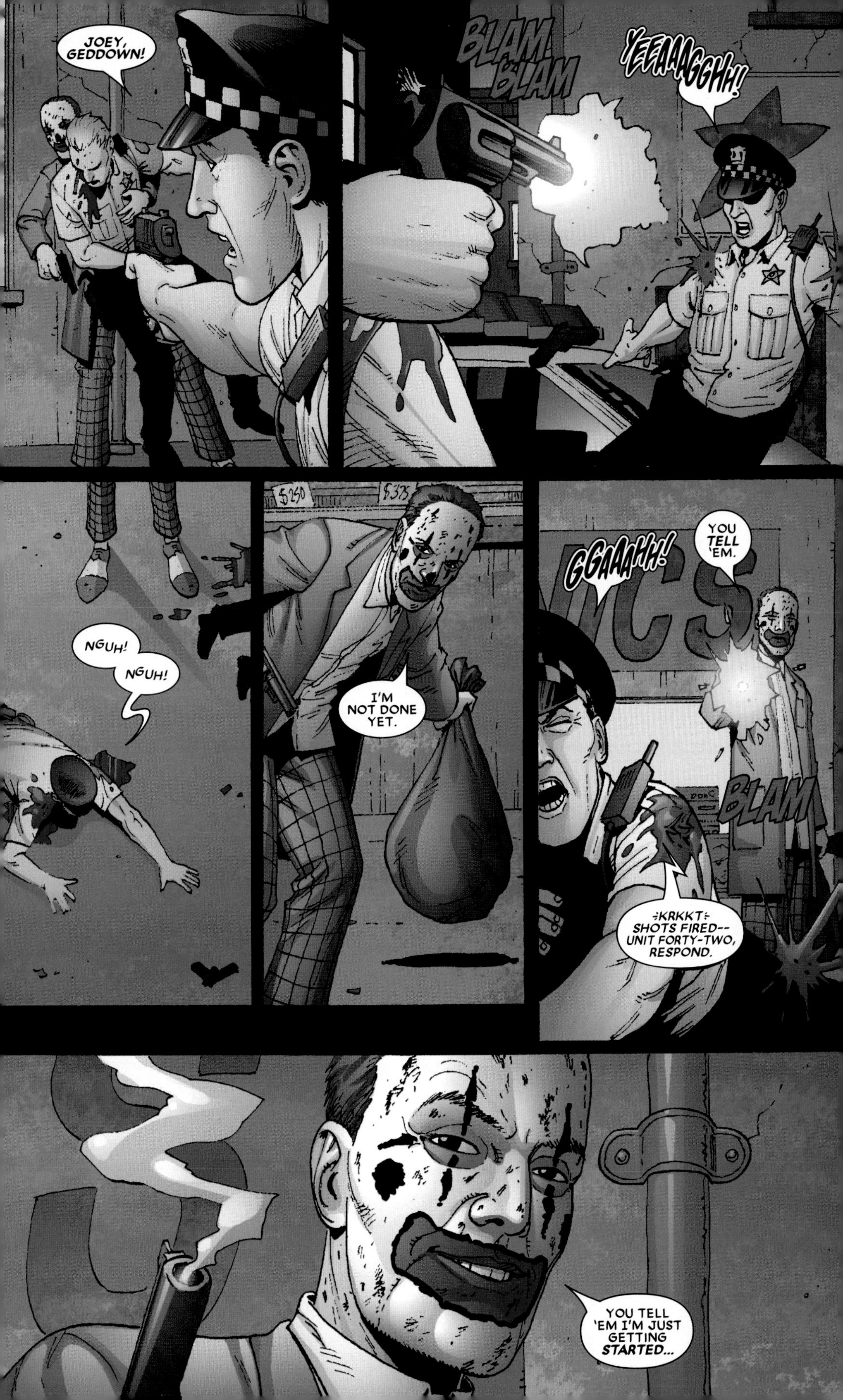

JOEY, GEDDOWN!
BLAM BLAM
YEEAAAAGGHH!
NGUH! NGUH!
I'M NOT DONE YET.
GGAAAHH!
YOU TELL 'EM.
BLAM
⇌KRKKT⇌ SHOTS FIRED-- UNIT FORTY-TWO, RESPOND.
YOU TELL 'EM I'M JUST GETTING *STARTED...*

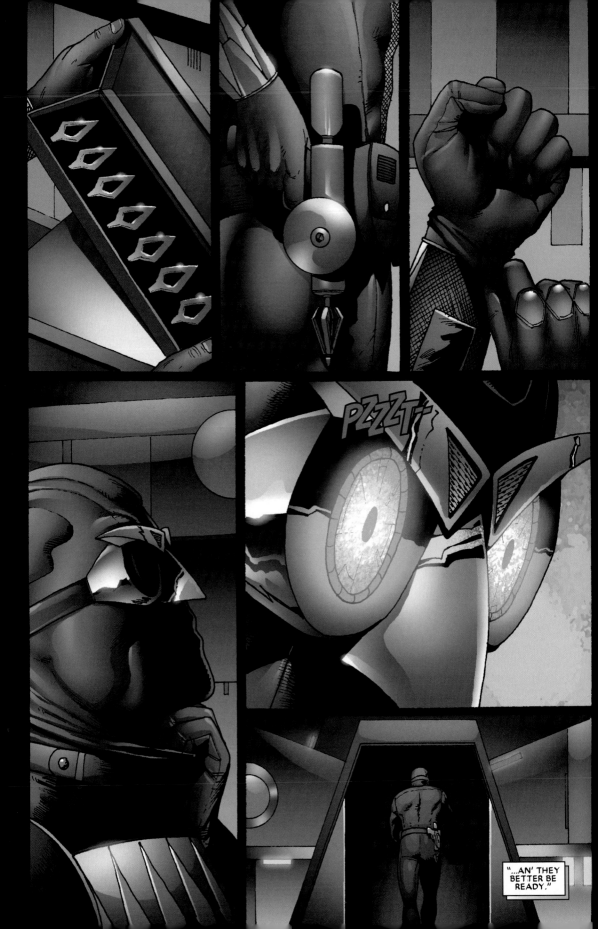

PZZZT

"...AN' THEY BETTER BE READY."

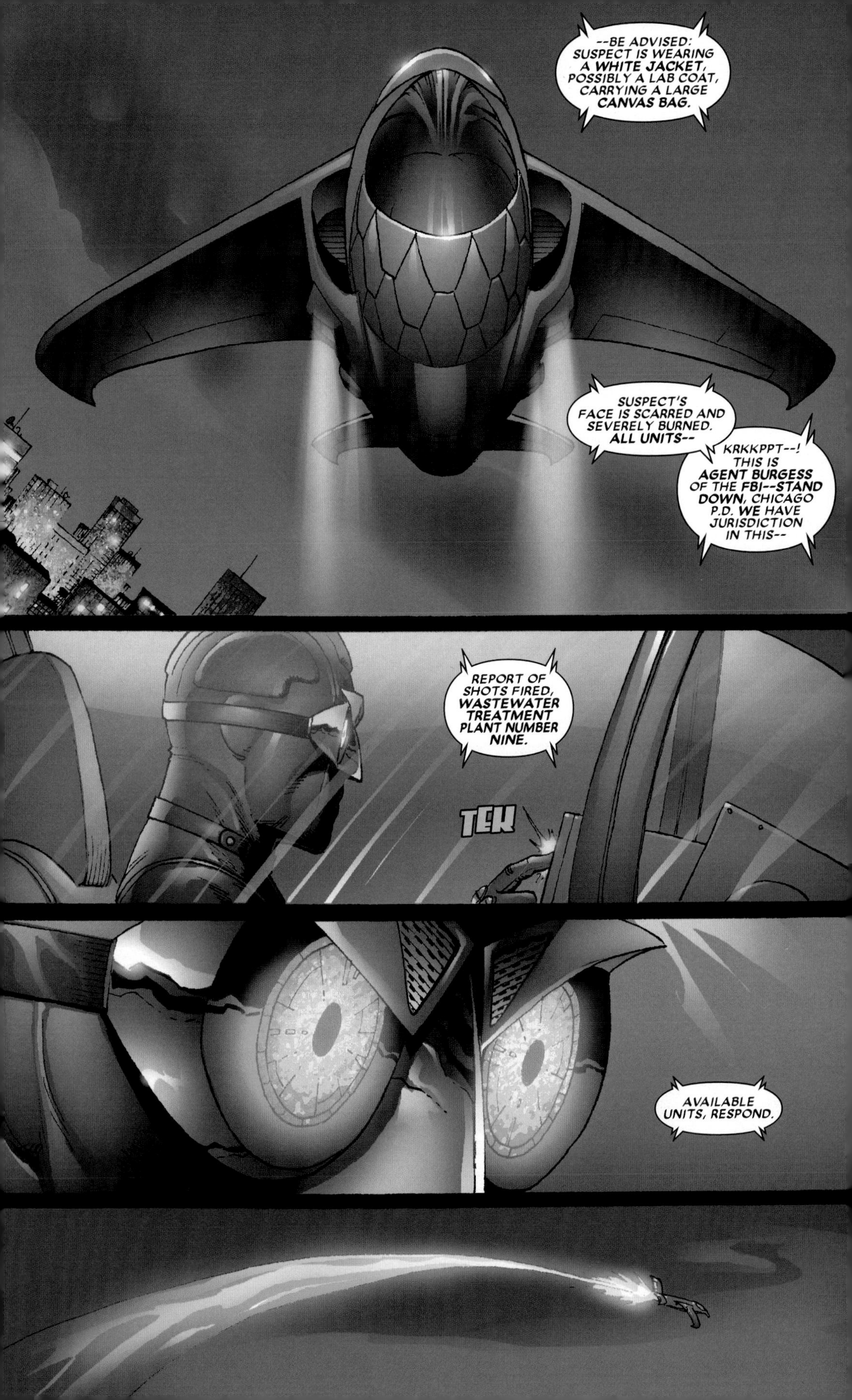
--BE ADVISED: SUSPECT IS WEARING A WHITE JACKET, POSSIBLY A LAB COAT, CARRYING A LARGE CANVAS BAG.
SUSPECT'S FACE IS SCARRED AND SEVERELY BURNED. ALL UNITS--
KRKKPPT--! THIS IS AGENT BURGESS OF THE FBI--STAND DOWN, CHICAGO P.D. WE HAVE JURISDICTION IN THIS--
REPORT OF SHOTS FIRED, WASTEWATER TREATMENT PLANT NUMBER NINE.
TEK
AVAILABLE UNITS, RESPOND.

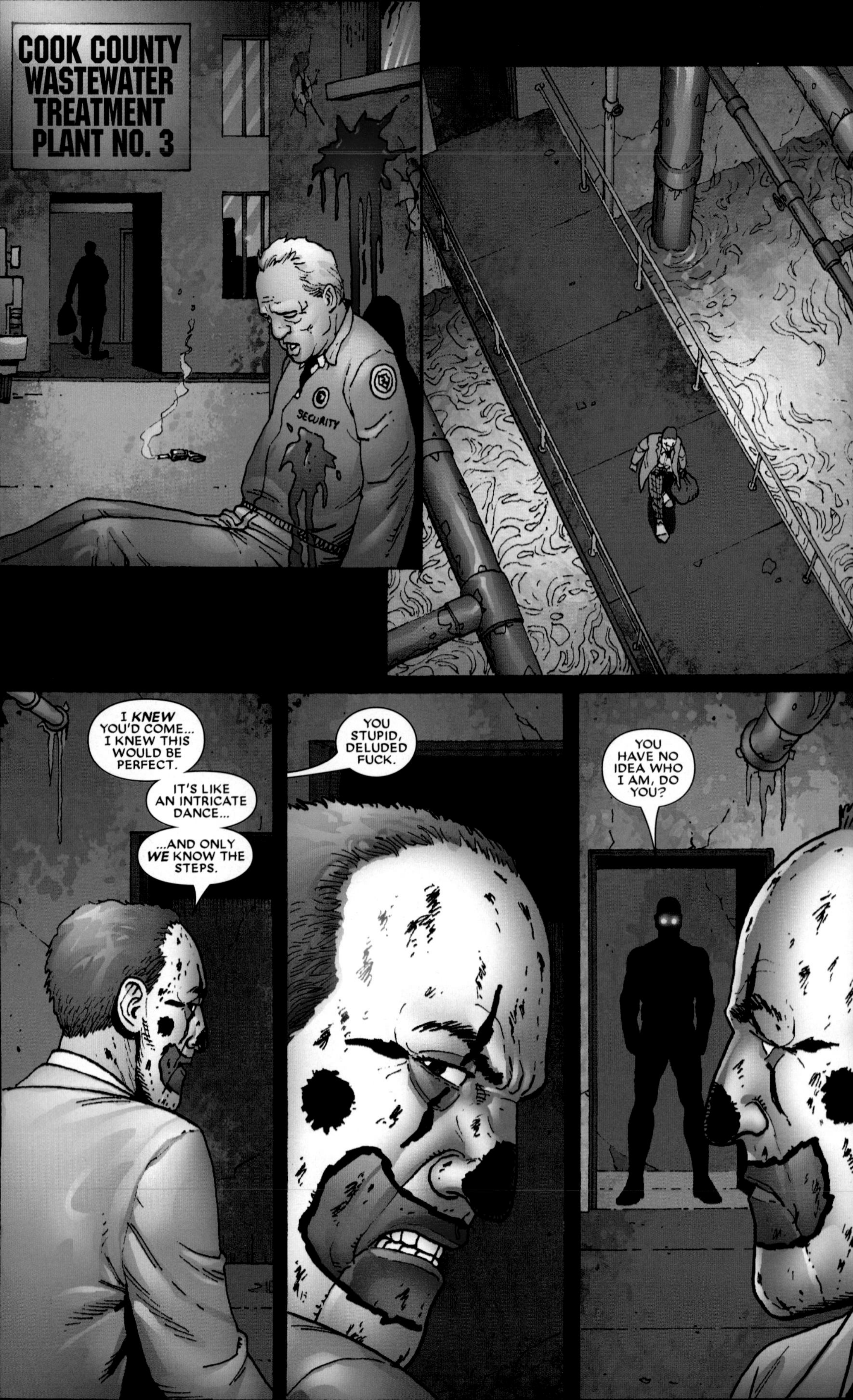
COOK COUNTY WASTEWATER TREATMENT PLANT NO. 3
SECURITY
I KNEW YOU'D COME... I KNEW THIS WOULD BE PERFECT.
IT'S LIKE AN INTRICATE DANCE...
...AND ONLY WE KNOW THE STEPS.
YOU STUPID, DELUDED FUCK.
YOU HAVE NO IDEA WHO I AM, DO YOU?

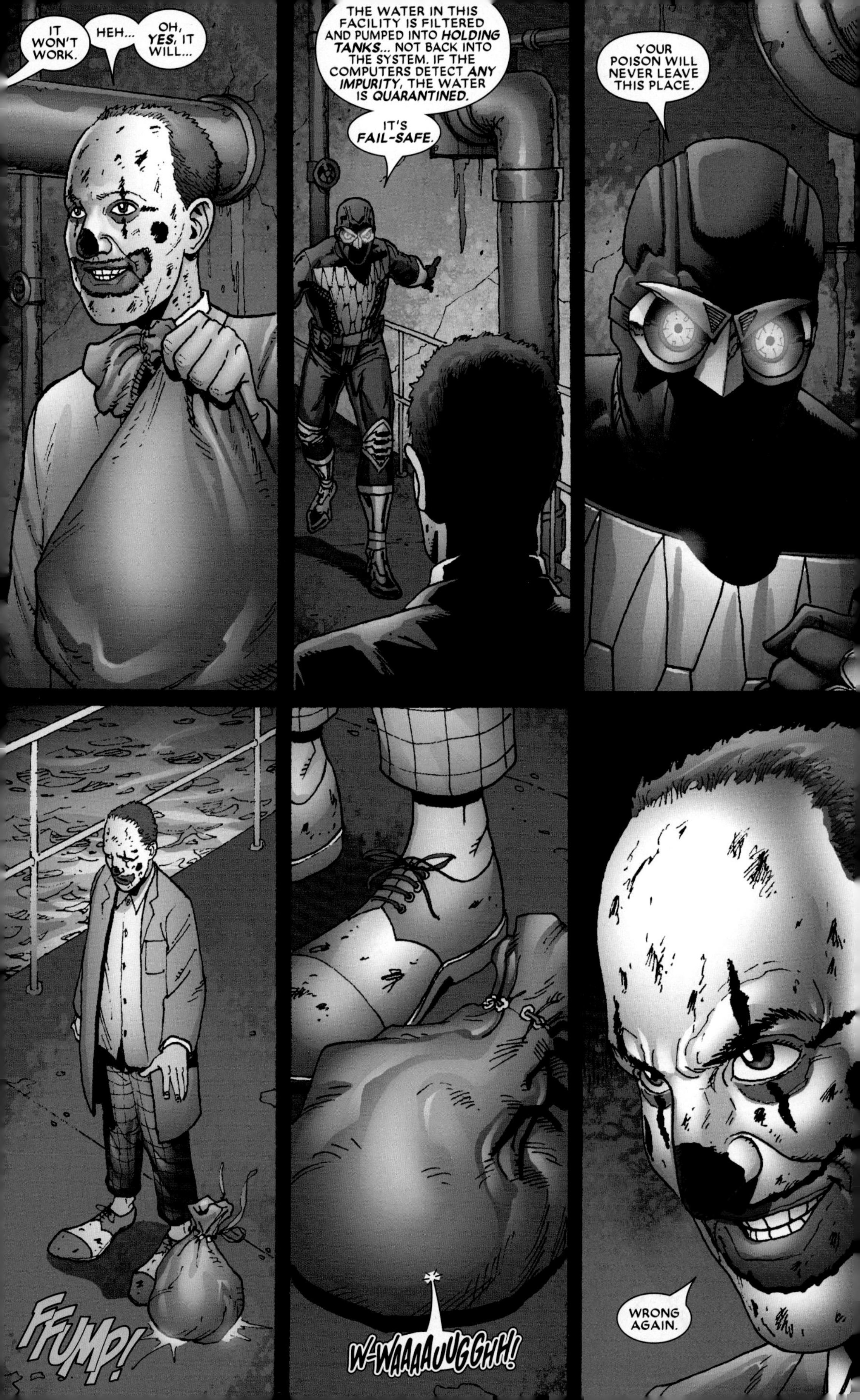
IT WON'T WORK.
HEH...
OH, YES, IT WILL...
THE WATER IN THIS FACILITY IS FILTERED AND PUMPED INTO HOLDING TANKS... NOT BACK INTO THE SYSTEM. IF THE COMPUTERS DETECT ANY IMPURITY, THE WATER IS QUARANTINED.
IT'S FAIL-SAFE.
YOUR POISON WILL NEVER LEAVE THIS PLACE.
FFUMP!
W-WAAAAUUGGHH!
WRONG AGAIN.

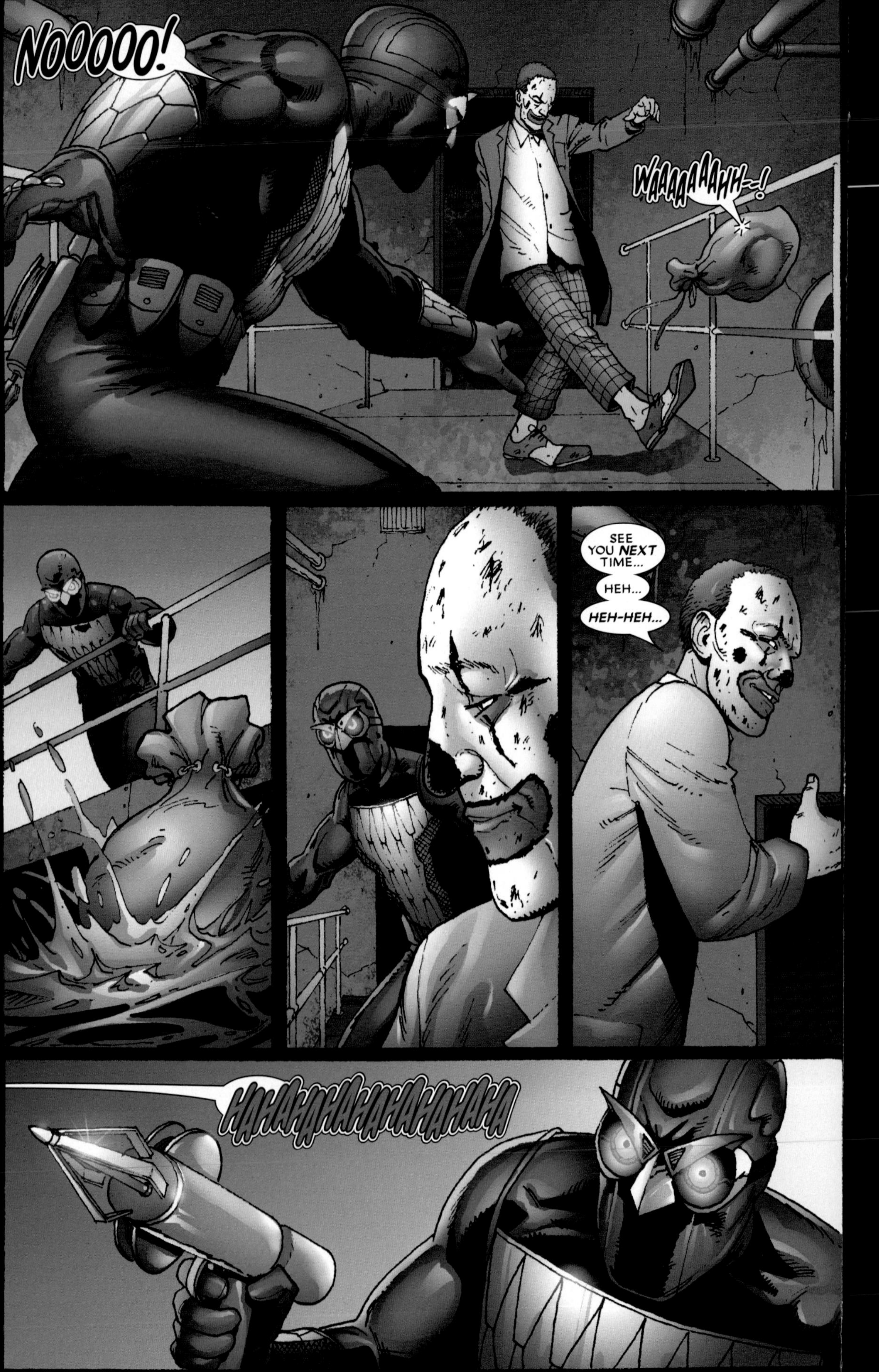
NOOOOO!
WAAAAAAAHH--!
SEE YOU NEXT TIME...
HEH...
HEH-HEH...
HAHAHAHAHAHAHAHAHAHA

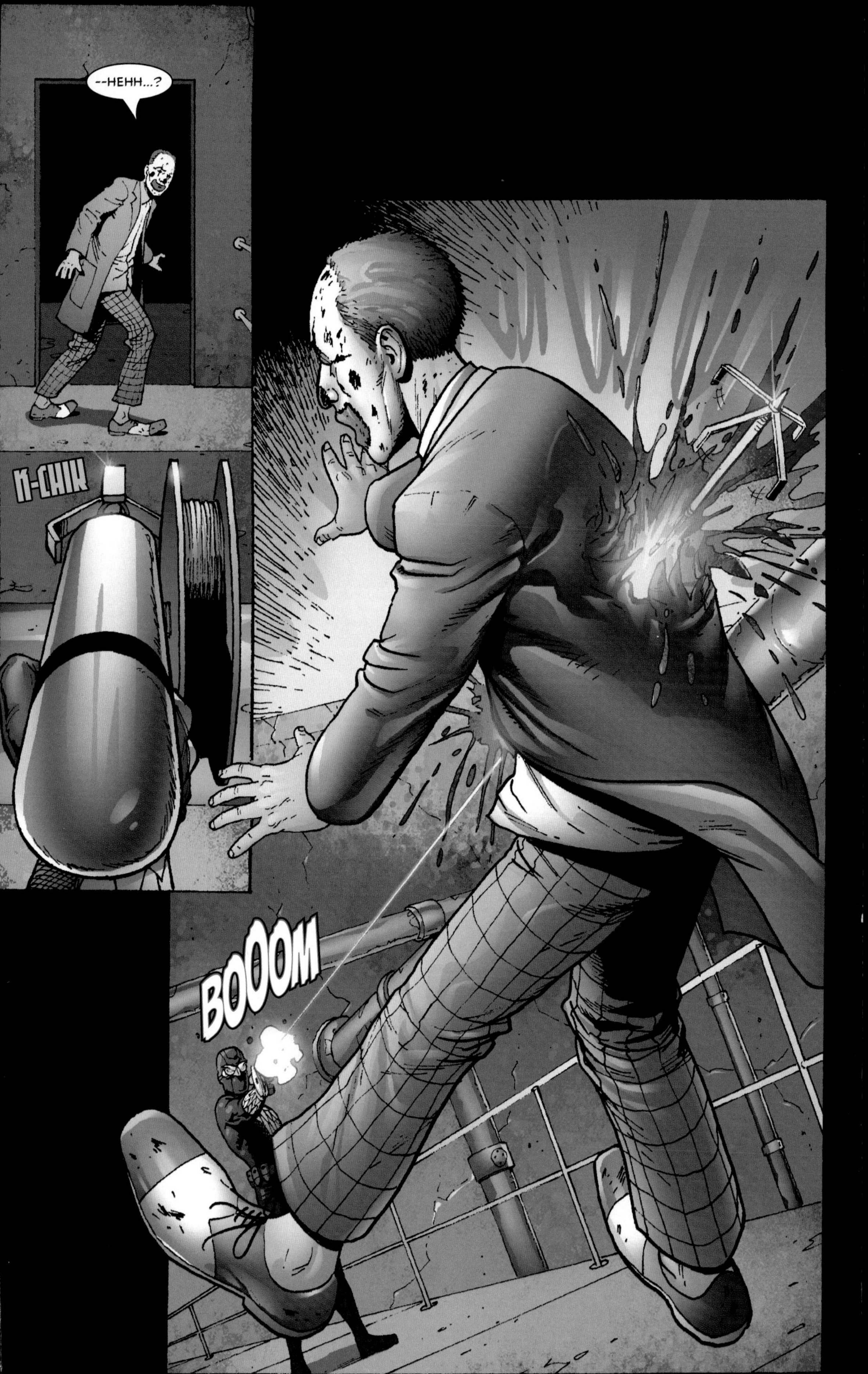
--HEHH...?
K-CHIK
BOOOM

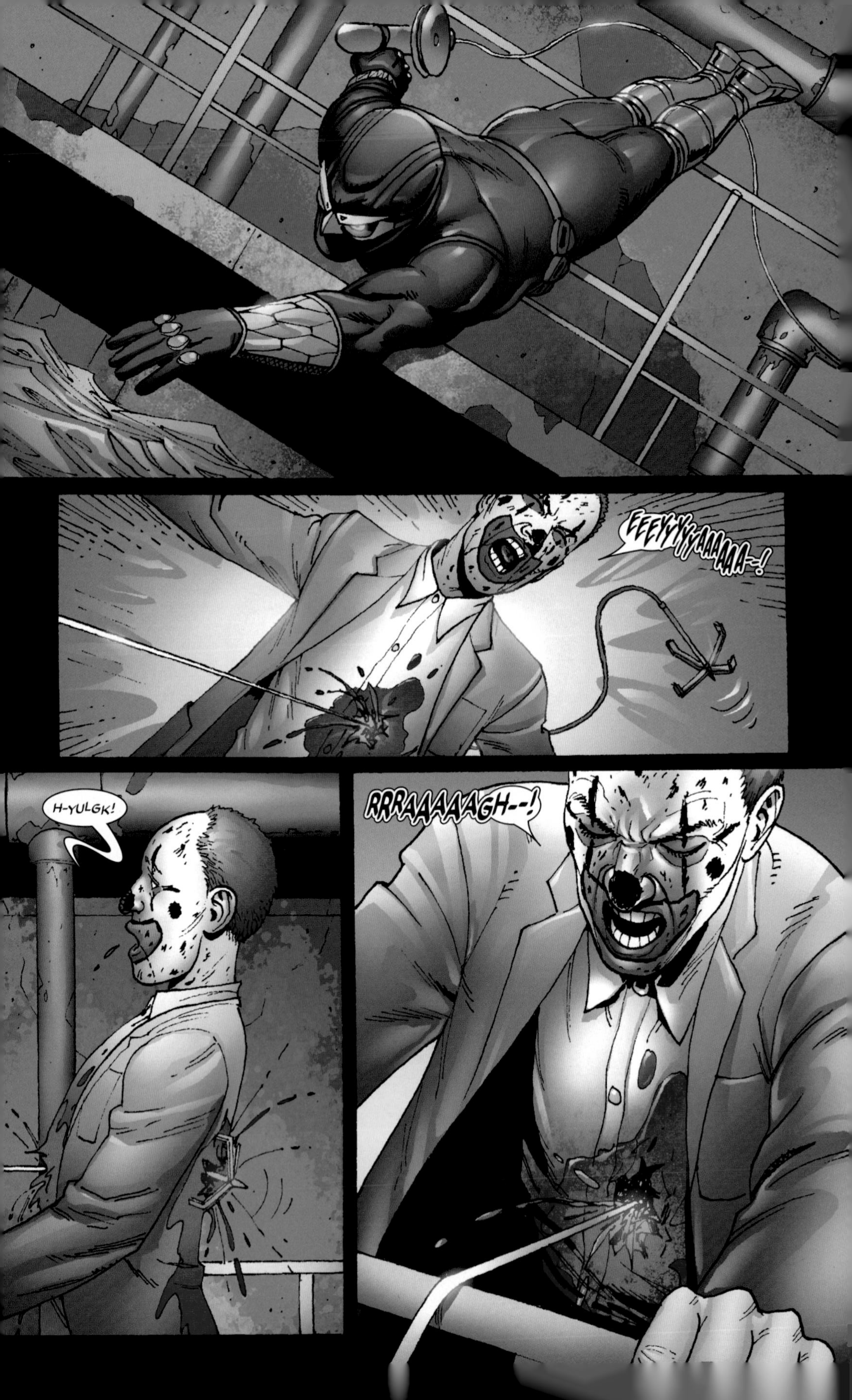
EEEYYYYYAAAAAA--!
H-YULGK!
RRRAAAAAAGH--!

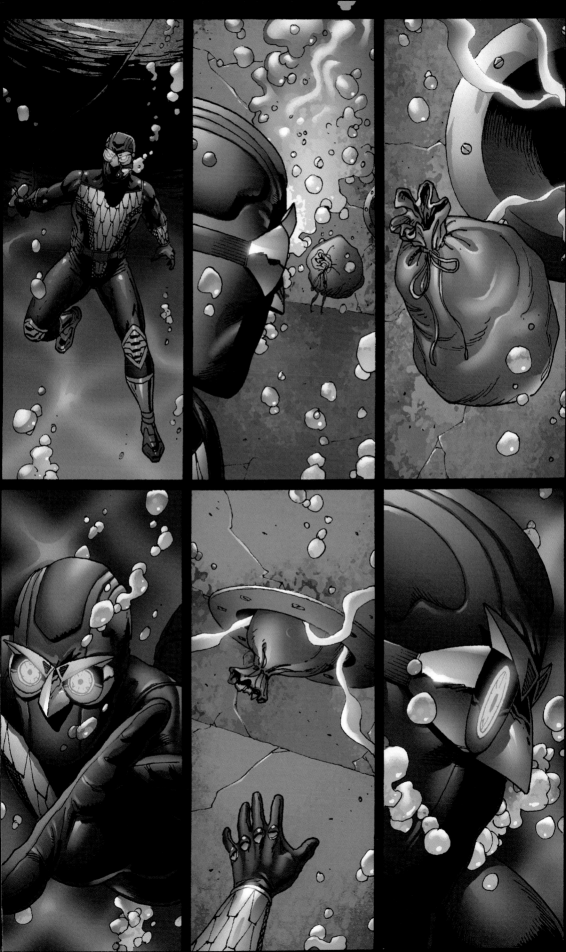

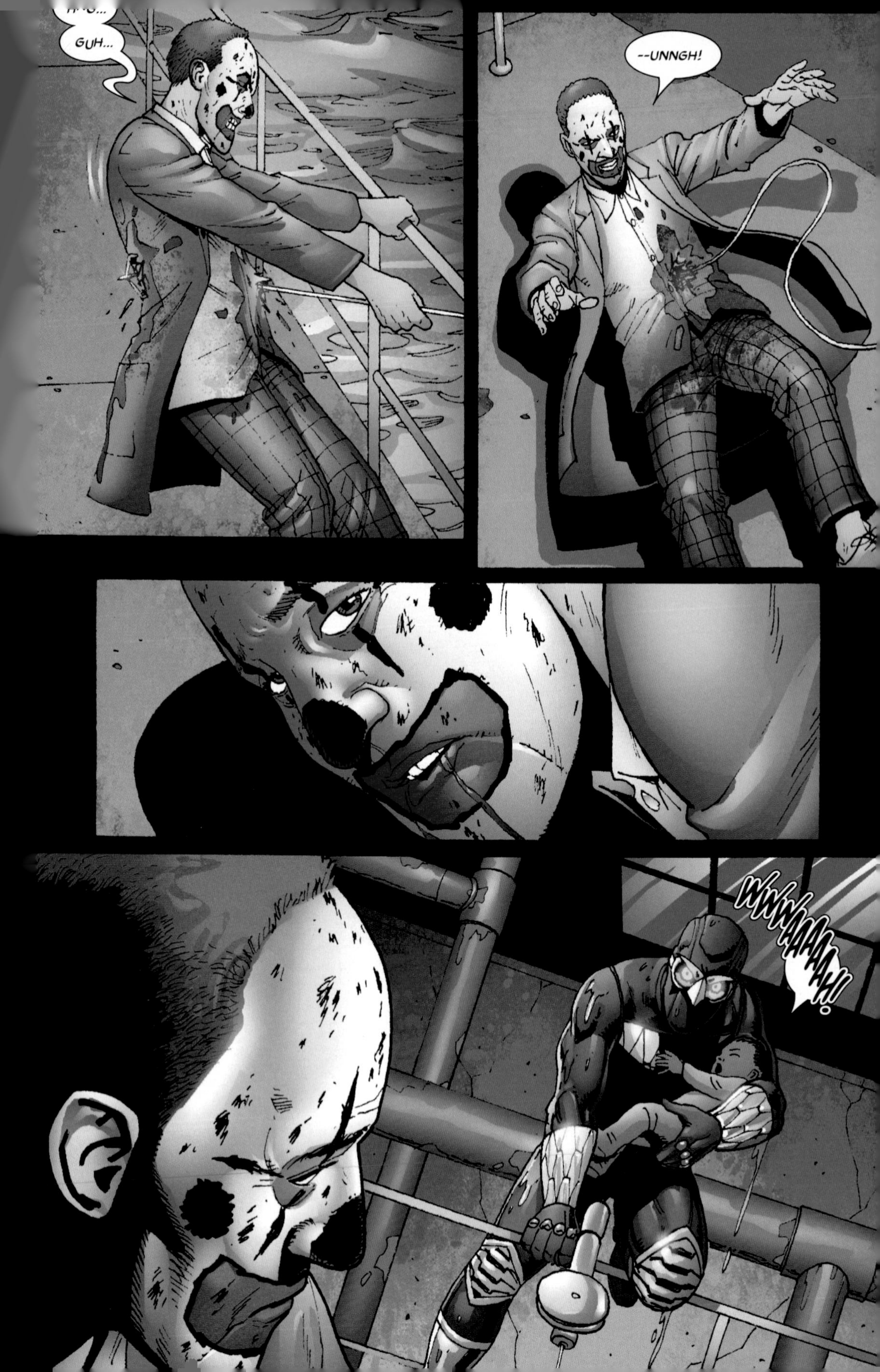
GUH...
--UNNGH!
WWWAAAAAH!

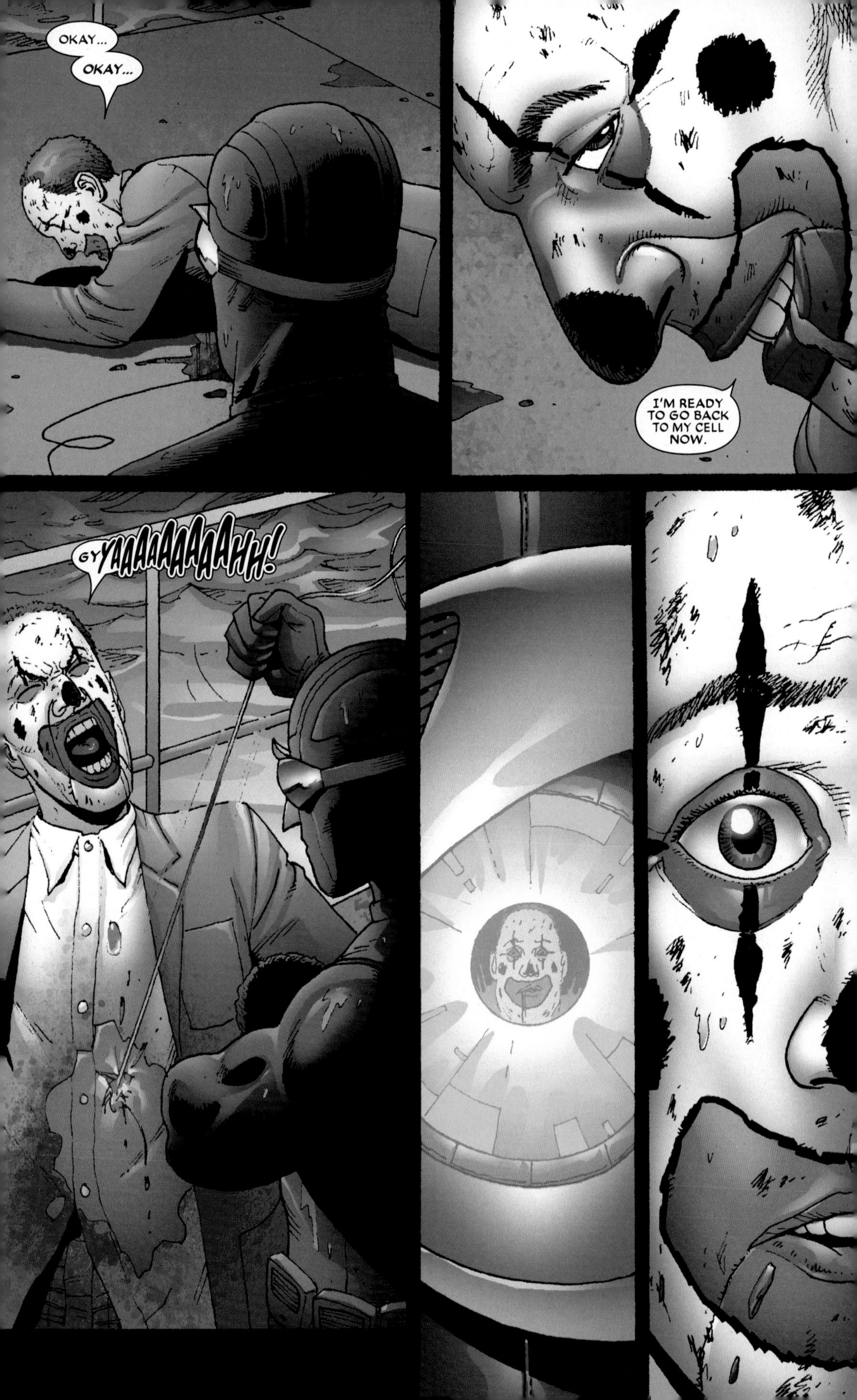
OKAY...
OKAY...
I'M READY TO GO BACK TO MY CELL NOW.
GYAAAAAAAAAHH!

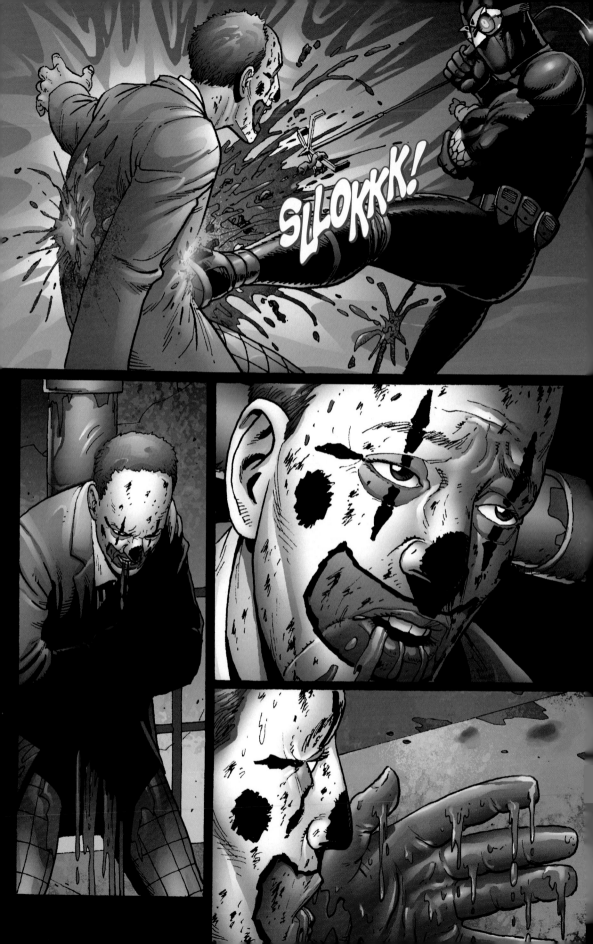

SLLOKKK!

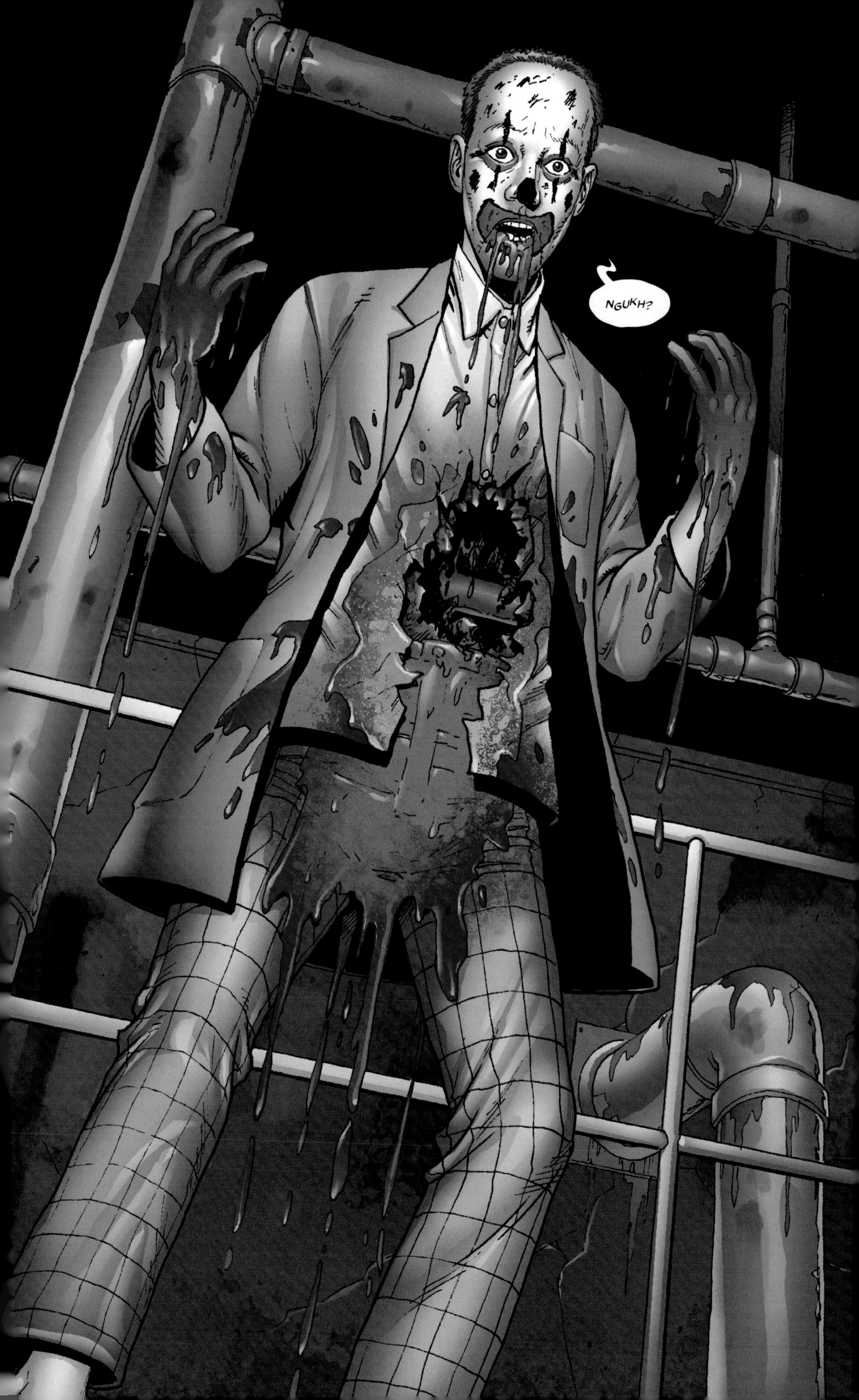
NGUKH?

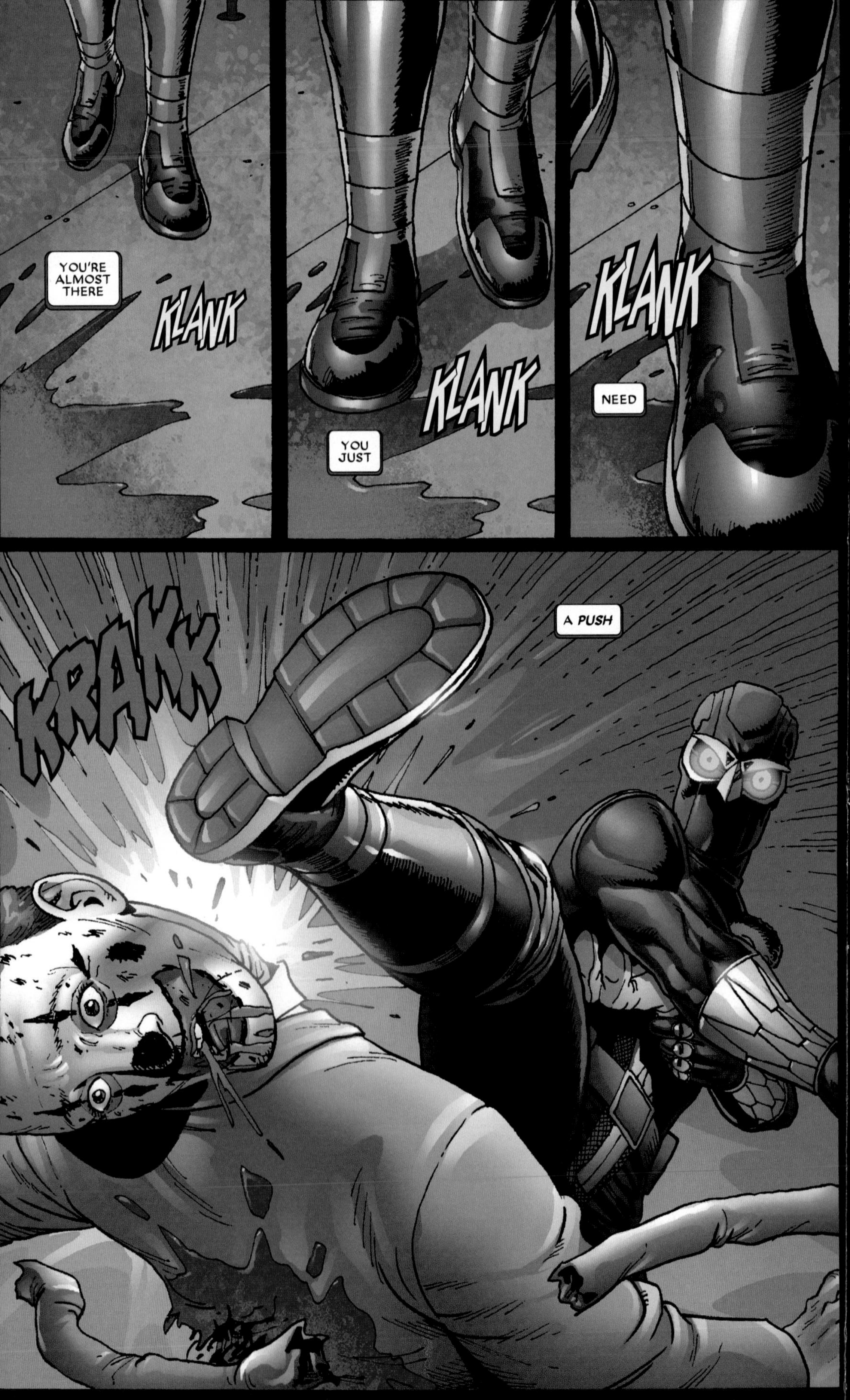
YOU'RE ALMOST THERE
KLANK
YOU JUST
KLANK
NEED
KLANK
KRAKK
A PUSH

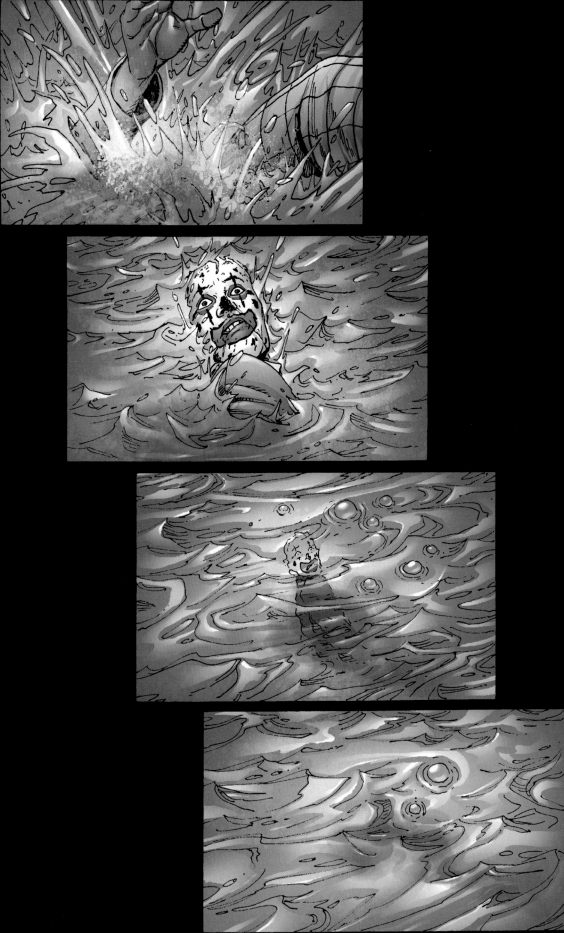

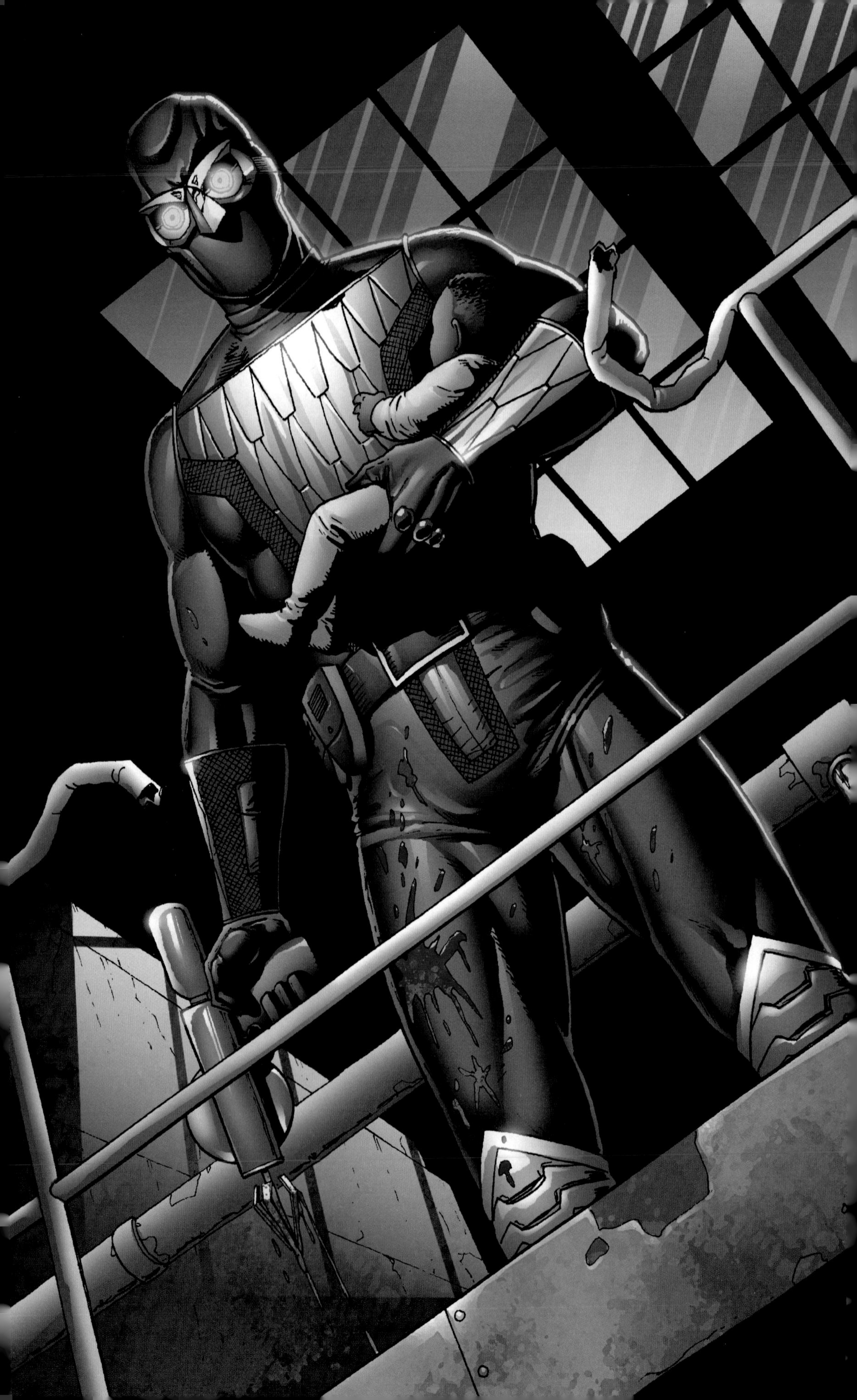

THE LAST LAUGH

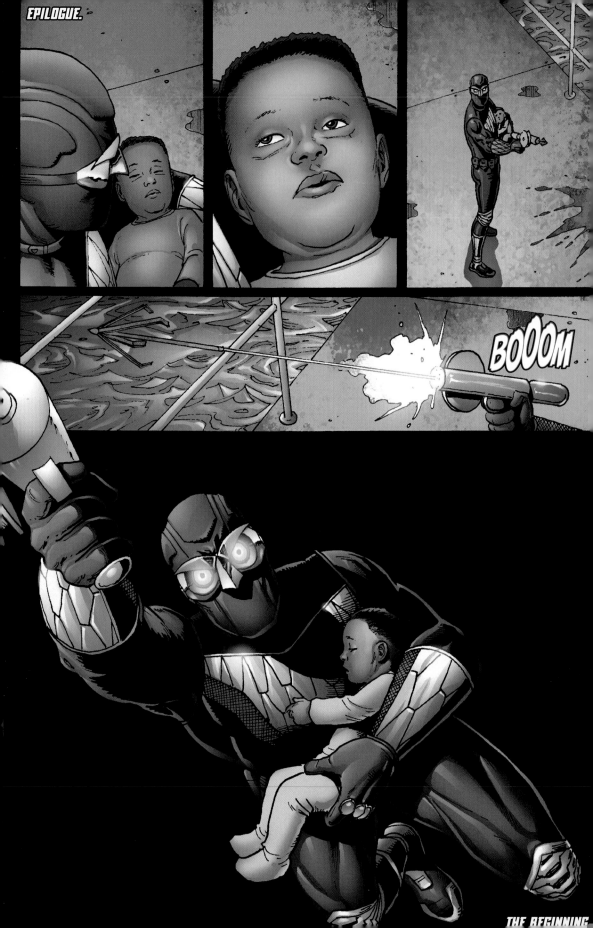

EPILOGUE.

BOOOM

THE BEGINNING

COVER #4 PROCESS BY STEVE DILLON

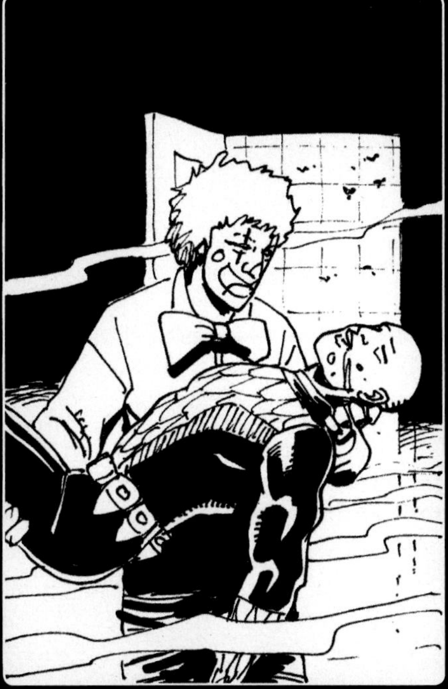

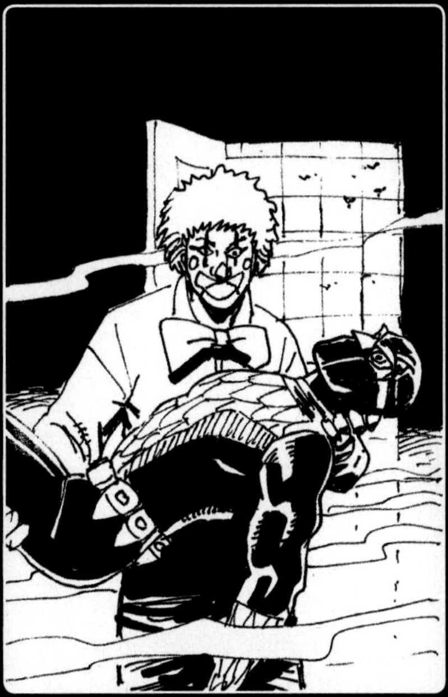

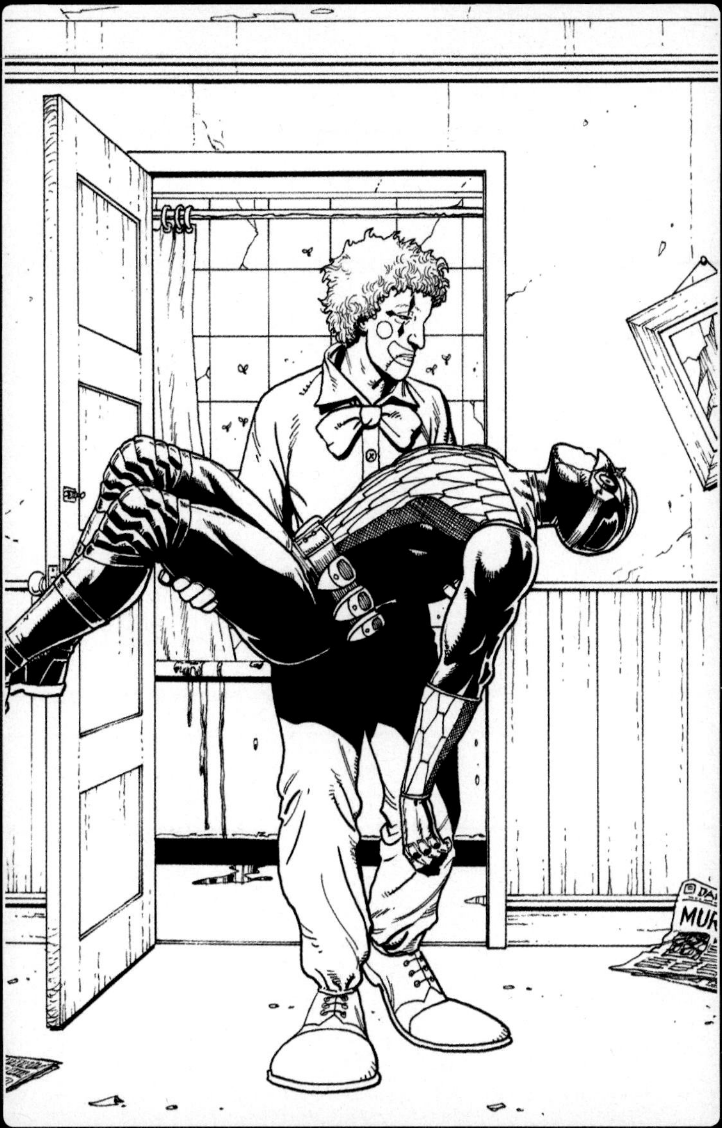

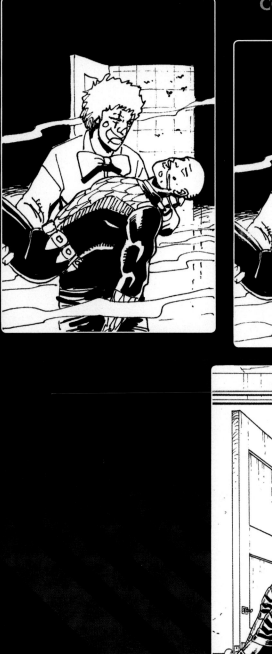

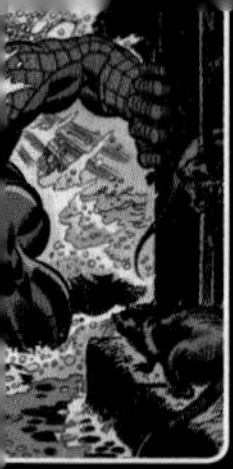

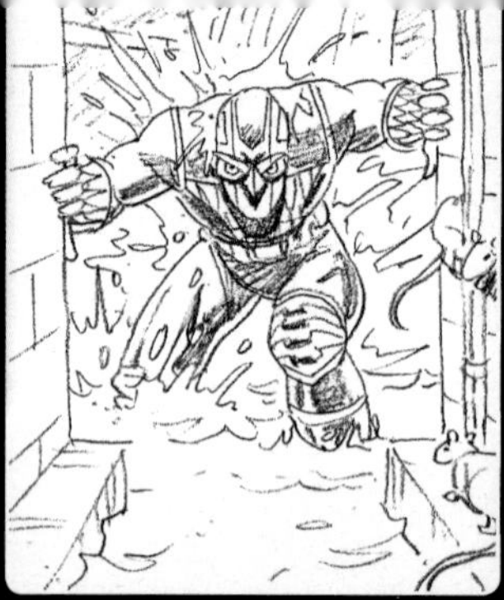

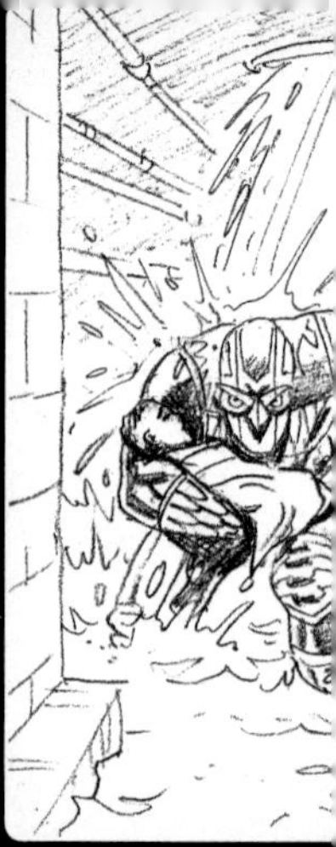

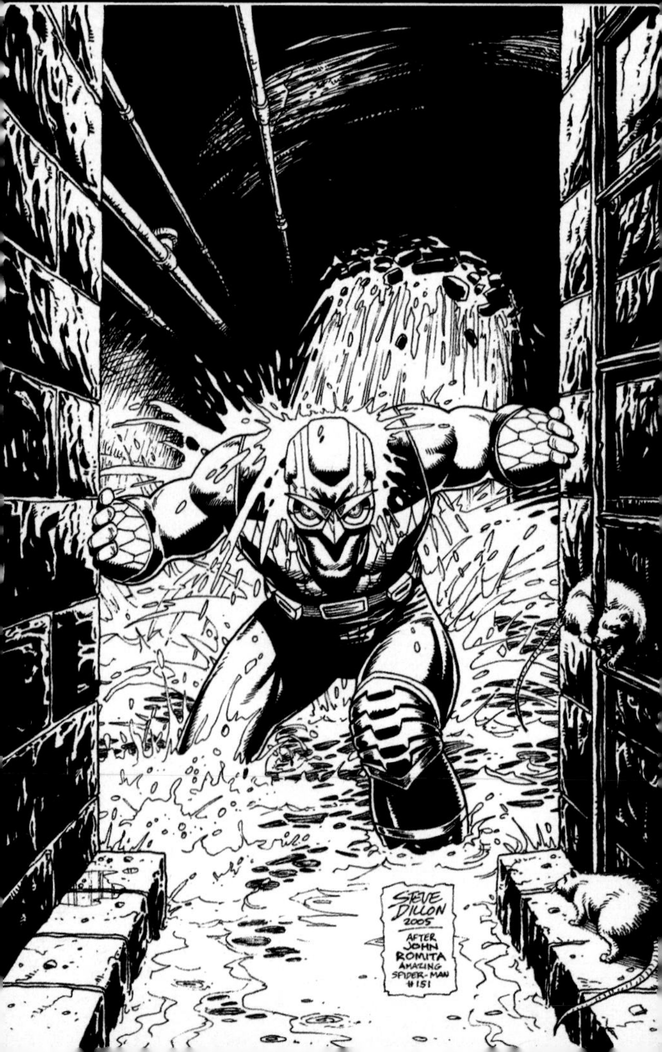
STEVE DILLON 2005
AFTER JOHN ROMITA AMAZING SPIDER-MAN #151

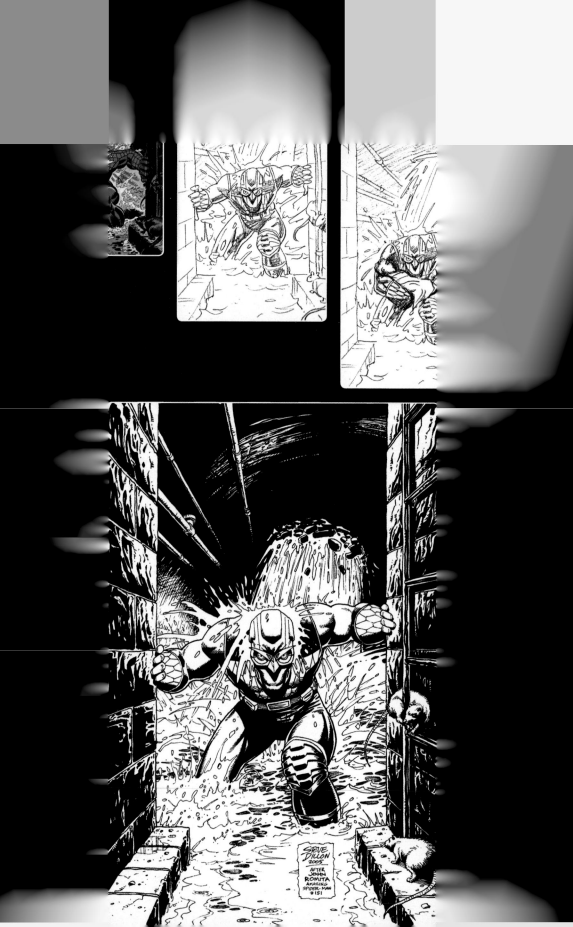